ENCYCLOPEDIA
OF
WORLD
GEOGRAPHY

SECOND EDITION

ENCYCLOPEDIA
OF
WORLD
GEOGRAPHY

SECOND EDITION

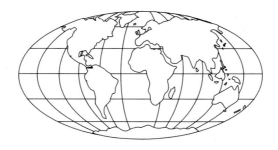

VOLUME FOUR
Central America and
The Caribbean

Marshall Cavendish
New York · Toronto · Sydney

2002 Reference Edition

Marshall Cavendish Corporation
99 White Plains Road
Tarrytown, New York 10591-9001

www.marshallcavendish.com

AN ANDROMEDA BOOK

Planned and produced by
Andromeda Oxford Ltd
11–13 The Vineyard, Abingdon,
Oxfordshire OX14 3PX, England

www.andromeda.co.uk

**Library of Congress
Cataloging-in-Publication Data**

Encyclopedia of world geography /
[general advisory editor, Peter
Haggett].-- 2nd ed.
p. cm.
Includes bibliographical references
and index.
ISBN 0-7614-7289-4 (set)
ISBN 0-7614-7293-2 (v. 4)
1. Geography--Encyclopedias.
I. Haggett, Peter.
G133 .E48 2001
910--dc21

2001028437

Printed by: L.E.G.O. S.p.A., Vicenza,
Italy

06 05 04 03 02 01   6 5 4 3 2 1

This page: Harvesting sugar cane for
immediate processing
Title page: Mount Gimie on St Lucia

CONTENTS

INTRODUCTION

Central America and the Caribbean

WITHIN THE NORTHERN TROPICS AND CONNECTING
North and South America are two arcs
of land. The western arc, Central
America, is dominated by Mexico; the
eastern arc is a chain of Caribbean
islands ranging from the Bahamas to
Trinidad and Tobago. The largest
islands in the chain (Cuba, Jamaica and
the other members of the Greater
Antilles) once formed part of the same
landmass as Central America, and continue its east–west
mountain chains. The smaller islands, the Lesser Antilles,
were created by volcanoes and are rich in endemic
species such as orchids and exotic parrots.

The western coast of Central America borders the
Gulf of Mexico, which leads to the Atlantic Ocean.
The waters in the Gulf are shallow and rich in oil
deposits. The east coast borders the deeper open
waters of the Pacific Ocean. Where Central America
tapers to its narrowest point in Panama, only 81.6 km
(50.7 mi) separate the deep waters of the Atlantic and
Pacific Oceans. In 1914 a channel, the Panama Canal,
was opened between them, revolutionizing patterns of
global communication.

Many different cultures have left their mark on the
region. The indigenous peoples of the mainland
(including Aztecs and Mayans, but all known
collectively as Amerindians) only survived European
conquest in societies of mestizos, people of mixed
European and Amerindian descent. In mestizo culture
the Spanish language and Roman Catholicism blend
with Amerindian languages and traditional religions.
Amerindians did not survive on the Caribbean islands,
whose modern societies are an ethnic blend of many
European peoples, former African slaves and South
Asian migrant workers. Today Caribbean island societies
are small and often divided; many are still dependencies
and territories of foreign countries.

The recent development of the region and its
potential for the future owes much to the proximity of
the United States, which dominates Central America's
political and economic life. Migrant workers circulate
between the United States and their homelands. Many
Central American and Caribbean countries, plagued by
external debt, seek to boost their economies by providing
their powerful northern neighbor with specialized
services and goods. However, any fragile economic
stability in Central America is threatened by war and
civil unrest. Refugees from the conflict often flee to the
United States, which has actively intervened in some
cases in order to prevent communist forces gaining
supremacy so close to its own borders.

North America

Central and South America

A	ALBANIA
AU	AUSTRIA
B	BELGIUM
BO	BOSNIA HERZEGOVINA
C	CROATIA
CZ	CZECH REPUBLIC
HUN	HUNGARY
M	MACEDONIA (FORMER YUGOSLAV REPUBLIC OF)
N	NETHERLANDS
R	RUSSIA
S	SLOVAKIA
SL	SLOVENIA
SW	SWITZERLAND
YU	YUGOSLAVIA

Europe

Asia

GREENLAND
(Denmark)

SVALBARD
(Norway)

ICELAND

RUSSIA

NORWAY

FINLAND

SWEDEN

ESTONIA

LATVIA

UNITED
KINGDOM

DENMARK

LITHUANIA

R

IRELAND

N

GERMANY

POLAND

BELARUS

LUXEMBOURG

B

CZ

S

UKRAINE

FRANCE

SW

AU

HUN

MOLDOVA

KAZAKHSTAN

MONGOLIA

ANDORRA

SL

C

BO

ROMANIA

YU

NORTH
KOREA

PORTUGAL

SPAIN

ITALY

A

M

BULGARIA

AZERBAIJAN

UZBEKISTAN

KYRGYZSTAN

SOUTH
KOREA

JAPAN

GREECE

GEORGIA

ARMENIA

TAJIKISTAN

CHINA

GIBRALTAR
(UK)

TUNISIA

MALTA

TURKEY

TURKMENISTAN

CYPRUS

SYRIA

MOROCCO

LEBANON

IRAQ

IRAN

AFGHANISTAN

TAIWAN

ISRAEL

KUWAIT

ALGERIA

LIBYA

EGYPT

JORDAN

QATAR

PAKISTAN

NEPAL

BHUTAN

WESTERN
SAHARA
(Morocco)

BAHRAIN

SAUDI
ARABIA

UNITED ARAB
EMIRATES

OMAN

BANGLADESH

NORTHERN
MARIANA
ISLANDS
(United States)

MAURITANIA

MALI

NIGER

CHAD

ERITREA

YEMEN

INDIA

MYANMAR

LAOS

CAPE
VERDE

DJIBOUTI

THAILAND

VIETNAM

PHILIPPINES

GUAM
(United States)

SENEGAL

BURKINA
FASO

BENIN

SUDAN

CAMBODIA

GAMBIA

GUINEA-
BISSAU

GUINEA

NIGERIA

PALAU

FEDERATED STATES
OF MICRONESIA

SIERRA LEONE

CÔTE
D'IVOIRE

TOGO

CENTRAL
AFRICAN
REPUBLIC

ETHIOPIA

BRUNEI

LIBERIA

GHANA

SOMALIA

SRI LANKA

MALAYSIA

EQUATORIAL GUINEA

CAMEROON

UGANDA

MALDIVES

NAURU

SAO TOME
& PRINCIPE

GABON

RWANDA

KENYA

SINGAPORE

INDONESIA

PAPUA
NEW GUINEA

SOLOMON
ISLANDS

REPUBLIC OF CONGO

DEMOCRATIC
REPUBLIC
OF CONGO

BURUNDI

CABINDA
(Angola)

TANZANIA

SEYCHELLES

COMOROS

ANGOLA

MALAWI

ZAMBIA

VANUATU

ZIMBABWE

MADAGASCAR

MAURITIUS

NAMIBIA

MOZAMBIQUE

REUNION
(France)

NEW
CALEDONIA
(France)

BOTSWANA

AUSTRALIA

SWAZILAND

SOUTH
AFRICA

LESOTHO

Africa

Australasia, Oceania and Antarctica

NEW
ZEALAND

Antarctica

Central America and the Caribbean

COUNTRIES IN THE REGION

MEXICO · GUATEMALA · BELIZE · EL SALVADOR

HONDURAS· NICARAGUA· COSTA RICA · PANAMA

CUBA · BAHAMAS · HAITI · JAMAICA

DOMINICAN REPUBLIC · SAINT KITTS-NEVIS

ANTIGUA AND BARBUDA · DOMINICA · SAINT LUCIA

SAINT VINCENT AND THE GRENADINES · BARBADOS

GRENADA · TRINIDAD AND TOBAGO

DEPENDENCIES IN THE REGION

TURKS AND CAICOS ISLANDS · BERMUDA

CAYMAN ISLANDS · PUERTO RICO

UNITED STATES VIRGIN ISLANDS

BRITISH VIRGIN ISLANDS · ANGUILLA

MONTSERRAT · ARUBA · THE NETHERLANDS

ANTILLES · GUADELOUPE · MARTINIQUE

Casting his net A fisherman in Haiti. This impoverished state occupies the western third of Hispaniola, the Caribbean island that was discovered by Christopher Columbus in 1492 and was the site of the first European landing in the Americas.

- ■ capital city
- ● major town

height of land (meters)

	3000
	2000
	1000
	500
	200
	0

▲ mountain peak

Gulf of Mexico

ATLANTIC
OCEAN

Great Abaco

Grand
Bahama
New Providence · Eleuthera

Nassau

Andros · BAHAMAS · Long Island

Caicos Islands

Acklins Island · Turks Islands

Tampico

Havana · CUBA · Camagüey · Great Inagua

Hispaniola

Puerto
Rico

Virgin Islands · Barbuda

Bay of Campeche

Mérida

Yucatán

Isla de la
Juventud

Guantánamo · DOMINICAN
REPUBLIC

San Juan

Basseterre

ANTIGUA AND BARBUDA

Antigua

ST KITTS

St John's

· Citlaltépetl
5699 · Veracruz

Cayman
Islands · Santiago
de Cuba

HAITI

Port-au-
Prince

Santo Domingo

NEVIS · Guadeloupe

G r e a t e r

Montego Bay · Kingston · Jacmel

A n t i l l e s

DOMINICA

Roseau · Martinique

Oriental

Isthmus
of
Tehuantepec

Usumacinta

JAMAICA

ST LUCIA · Castries · BARBADOS

del Sur

Gulf of
Tehuantepec

Sierra Madre

Belmopan

BELIZE

GUATEMALA · San Pedro Sula

Cape Gracias a Dios

Caribbean Sea

Lesser Antilles

Bridgetown

ST VINCENT
AND THE
GRENADINES · Kingstown

GRENADA · St George's

Lesser Antilles

Tobago

Guatemala · HONDURAS

Coco

Tegucigalpa

San Salvador

EL SALVADOR · NICARAGUA

Lake
Managua · Managua

Lake
Nicaragua

Aruba · Curaçao · Bonaire

Port of Spain · TRINIDAD
AND TOBAGO

Trinidad

COSTA
RICA · San José

· Chirripó
3820 · Gatún Lake · Panama

Panama
Canal

PANAMA

Mexico

UNITED MEXICAN STATES

MEXICO IS ONE OF THE LARGEST OF THE Latin American states, possessing a colorful diversity of cultures. However, rich natural resources and swift economic growth have been largely offset by the rapid rise in population.

ENVIRONMENT

Mexico forms a large tongue of mountainous land between the Pacific Ocean and the Gulf of Mexico. The southern half of the country, which lies within the tropics, has a wide variety of landscapes.

The land

Mexico lies in a geologically unstable part of the world. Many areas are subjected to frequent earthquakes and volcanic eruptions; a major earthquake in 1985 devastated Mexico City.

Much of the northern border with the United States is formed by the Rio Bravo del Norte (Rio Grande). From here the land arcs southeast toward the borders with Guatemala and Belize. The low-lying Yucatán Peninsula extends northward from the Belize border. The long and mountainous peninsula of Baja California runs parallel to the west coast of the Mexican mainland. Some 500 km (300 mi) out to sea is a group of volcanic islands called the Islas de Revillagigedo.

The broad coastal plain along the Gulf of Mexico is fringed by swamps, lagoons and sandbars, while the Pacific coastal plain is narrower and more interrupted. The area in between is occupied by the massive central plateau. This rises in the south to the Mesa Central, which is crossed by a series of mighty volcanoes, including Citlaltépetl and Popocatépetl. The plateau is bounded to the east, west and south by the mountain ranges of the Sierra Madre. In the south, beyond the Sierra Madre del Sur, the Isthmus of Tehuantepec links these highlands to the mountains on the Guatemalan border.

Climate

The climate varies both with latitude and altitude. In the far north low rainfall and extremes of temperature create desert landscapes. In the south most rain falls between May and August. Rainfall increases southeastward, with the heaviest falls along the Gulf coast and in the south.

The coastal plains and the foothills of the Sierra Madre are the *tierra caliente* ("hot land"), where temperatures are mostly uniformly high. Between August and October these areas are vulnerable to tropical hurricanes from the Gulf of Mexico and the Pacific. Above 1,000 m (3,000 ft) is the *tierra templada* ("temperate land"), which extends over much of the central plateau. The Mesa Central often reaches into the *tierra fria* ("cold land") above 2,000 m (6,000 ft). Above about 4,000 m (13,000 ft) is the *tierra helada* ("frozen land"), where temperatures are always below 10°C.

Plants and animals

Desert scrub predominates in the deserts of the north, with grasses, shrubs and succulents on higher ground. Farther south settlers have destroyed most of the ancient forests, but stands of conifers still remain on the higher slopes of the western mountains. Much of the central plateau is covered with grassland. Higher rainfall in the east allows tropical rainforest to flourish there, with temperate rainforest growing at higher altitudes. In southwestern areas, deciduous and semideciduous woodland grows along the Pacific coastline.

The rainforests of the south support a great diversity of animals, such as monkeys, parrots, jaguars, tapirs and anteaters. In the north, and in settled areas of the central plateau, domestic livestock have been introduced, taking the place of the native species. However, in the deserts and steppes native animals such

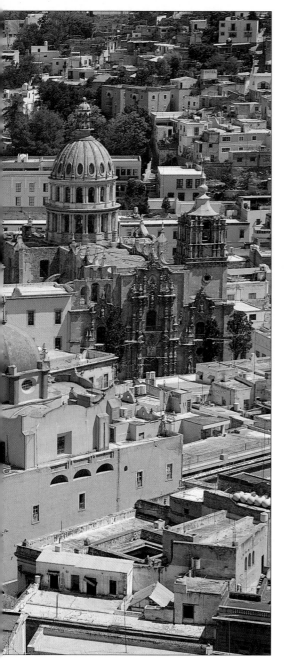

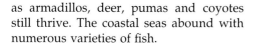

as armadillos, deer, pumas and coyotes still thrive. The coastal seas abound with numerous varieties of fish.

SOCIETY

The cultural diversity and racial mix of modern Mexico owes much to its complex, colorful and often violent history.

History

Mexico had a succession of highly sophisticated early civilizations. The Olmecs reached their peak from 900–400 BC. They built impressive ceremonial centers elaborately decorated with mosaics and stone carvings. The Mayas rapidly expanded into the forests of southeastern Mexico from Guatemala, where they originated, in about 300 AD. They were a highly sophisticated, wealthy people; archaeological remains include not only majestic stone buildings and stepped

pyramids, but also intricate jewelry, carved figures and hieroglyphic manuscripts that are not yet fully understood.

The Aztecs, originally a nomadic people from the arid northern highlands, migrated to Mexico's great Central Valley in about 1200. Here they became the dominant power and built their capital, Tenochtitlán, on the site of modern Mexico City, from which they established a vast empire. Their architecture, jewelry and textiles were outstanding; they used a complex calendar for time-keeping; and they practiced ritual human slaughter on a grand scale to propitiate their gods. The Aztec empire was largely destroyed by the 16th-century Spanish adventurer Hernán Cortés (1485–1547). Tenochtitlán fell in 1521, and in 1535 the conquered territory became New Spain.

Spanish rule was often harsh, especially in the 18th century, and independence was not achieved until 1821. Mexico then became a republic, adopting a federal constitution in 1824.

In 1845 Mexico tried and failed to resist the United States' annexation of Texas. A bitter war was to follow, and further territories were ceded by the Treaty of Guadalupe Hidalgo in 1848. In 1857 the introduction of a reformed constitution brought civil war. The reformers, led by Benito Juárez (1806–72), were victorious.

In 1910, following the overthrow of the dictatorial president Porfirio Díaz (1830–1915), there began a long power struggle by various revolutionary groups, who eventually formed a single National Revolutionary Party in 1929. In 1946 it

One for the road (*above*) Farm workers wearing traditional ponchos refresh themselves with a cup of pulque – a cloudy white beer made from the agave, a succulent plant.

Colonial riches (*left*) For centuries, gold and silver mines made the beautiful city of Guanajuato, with its fine baroque churches and colonial buildings, the wealthiest in Mexico. Today it is an important university town and cultural center.

NATIONAL DATA – MEXICO

Land area 1,958,201 sq km (756,066 sq mi)

Climate	Altitude m (ft)	Temperatures January °C(°F)	July °C(°F)	Annual precipitation mm (in)
Mexico City	2,306 (7,564)	12 (54)	16 (61)	726 (28.6)

Major physical features highest point: Citlaltépetl 5,699 m (18,700 ft); longest river: Rio Grande (part) 2,100 km (1,300 mi)

Population (2000 est.) 100,349,766

Form of government federal multiparty republic with two legislative houses

Armed forces army 130,000; navy 37,000; air force 8,000

Largest cities Mexico City (capital – 8,591,309); Guadalajara (1,647,000); Ecatepec (1,619,000); Puebla (1,270,989); Nezahualcóyotl (1,224,500)

Official language Spanish

Ethnic composition Mestizo 60.0%; Amerindian 30.0%; White 9.0%; others 1.0%

Religious affiliations Roman Catholic 92.6%; Protestant 3.3%; nonreligious 3.1%; Jewish 0.1%; others 0.9%

Currency 1 New Mexican peso (Mex $) = 100 centavos

Gross domestic product (1999) US $865.5 billion

Gross domestic product per capita (1999) US $8,500

Life expectancy at birth male 69.0 yr; female 75.2 yr

Major resources petroleum, silver, copper, gold, lead, zinc, natural gas, timber, coffee, sugar, cotton

was renamed the Party of the Institutionalized Revolution (PRI). This party carried out many important reforms, and remained the dominant political force during subsequent decades.

Government

According to the 1917 constitution, voting is mandatory for all adults over 18 years of age. The president is elected for one six-year term only. There are two legislative houses: a 500-member chamber of deputies and a 64-member senate. The deputies are elected for a three-year term – three-quarters of them directly and the rest according to the votes cast for individual parties. Senators are elected for a six-year term – two for each of the 31 states and two for the Federal District. Each state elects its own governor and legislature, but the appointment of the governor of the Federal District is the prerogative of the president.

People

About one-third of Mexico's population are Amerindians, while over half are mestizos of mixed European and native descent; there are several other minority groups. The official language is Spanish, but some 50 Amerindian languages are also spoken. Most of the population is Roman Catholic.

More than two-thirds of Mexicans live in or around the three major cities of Mexico City, Guadalajara and Monterrey. Mexico City, the capital, is probably the world's most populous city. Large-scale emigration across the northern border has caused difficulties with the United States, Mexico's chief trading partner.

ECONOMY

Mexico has little good agricultural land, and much food has to be imported. Its struggle for economic growth has been hampered by falling oil prices, the 1985 Mexico City earthquake and massive foreign debt. Inflation remains high, and economic controls have been only moderately successful.

Agriculture

Most agricultural land is on the central plateau, though irrigation projects in the north have created new farmlands there. Since 1910 much of this land has been occupied by small subsistence farms. Export crops include coffee, sugar cane and cotton, while staples include maize, squash and kidney beans. Cattle ranching is largely concentrated in the north, and

some meat is exported. Fishing is largely an export industry, the most important catches being tuna, anchovies, sardines and shrimps.

About one-fifth of Mexico is forested, mostly in the east and south. These forests are exploited for hard and fragrant woods, and for chicle, the base material for chewing gum. Many forested areas, however, are threatened by large-scale clearance for agriculture.

Industry

Mexico is the world's leading source of silver; other commercial minerals include zinc, copper and lead. Ore from Durango

Cultural revival (*above*) A member of an Aztec dance troupe helps to keep ancient traditions alive. Mexico's rich Amerindian culture inspires many modern artists, sculptors and architects.

Monte Albán (*left*), the center of ancient Zapotec culture, was built on a flattened hilltop rising 300 m (1000 ft) from the valleys below. This impressive site is a lasting tribute to the sophistication and skill of Mexico's indigenous civilizations.

in and around Mexico City. Products include industrial chemicals, machinery and transportation equipment.

Transportation and communications

Tourism is an important foreign-currency earner, and has stimulated the development of both road and air networks. The extensive railroad system is slow and unreliable, but the road network has almost doubled in extent since the 1940s and is continuing to expand. There are two state-owned airlines, Aeroméxico and Mexicana, with more than 75 airports serving major cities, resorts and international destinations.

Mexico has a free press, with several hundred daily newspapers.

Health and education

Subsidized health care is available to many, but poor facilities in rural areas are reflected in higher rates of death and disease, particularly malaria. Adequate housing is a major problem, particularly in the cities. There are minimum-wage laws, but rural poverty is widespread.

Education is free, and literacy levels are high as a result of an extensive campaign. However, rural areas lack facilities, and there are few secondary schools outside the cities.

in the west of the country is used for iron and steel production at Monterrey in the northeast, fueled by coking coal from the nearby Sabinas fields. Mexico's massive hydrocarbon resources now provide the majority of foreign-exchange earnings. The state-owned company Pemex, Mexico's largest employer, controls the ex-

ploration, production and marketing of natural gas and petrochemical products.

Petrochemicals are the chief energy source. Hydroelectricity is also significant, however, and geothermal energy is being increasingly exploited. There is a nuclear power plant at Laguna Verde. Manufacturing industry is concentrated

Guatemala

REPUBLIC OF GUATEMALA

Tʜᴇ ʀᴇᴘᴜʙʟɪᴄ ᴏꜰ ɢᴜᴀᴛᴇᴍᴀʟᴀ ʟɪᴇꜱ ᴏɴ ᴛʜᴇ southwestern border of Mexico, with coastlines on both the Atlantic and the Pacific. It also shares frontiers with Belize to the northeast, and Honduras and El Salvador to the southeast.

ENVIRONMENT

The heart of the country is crossed by two main mountain ranges. The Altos Cuchumatanes to the north are older and more eroded. The younger Sierra Madre range in the south includes 33 volcanoes, three of them active. The soils here are enriched by volcanic ash, making it the most fertile part of the country. In the north the highlands fall away to a large, flat, forested area called the Petén, and to the plains bordering the Gulf of Honduras.

The climate is mostly tropical with seasonal rains, though the mountains are both cooler and wetter. The lowland rainforests are rich in tropical hardwoods and rubber trees, with oaks and conifers higher up, and some mangroves along the coasts. Typical wildlife includes jaguars, peccaries and monkeys, while the rivers support crocodiles and manatees. There is also a tremendous variety of birds.

SOCIETY

For many centuries the area that is now Guatemala formed the heart of the ancient Maya civilization, which reached its peak from 300 to 900 AD. The empire then fell into decline, and the ruins of the Mayas' great stone cities can still be found in the remote northern lowlands. In 1523 the country was overrun by Spanish conquistadors under Pedro de Alvarado (c. 1485–1541). They set up large agricultural estates that were worked by Amerindian laborers. Between 1821 and 1847 the ruling landowners established Guatemala's independence. Their leader, Rafael Carrera (1841–65), became the first of a series of powerful dictator-presidents. A few were relatively liberal reformers whose aims were to modernize the country; Jorge Ubico (1878–1946), who ruled in the 1930s, was a protector of the Amerindians, but there were often periods of political repression.

The effects of World War II caused an economic decline, and subsequent decades were characterized by political extremism and constant divisive military coups. Guatemala finally achieved a level of stability following elections in 1996 and the signing of a peace treaty between government and rebel forces which ended 40 years of civil war.

Over 50 percent of the population are of mixed Amerindian and Hispanic descent, and Roman Catholicism is the dominant religion in Guatemala.

ECONOMY

Guatemala's economy is still largely agricultural. Coffee is the main crop as well as the principal export. Bananas, cotton, sugar cane and maize are also important. Large numbers of cattle are raised on the Pacific coastal pastures. The forests provide timber and chicle, the main ingredient in chewing gum. Guatemala has few mineral or energy reserves apart from small quantities of petroleum, copper and other metals. Industry is mostly confined to the processing of timber, sugar, tobacco and other agricultural products. Education is free, but resources are insufficient to provide adequate schooling or health care in rural areas.

NATIONAL DATA – GUATEMALA

Land area	108,889 sq km (42,042 sq mi)		

Climate		Temperatures		Annual
	Altitude m (ft)	January °C(°F)	July °C(°F)	precipitation mm (in)
Guatemala	1,480 (4,856)	17 (63)	21 (69)	1,316 (51.8)

Major physical features	highest point: Tajumulco ken

Population	(2000 est.) 12,639,939

Form of government	multiparty republic with one legislative house

Armed forces	army 38,500; navy 1,500; air force 700

Largest cities	Guatemala City (capital – 823,301); Mixco (209,791); Villa Nueva (101,295)

Official language	Spanish

Ethnic composition	Ladino (Mestizo) 56.0%; Amerindian 44.0%

Religious affiliations	Roman Catholic 75.0%; Protestant 25.0%

Currency	1 quetzal (Q) = 100 centavos

Gross domestic product	(1999) US $47.9 billion

Gross domestic product per capita	(1999) US $3,900

Life expectancy at birth	male 63.8 yr; female 69.2 yr

Major resources	coffee, sugar, bananas, cardamom, beef, rare woods, fish, chicle

Thriving Maya culture (*above*) Guatemala is famous for the colorful dress, folk art, village markets and religious festivals – which mingle traditional and Christian practices – of its large Maya population.

Lake Atitlán (*right*), fringed by three volcanoes, is one of Guatemala's most beautiful sights. On market days, people from miles around bring their goods in brightly colored bundles to sell in the villages along the lakeside.

Belize

BELIZE, FORMERLY BRITISH HONDURAS, IS A small country on the Caribbean coast of Central America, bordered by Mexico and Guatemala.

ENVIRONMENT

Northern Belize is mostly a low-lying and often swampy plain drained by the Belize and Honda rivers; the latter forms the Mexican border. Southern Belize rises sharply from a narrow coastal strip to the Maya Mountains – a fragmented plateau of serrated ranges; the highest point is Victoria Peak. Along the coast a chain of small coral islands forms a long barrier reef, second only to Australia's.

The climate is subtropical with marked seasonal rains, usually between June and November. The coastal area is particularly vulnerable to hurricanes; in 1961 Belize City was destroyed, and the capital was moved inland to Belmopan. Dense tropical rainforests cover nearly half the country, while drier areas are characterized by open forest and savanna. The abundant wildlife includes pumas, jaguars, crocodiles and manatees.

SOCIETY

Belize was once part of the ancient Maya empire, whose remains are still to be found there. Spanish settlement did not extend into this area, and the first recorded European colonists were British logwood cutters in the 17th century. They gradually migrated into the interior, clashing with the indigenous Amerindian peoples and repelling Spanish incursions from Guatemala. Sugar plantations were later established, worked by imported African slaves. British Honduras was declared a crown colony in 1862, but newly independent Guatemala continued to claim the country. The colony became

City on water Many of the buildings in Belize are wooden and raised on stilts above the mangrove swamps that surround the town. Once the capital, Belize is still the major port and commercial center.

independent as Belize in 1981; Britain relinquished responsibility for external defense in 1993. The country remains within the Commonwealth, and has parliamentary government on British lines.

The official language is English, but the majority of people speak a Creole dialect that reflects the complex racial mix. The largest element are descendants of black Africans. Then there are Maya Indians, Black Caribs of mixed black and Amerindian descent, and a variety of Europeans and North Americans, including farmers of the Mennonite religious sect.

ECONOMY

Agriculture is the mainstay of the economy, employing more than one-quarter of the labor force, and is being actively developed. Sugar cane is the main crop, while citrus fruits and bananas are also important. Maize, rice, kidney beans and sweet potatoes are the main domestic staples. Livestock is less important, except for beef and dairy cattle, especially on Mennonite farms.

Forestry, once the principal activity, is today less important but still yields valuable rosewood, mahogany and chicle, used in chewing gum. A great deal of timber is produced not only for export but also as a chief source of fuel, and reforestation schemes are encouraged. Cooperative fisheries provide some items such as lobsters and shrimps for export.

Mineral and fuel reserves (with the exception of timber) are scanty, so both have to be imported in quantity. Manufacturing industry is small but growing, producing food products, furniture and some clothing for export. There are virtually no railroads, but there is a good road network in the north. Education, though government-funded, is mostly run by the Roman Catholic church; literacy levels are relatively high. Medical care is free, and extensive social-security schemes are in operation.

NATIONAL DATA – BELIZE				
Land area 22,965 sq km (8,867 sq mi)				
Climate		**Temperatures**		**Annual**
	Altitude m (ft)	January °C(°F)	July °C(°F)	precipitation mm (in)
Belmopan	41 (135)	23 (74)	27 (81)	1,890 (74.4)
Major physical feature highest point: Victoria Peak 1,122 m (3,681 ft)				
Population (2000 est.) 249,183				
Form of government multiparty constitutional monarchy with two legislative houses				
Armed forces total 1050				
Largest cities Belize City (49,050); Orange Walk (13,483); San Ignacio (13,260)				
Official language English				
Ethnic composition Mestizo 44.0%; Creole 30.0%; Manja 11.0%; Garifuna 7.0%; other 8.0%				
Religious affiliations Roman Catholic 61.7%; Protestant 28.9%; Baha'i 2.5%; Jewish 1.2%; other 5.7%				
Currency 1 Belize dollar (Bz$) = 100 cents				
Gross domestic product (1999) US $740 million				
Gross domestic product per capita (1999) US $3,100				
Life expectancy at birth male 67.23 yr; female 71.26 yr				
Major resources sugar cane, fruit crops, tourism, timber				

El Salvador

REPUBLIC OF EL SALVADOR

The dangers of earthquakes Heavy debris from a collapsing building landed on a car during this quake in January 2001 in El Salvador. Like the rest of Central America, the country is prone to earthquakes.

THE SMALLEST AND MOST DENSELY POPU-lated country in Central America, El Salvador lies between Guatemala to the west and Honduras to the northeast.

ENVIRONMENT

In the south a narrow Pacific coastal plain rises to a mountain range including more than 20 volcanoes. Beyond a central plain, cut by the river valleys of the Lempa, are the Metapán and Chalatenango mountain chains near the Honduran border. The climate is mainly hot, with heavy rains between May and October. Temperatures are lower in the mountains, and rainfall there is generally much higher.

The coastal plains and foothills are covered in savanna grasslands or decid-uous forest. The trees become sparser in the valleys and the central plains. Higher up the mountains there are temperate grasslands, with scattered areas of pine and deciduous forest. Large areas of the land are cultivated, and mammals are therefore less prolific than elsewhere in Central America.

SOCIETY

Between 1524 and 1539 Spanish invaders overran the Pipil Indian kingdom of Cuzcatlán, creating the territories of San Salvador and Sonsonate. In 1821 the area became independent as part of the Mexican empire. On the empire's collapse in 1823, San Salvador and Sonsonate were united to form the state of El Salvador. However, even after independence, inter-nal strife remained, and in 1931, when there was a brief move toward democ-racy, there followed a succession of mili-tary dictatorships.

From 1979 to 1992 the left-wing Fara-bundo Martí Front for National Libera-tion (FLMN) fought a guerrilla war against successive governments. The con-flict led to the deaths of tens of thousands of people. A new constitution in 1983 brought in direct elections to a 60-member legislative assembly but failed to end the civil war. The FLMN boycotted the 1989 elections, which were won by the right-wing Arena party. In January 1992 the United Nations sponsored a successful peace conference in Mexico, and in the following January the last FLMN troops were demobilized.

Most of the population are mestizos of mixed Amerindian and European ances-try, and the majority are Roman Catholic. The church played a leading role in anti-government movements in the early 1980s. The official language is Spanish.

ECONOMY

The economy is predominantly agricul-tural; the land has, in the main, been owned by a small elite of white people, but is now being slowly redistributed by the government. Coffee is a vital export crop, along with cotton, maize and sugar cane.

There are few important mineral re-sources. Most power comes from a hydro-electric project on the Lempa river, east of the capital, San Salvador. Massive investment in the 1970s brought a host of new manufacturing industries, but the civil war caused much damage to the infrastructure and the economy. In the early 1990s, fuel oil, petroleum and food processing were the major industries.

The El Salvador National Railroad oper-ates a narrow-gauge railroad system. There are three Pacific ports, and a road and rail link to Puerto Barrios in Guatemala.

The welfare system protects those in paid employment, but unemployment is high. Health and sanitation are often poor, and disease is common in many rural areas, where there are few trained medical personnel.

Primary education is free and compul-sory. There are three state universities and adult literacy had risen to 71.5 percent in 1995.

NATIONAL DATA – EL SALVADOR				
Land area 21,041 sq km (8,124 sq mi)				
Climate		**Temperatures**		**Annual**
	Altitude m (ft)	January °C(°F)	July °C(°F)	precipitation mm (in)
San Salvador	682 (2,238)	22 (71)	24 (75)	1,775 (69.9)
Major physical features highest point: Izalco 2,386 m (7,828 ft); longest river: Lempa 320 km (200 mi)				
Population (1999 est.) 5,839,079				
Form of government multiparty republic with one legislative house				
Armed forces army 28,000; navy 700; air force 2,000				
Largest cities San Salvador (capital – 1,522,000); Santa Ana (239,000); San Miguel (192,000)				
Official language Spanish				
Ethnic composition Mestizo 94.0%; Amerindian 5.0%; White 1.0%				
Religious affiliations Roman Catholic 75.0%; others 25.0%				
Currency 1 colón = 100 centavos				
Gross domestic product (1999) US $18.1 billion				
Gross domestic product per capita (1999) US $3,100				
Life expectancy at birth male 66.7 yr; female 73.5 yr				
Major resources coffee, cotton, corn (maize), sugar cane, hydroelectric power				

Honduras

REPUBLIC OF HONDURAS

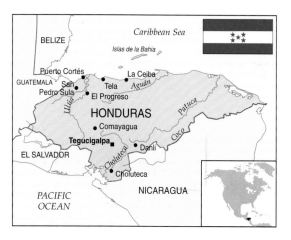

M OUNTAINOUS HONDURAS LIES BETWEEN Guatemala and El Salvador to the west, and Nicaragua to the southeast.

ENVIRONMENT

From the Caribbean coastal plain in the north, several deep river valleys cut southwestward into the central uplands; the coastal plains become broader toward the east. South of the mountains, a narrow lowland strip borders the very short Pacific coastline.

The hot, humid climate is moderated by altitude inland. The mainly seasonal rainfall is highest in the north and east, where destructive summer hurricanes may also strike, and is lowest in sheltered inland valleys and basins.

In the east, coastal mangroves and palms give way to sandy plains, pine-savanna and dense rainforest near the Nicaraguan border. The highland areas support grassland and broadleaf forests, with further savanna forest and mangroves on the Pacific coast. Although many forest areas have been cleared for agriculture, there is still a profusion of wildlife: insects, birds and reptiles as well as peccaries, pumas, jaguars and tapirs.

SOCIETY

Honduras was once an important center of the Maya civilization. It was first settled by Europeans in 1522. After a savage war with the indigenous Amerindians, the Spanish made Honduras part of Guatemala. Independence as part of Mexico came in 1821, and full independence in 1838. Government became increasingly unstable in the early 20th century, and the United States sent in marines to protect their investments, particularly in the banana trade. The 1932 election produced a dictator, General Tiburcio Carlas Andino (1876–1969), who ruled until 1949 despite the frequent uprisings. Later governments have been generally short-lived, and the military has often kept effective control. Until 1989 Honduras sheltered the Contra rebels who, with American backing, were fighting the Nicaraguan government.

The Honduran constitution has been rewritten at least 16 times since 1821. That of 1982 provides for a 128-member legislative assembly and a president, both directly elected. In practice ultimate power rests with the army. The population is still mostly rural, consisting of mestizos of mixed Amerindian and European ancestry. The official language is Spanish, and the majority are Roman Catholic.

ECONOMY

Just over one third of the work force are farmers. Bananas and coffee are the major export crops, but Hurricane Mitch caused extensive damage in Honduras in 1998, affecting economic recovery and future growth badly. Maize, beans and rice are important staples, but the majority of the population is still affected by malnutrition. Mineral resources are quite considerable, but have remained largely unexplored. Energy comes mainly from hydroelectricity; a small amount is from imported fuels. Small-scale manufacturing produces a variety of goods such as furniture, textiles, footwear, chemicals and cement.

There are few railroads and freight and passengers rely mostly on the extensive road network, reducing the importance of domestic air services. Welfare benefits are mostly limited to urban workers. Health and sanitation are often poor, and tropical diseases are common, with few doctors on hand to treat them. Education is free and compulsory, but often inaccessible to rural communities; there are too few teachers, and illiteracy is relatively high.

Legacy of the Maya (*above*) A carved head at the ruins of Copán. This great city, first inhabited in 2000 BC, was the heart of Honduras' Maya civilization.

"The last paradise" (*left*) So-named by enchanted tourists, the Islas de la Bahía, 50 km (30 mi) off the coast of Honduras, were once a base from which pirates launched their attacks on Spanish ships.

NATIONAL DATA – HONDURAS			
Land area 112,088 sq km (43,277 sq mi)			

Climate		**Temperatures**		**Annual**
	Altitude m (ft)	January °C(°F)	July °C(°F)	precipitation mm (in)
Tegucigalpa	1,004 (3,294)	19 (66)	23 (74)	1,621 (63.8)

Major physical features highest point: Cerro Las Minas 2,827 m (9,275 ft); longest river: Coco (part) 685 km (425 mi)

Population (1999 est.) 5,997,327

Form of government multiparty republic with one legislative house

Armed forces army 14,000; navy 1,000; air force 1,800

Largest cities Tegucigalpa (capital – 775,000); San Pedro Sula (368,500)

Official language Spanish

Ethnic composition Mestizo 89.9%; Amerindian 6.7%; Black 2.1%; White 1.3%

Religious affiliations Roman Catholic 97.0%; others 3.0%

Currency 1 lempira (L) = 100 centavos

Gross domestic product per capita (1999) US $2,050

Gross domestic product (1999) US $14.1 billion

Life expectancy at birth male 63.2 yr; female 66.3 yr

Major resources bananas, coffee, shellfish, timber, gold, silver, copper, lead

Nicaragua

REPUBLIC OF NICARAGUA

THE CENTRAL AMERICAN STATE OF NICA-ragua lies between Honduras to the northwest and Costa Rica to the south.

ENVIRONMENT

Its eastern plains are bordered with lagoons and swamps along the Caribbean or Mosquito Coast. The land rises westward toward a roughly triangular highland area bordering Honduras. Westward again are Lake Nicaragua and Lake Managua, and beyond them is a second, smaller range of about 40 volcanoes, flanked to the west by a narrow lowland belt. Some volcanoes are still active, and the area is subject to severe earthquakes.

Nicaragua's tropical climate is hotter and drier on the Pacific side, where the rainy season lasts from May to November. On the Caribbean side it lasts for at least nine months, and there is a greater risk of hurricanes. Temperatures are lower on the northern mountains. Most of the western half of the country is covered in savanna, and the eastern half in tropical rainforest. Wildlife includes crocodiles, pumas and peccaries.

SOCIETY

Nicaragua, like its neighbors, was conquered by Spain in the 16th century, and gained full independence in 1838. Later politics were dominated by Conservatives (the coffee and sugar plantation owners) and Liberals (artisans and small landowners). Great Britain and the United States both had strategic interests in Nicaragua, and the United States sent in military forces on two occasions to support Conservative regimes.

From 1934-1979 Nicaragua was ruled by a military regime dominated by the Somoza family. In 1979 rebel forces seized power in a country devastated by war and formed the left-wing Sandinista government. Until 1990 the United States supported the guerrilla opponents (Contras) of the new Sandinista regime. US advisors trained them in neighboring Honduras. Elections followed their withdrawal in 1990, in which the opposition coalition, the National Opposition Union (UNO), came to power. The president is elected by a majority, and the 92-member national assembly on a proportional basis. Constitutional deadlock ensued after the president blocked reforms passed by the national assembly in 1994.

Most of the population are mestizos of mixed Amerindian and European descent. Spanish is the official language, and most people are Roman Catholic.

ECONOMY

At the end of the 1990s, Nicaragua was showing signs of economic recovery from the effects of the civil war, but was devestated by Hurricane Mitch in 1998, estimated to cause US$ 1bn damage. Despite international aid, growth will take some time to resume. The chief crops are cotton, coffee and bananas. Mineral resources are plentiful, but only gold and silver are intensively mined. Food processing, chemicals and textiles are the chief industries. Industrial development is limited.

Communications are poor except in the west, and even here only half the roads are passable when it rains. Railroads are also limited to the west, leaving eastern areas dependent on water and air transportation. Housing, sanitation and water supplies are inadequate, with tropical diseases common. Health care is difficult to obtain despite reforms by the Sandinistas, and there are few trained doctors. There is limited social security for workers in Managua. Primary education is free, and enrollment is high. Few receive secondary education, but literacy levels are on the increase.

A fertile land Crops flourish on the rich volcanic soils of Nicaragua. Some volcanoes are active, but earthquakes are a worse threat; the capital Managua was almost totally destroyed in 1972.

NATIONAL DATA – NICARAGUA

Land area	120,349 sq km (46,467 sq mi)		

Climate	Altitude m (ft)	Temperatures January °C(°F)	July °C(°F)	Annual precipitation mm (in)
Managua	55 (180)	26 (79)	30 (86)	1,140 (44.9)

Major physical feature	highest point: Cerro Mogotón 2,107 m (6,913 ft)

Population	(2000 est.) 4,812,569

Form of government	multiparty republic with one legislative house

Armed forces	army 13,500; navy 500; air force 1,200

Capital city	Managua (864,201)

Official language	Spanish

Ethnic composition	Mestizo 69.0%; White 17.0%; Black 9.0%; Amerindian 5.0%

Religious affiliations	Roman Catholic 95.0%; Protestant 5.0%

Currency	1 gold córdoba (C$) = 100 centavos

Gross domestic product	(1999) US $12.5 billion

Gross domestic product per capita	(1999) US $2,650

Life expectancy at birth	male 64.7 yr; female 69.6 yr

Major resources	cotton, coffee, gold, silver, copper, tungsten, lead, zinc, timber, fish

Costa Rica

REPUBLIC OF COSTA RICA

COSTA RICA LIES ON THE CENTRAL AMERICAN isthmus between Nicaragua to the north and Panama to the east.

ENVIRONMENT

From the Caribbean lowlands in the northeast the land rises gently to a mountainous backbone. The Cordillera de Guanacaste, including four major volcanoes, runs southeastward from the Nicaraguan border to meet the much higher Cordillera Central. Between this and the volcanic Cordillera de Talamanca in the southeast lies the Meseta or Valle Central, where the capital, San José, lies in an area also subject to both volcanic eruptions and earthquakes. The narrow Pacific coastal belt and the Caribbean coast are lined with mangrove swamps and white, sandy beaches.

The climate is generally hot and rainy, but there is a marked dry season on the Pacific coast, whereas the Caribbean lowlands have rain throughout the year. Both areas are heavily forested, with an enormous variety of birds, insects and reptiles, and a mixture of South and North American mammals. The higher Central and Talamanca ranges are warm and temperate, with dry seasons on the more sheltered southern slopes.

SOCIETY

Costa Rica was not fully controlled by Spain until 1570. Its later history was broadly similar to that of the rest of Central America until independence in 1838. Coffee exports put the country on a sound financial footing, and its isolation largely protected it from the more dramatic events in neighboring lands. In 1890 the free election of President José Joaquin Rodríguez set a pattern of democracy that survived revolutions in 1917 and 1948. The new constitution of 1949 disbanded the army to prevent any future military coups. The president and the 57-member legislative assembly are each directly elected for a four-year term. More recently Costa Rica has suffered the effects of eathquake damage, falling coffee prices, foreign debt and an influx of refugees from its troubled neighbors.

The population profile is unusual for Central America in that most people are of European descent, with only a minority of mestizos of mixed Amerindian, European and African extraction. Most are Roman Catholic, and Spanish is the official language.

ECONOMY

The main cash crops are coffee and bananas. Maize, beans and rice are the chief staples, but food still has to be imported. Timber resources have enormous potential, and there are significant bauxite deposits. Hydroelectricity is being increasingly developed, but much electrical power still comes from diesel plants. Manufactures for export include medicines, paper products, sheet metal and electrical machinery.

Apart from the Pan-American Highway, the limited road network, centers on the Valle Central, which is also linked by railroad to ports on the Pacific and Caribbean coasts. There is an international airport at Juan Santa Maria, near the capital, and a few other airports serve domestic flights. There are five daily

A craftsman at work in Sarchí, Costa Rica's handicrafts center. This prosperous and peaceful country – it has no army – has largely managed to avoid the political conflict that has troubled so much else of Central America.

newspapers and a single television network; there is no government censorship.

Welfare benefits are provided for those in employment, and a preventive health program is in place. Rural areas, however, are less well served and malnutrition and disease are a problem. Education is free and compulsory, enrollment is high, and so are literacy levels.

NATIONAL DATA – COSTA RICA			
Land area 51,100 sq km (19,730 sq mi)			

Climate		Temperatures		Annual
	Altitude m (ft)	January °C(°F)	July °C(°F)	precipitation mm (in)
San José	1,146 (3,760)	19 (66)	21 (69)	1,793 (70.6)

Major physical feature highest point: Chirripó 3,820 m (12,533 ft)	
Population (2000 est.) 3,710,558	
Form of government multiparty republic with one legislative house	
Armed forces civil guard 3,000	
Capital city San José (341,708)	
Official language Spanish	
Ethnic composition European 87.0%; Mestizo 7.0%; Black/Mulatto 3.0%; Eastern Asian 2.0%; Amerindian 1.0%	
Religious affiliations Roman Catholic 95.0% (official religion); others 5.0%	
Currency 1 Costa Rican colón = 100 céntimos	
Gross domestic product (1999) US $26 billion	
Gross domestic product per capita (1999) US $7,100	
Life expectancy at birth male 73.6 yr; female 78.6 yr	
Major resources coffee, bananas, timber, hydroelectric power	

Panama

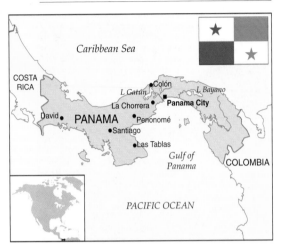

PANAMA IS A STRATEGICALLY POSITIONED country forming an S-shaped neck of land that links together Central and South America.

ENVIRONMENT

At its narrowest point, in the center of the country, the Panama Canal links the Caribbean Sea and the Pacific Ocean. West of the canal the mountains of the Serrania de Tabasara are flanked by narrow coastal plains on either side. In the southeast of this area the land rises once again to the mountains of the Azuero Peninsula. East of the canal, two mountain arcs run parallel to the Pacific and Caribbean coastlines.

The climate is generally hot and wet throughout the year, but the mountains are cooler, and there is a marked dry season along the Pacific coast. Most of the country is forested, with tropical rainforest predominating. Plant and animal life are rich and abundant except in the mainly deforested Canal Zone.

SOCIETY

After 300 years of Spanish rule, Panama achieved freedom from Spain in 1821, though it remained a part of neighboring Colombia. The California Gold Rush of 1849 provided the incentive for building a canal across the Central American isthmus that would make the journey from the eastern United States to the booming western states easier and faster than overland travel. The project finally got under way in 1879, but foundered ten years later. In 1903 the United States helped Panama to secure independence from Colombia in return for perpetual control of the 16 km (10 mi) wide Canal Zone. The canal was finally opened to traffic in 1914.

In 1977, after many years of unrest, a

The Panama Canal (*above*) links the Pacific and the Atlantic Oceans. The trade generated by this great feat of engineering – a tourist attraction in itself – is the mainstay of the Panamanian economy.

"The valley of the moon" (*left*) is the meaning of Chiriqui province's name. This fertile area is famous for its Swiss-style mountain chalets, and for cattle and horse-breeding ranches on the coastal plain.

process began whereby formal control of the Canal Zone was gradually to be returned to Panama. Ownership of the canal itself was transferred in 2000. The 1983 constitution provided for the election of a president, two vice-presidents and a 67-member legislative assembly, all of these for a five-year term. However, political unrest continued, and in 1989 General Manuel Noriega (b. 1940), who had assumed effective power, was ousted by the United States, accused of drug-running and election rigging.

Most Panamanians are mestizos or mulattos of mixed Amerindian, European and African descent; the official language is Spanish. The birth rate is the lowest in Central America, but economic growth is slower than population growth.

ECONOMY

The chief export crops are bananas, coffee, and sugar. Rice, beans and corn are the main staples. Livestock is also important, and Panama is largely self-sufficient in food. Fishing is encouraged, and shrimps are now a major export. Mineral resources are scanty except for copper ore, and power comes largely from hydroelectricity. The industrial base around Panama City manufactures consumer goods, building materials and also petroleum products, as a result of the construction of a trans-Panamanian oil pipeline.

Most of the country's revenue comes from the service industries, including finance, trade and tourism. The main earners are the Panama Canal and the Colón Free Zone, which is one of the largest trading centers in the world. There is an extensive road system, and a railroad runs parallel to the canal. There are good port facilities on both coasts, and more than 100 airports.

Welfare services are well developed, and medical facilities are adequate in most parts of the country, though tuberculosis is common in urban slum areas. Education is free and compulsory, and higher education is available.

NATIONAL DATA – PANAMA				
Land area 77,082 sq km (29,762 sq mi)				

Climate		**Temperatures**		**Annual**
	Altitude m (ft)	January °C(°F)	July °C(°F)	precipitation mm (in)
Panama	36 (118)	26 (79)	27 (81)	1,770 (69.7)

Major physical features highest point: Volcán Barú 3,475 m (11,400 ft); largest lake: Gatún 430 sq km (166 sq mi)

Population (2000 est.) 2,808,268

Form of government multiparty republic with one legislative house

Armed forces army abolished; National Maritime service 400

Capital city Panama (463,093)

Official language Spanish

Ethnic composition Mestizo 70.0%; Other 14%; White 10.0%; Amerindian 6.0%

Religious affiliations Roman Catholic 84.0%; Protestant 4.8%; Muslim 4.5%; others 6.7%

Currency 1 balboa (B) = 100 centesimos

Gross domestic product (1999) US $21 billion

Gross domestic product per capita (1999) US $7,600

Life expectancy at birth male 71.9 yr; female 77.5 yr

Major resources bananas, sugar cane, coffee, timber (mahogany), shrimp, copper ore, tourism

Cuba

REPUBLIC OF CUBA

CUBA IS AN ISLAND STATE IN THE CARIBBEAN lying directly south of Florida. It consists of a single long island, flanked by the much smaller Isla de la Juventud (Isle of Youth) to the south.

ENVIRONMENT

The main island of Cuba is characterized by wide stretches of lowland divided by three main mountain areas. The largest of these, in the east, comprises the Sierra del Cristal and the Sierra Maestra along the southeast coast, the highest point being Pico Turquino. The lower central chain crosses the island to the east of Cienfuegos, while the Sierra de Los Organos runs along the northwestern tip beyond the capital, Havana. The coastline is irregular, and is lined with numerous mangroves, beaches and coral reefs.

The climate is semitropical, with heavy seasonal rainfall and a tendency to hurricanes. Rivers also vary with the seasons, and only a few are navigable. Although there has been considerable deforestation, the island's forests are still extensive, including tropical near-jungle.

SOCIETY

Cuba was among the earliest Spanish settlements after Christopher Columbus (1451–1506) landed there in 1492. From the early 16th century it was divided into large estates, worked at first by enslaved Amerindians, then by African slaves until slavery was finally abolished in 1886. Independence from Spain was achieved in 1899 after two uprisings, the latter led by José Martí (1853–95) and in which US troops became involved – they finally left in 1902. In 1959 the decaying regime of Fulgencio Batista (1901–73) was ousted by the communist revolutionary movement led by Fidel Castro (b.1927). Castro remodeled the Cuban state as a personal dictatorship on Soviet lines, but significantly improved the living standards of the poor. The United States imposed a trade embargo which lasted into the 2000s, and supported an unsuccessful countercoup in the Bay of Pigs on Cuba's south coast in 1961. From then on, Cuba became increasingly dependent on the Soviet Union. Cuba's first direct elections were held in 1994, but only approved Communist Party candidates were allowed to run. Further relaxation of Castro's hard-line policies was seen in January 1998 when the Pope visited Cuba.

ECONOMY

The suspension of Soviet financial aid and technical advice in the early 1990s severely affected the Cuban economy. GDP declined by 35 percent during the period 1989-93 and growth was only slowly resumed in 1994. However, severe hurricanes in 1993, 1994 and 1996 devastated the sugar cane harvest and the economy slumped badly. The main cash crops are sugar cane, tobacco, citrus fruits and coffee. There has been some relaxation of state control of agriculture and limited free trading is allowed. Food has to be imported to meet domestic needs. Fishing, chiefly for tuna, has been developed with government support.

Large nickel deposits supply Cuba's other main export. Other reserves include copper, chromite and iron ore. Some petroleum has been found, but most fuel has to be imported. The traditional industries are food and tobacco processing, but this sector has been greatly diversified to include such items as steel, fertilizers, machinery and electrical goods.

The transportation network is well developed, with an emphasis on public service. Social benefits and health care are available, and literacy is high.

NATIONAL DATA – CUBA				
Land area 110,861 sq km (42,804 sq mi)				
Climate		**Temperatures**		**Annual**
	Altitude m (ft)	**January** °C(°F)	**July** °C(°F)	**precipitation** mm (in)
Havana	49 (161)	21 (70)	27 (81)	1,167 (45.9)
Major physical features highest point: Turquino 2,005 m (6,578 ft); longest river: Cauto 249 km (155 mi)				
Population (2000 est.) 11,141,997				
Form of government one-party republic with one legislative house				
Armed forces army 38,000; navy 5,000; air force 10,000				
Largest cities Havana (capital – 2,143,406); Santiago de Cuba (443,149); Camagüey (288,760); Holguín (241,060); Guantánamo (217,484); Santa Clara (207,000)				
Official language Spanish				
Ethnic composition Mulatto 51.0%; White 37.0%; Black 11.0%; Chinese 1.0%				
Religious affiliations nonreligious 55.2%; Roman Catholic 39.7%; Afro-Cuban 1.7%; Protestant 3.4%				
Currency 1 Cuban peso (CuP) = 100 centavos				
Gross domestic product (1999) US $18.6 billion				
Gross domestic product per capita (1999) US $1,700				
Life expectancy at birth male 73.4 yr; female 78.3 yr				
Major resources sugar cane, tobacco, timber, fisheries, citrus fruits, coffee, nickel				

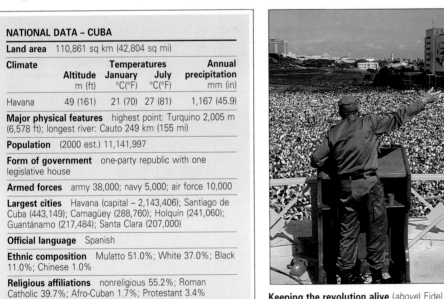

Keeping the revolution alive (*above*) Fidel Castro – Central America's most charismatic and durable leader – holds the local crowd spellbound with his oratory.

Money to spend (*right*) Automobiles parked proudly outside their owners' homes attest to good wages; yet despite many advances in living standards, Cuba has failed to industrialize and diversify its economy.

Bahamas

COMMONWEALTH OF THE BAHAMAS

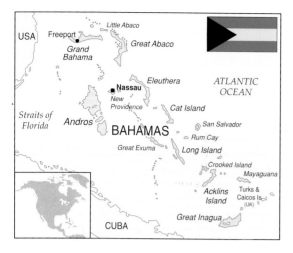

T HE BAHAMAS ARE A LONG ARCHIPELAGO OF some 700 islands and cays (reefs) lying in the Caribbean Sea southeast of Florida, in the United States, and north of Cuba.

ENVIRONMENT

The islands are very much alike; they are all exposed segments of a single coralline limestone shelf. They are low-lying, apart from a few hills formed by windblown sand, and their coastlines are fringed with mangroves, lagoons and coral reefs. The climate is mild and humid, but the porous limestone of the landscape means that rainfall is easily lost. Caribbean pine forest covers much of the larger islands, such as New Providence, Grand Bahama, Great Abaco and Andros. The teeming birds and colorful sea life along the reefs attract numerous tourists, who create considerable conservation problems.

SOCIETY

The native Arawak people were forcibly removed by Spanish slave raiders, who put them to work on Hispaniola. In the 17th century British settlers arrived from Bermuda, but the colony degenerated into a pirate haven. Numbers were later swelled by Loyalist refugees from the American War of Independence (1775–83). The islands thrived briefly on illicit trade with the United States during the Civil War (1861–67) and later during Prohibition in the 1920s, but they gained more lasting prosperity from tourism following World War II. Internal self-government was granted by Britain in 1967, and full independence in 1973. Government is along British lines, with a governor-general representing the sovereign as head of state. There is a prime minister and a two-chamber parliament. Most Bahamians are of African descent, and English is the dominant language.

Opulent cruise ships line up in Nassau harbor, bringing the wealthy North American tourists upon whom the Bahamian economy depends Nassau is also an important banking center

ECONOMY

Since only a tiny percentage of the land is arable, there is little agriculture beyond fruit and vegetable growing. Salt is the main mineral produced, although refining of imported petroleum for export is a major industry; others include pharmaceuticals, rum distilling and fruit canning. New legislation in the financial sector has made way for the development of international banking.

Tourism, however, is the country's economic mainstay, and has been developed on a huge scale; visitors flock to the golden palm-fringed beaches, warm waters and sunshine. Poor road provision is offset by good air and sea communications. Education, social benefits and health care are widely available, and living conditions are good.

NATIONAL DATA – BAHAMAS

Land area	13,939 sq km (5,382 sq mi)		

Climate		**Temperatures**		**Annual**
	Altitude m (ft)	January °C(°F)	July °C(°F)	precipitation mm (in)
Nassau	4 (13)	22 (71)	27 (81)	1,179 (46.4)

Major physical features   highest point: Cat Island 63 m (206 ft); largest island: Andros 5,957 sq km (2,300 sq mi)

Population   (2000 est.) 294,982

Form of government   multiparty constitutional monarchy with two legislative houses

Armed forces   paramilitary coastguard 830

Capital city   Nassau (178,000)

Official language   English

Ethnic composition   Black 72.3%; Mixed 14.2%; White 12.9%; others 0.6%

Religious affiliations   Baptist 32.1%; Anglican 20.1%; Roman Catholic 18.8%; Methodist 6.1%; other Christians 17.0%; others 5.9%

Currency   1 Bahamian dollar (B$) = 100 cents

Gross domestic product (1999) US $5.58 billion

Gross domestic product per capita   (1998) US $20,000

Life expectancy at birth   male 70.94 yr; female 77.64 yr

Major resources   tourism, salt, timber

Haiti

REPUBLIC OF HAITI

HAITI, ONE OF THE POOREST COUNTRIES IN the world, occupies the western third of the island of Hispaniola in the central Caribbean east of Cuba. The Dominican Republic occupies the eastern part.

ENVIRONMENT

Two mountainous peninsulas enclose the central plain of the Artibonite river. The northern range, called the Massif du Nord, extends into the heart of the Dominican Republic, where it becomes the Cordillera Central.

The climate is generally hot with seasonal rains, but temperature and rainfall patterns vary. Some areas are practically desert; others, chiefly on mountain slopes, were once densely forested. Centuries of deforestation, however, have greatly reduced this, and there has been little attempt at conservation. Bird life is rich and varied, but land animals are scarce; crocodiles are found in the rivers.

SOCIETY

Hispaniola's indigenous Arawak peoples were wiped out by the first Spanish conquistadors, through enslavement and disease. This left the western part of the island largely unsettled, and it came to be used as a base by French freebooters and traders. In the 17th century it became the French colony of Saint Domingue. The plantations, worked by African slaves imported in hundreds of thousands, were immensely profitable. The majority of today's population are Creole-speaking descendants of these Africans. Their animist religions mixed with elements of the official Roman Catholic faith, giving rise to the syncratic religious cult, known as Voodoo, which involves the worship of their ancestors.

The French Revolution inspired bloody slave revolts, led by Pierre Toussaint-L'Ouverture (1746–1803), himself a former slave. He was betrayed by Napoleon (1769–1821), who reimposed slavery, but his successor Jean–Jacques Dessalines (1758–1806) drove out the French. Dessalines and his successors sought to modernize Haiti. They even gained temporary control of eastern Hispaniola (then Santo Domingo), but they were brought down by internal strife. A series of brutal dictatorships followed, interrupted by United States control from 1915 to 1934.

Further dictatorships followed until 1957, when François Duvalier ("Papa Doc", 1907–71) was elected president. The secret police, the "Tontons Macoutes," dominated the country during Papa Doc's regime. He was succeeded in 1971 by his son Jean-Claude ("Baby Doc", b.1951) who was forced to flee the country in 1986. In 1990 Fr. Jean-Bertrand Aristide (b.1953), a radical Roman Catholic priest, became Haiti's first left-wing president. He was deposed by a military coup in 1991 but reinstated in 1994 following a UN naval blockade and peaceful invasion by 20,000 US troops. In 1995 a UN peacekeeping force took over and Aristide was succeeded by Renee Préval.

ECONOMY

Haiti's impoverished population depends largely on subsistence agriculture. Rice, corn and various fruits are the main staple crops, while coffee and some sugar cane are grown for export. Small amounts of bauxite, copper and other metals are mined, and power is drawn mostly from hydroelectric plants. Unrest has discouraged tourism, once a major earner, and the country depends on foreign aid. Social services and health care are poor, and education, though free and compulsory, is poorly resourced outside the capital, Port-au-Prince.

Echoes of Africa Over 90 percent of Haiti's people are descendants of African slaves. Haiti became the world's first black republic in 1804 after the slaves revolted against their French masters.

NATIONAL DATA – HAITI				
Land area 27,400 sq km (10,569 sq mi)				
Climate	Altitude m (ft)	Temperatures January °C(°F)	July °C(°F)	Annual precipitation mm (in)
Port-au-Prince	37 (121)	25 (77)	29 (84)	1,321 (52.0)
Population (2000 est.) 8,867,995				
Form of government multiparty republic with two legislative houses				
Armed forces interim public security force 3,000				
Capital city Port-au-Prince (917,112)				
Official languages Haitian Creole, French				
Ethnic composition Black 95.0%; Mulatto 4.9%; White 0.1%				
Religious affiliations Roman Catholic 80.3%; Protestant 15.8%; others 3.9% (Voodoo is practiced by many people)				
Currency 1 gourde (G) = 100 centimes				
Gross domestic product (1999) US $9.2 billion				
Gross domestic product per capita (1999) US $1,340				
Life expectancy at birth male 49.5 yr; female 53.9 yr				
Major resources coffee, sugar cane, bauxite, copper				

Jamaica

JAMAICA

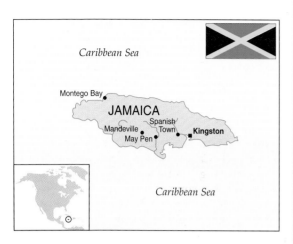

THE LUSH, TROPICAL ISLAND STATE OF Jamaica lies in the Caribbean south of Cuba and west of Haiti.

ENVIRONMENT

Apart from the irregular coastal plains and several fertile river basins, mostly in the south and west, the land rises sharply to a limestone plateau, whose rugged, fragmented landscape was created by both heavy faulting and erosion. This is especially true of the Cockpit Country toward the northwest, with its typical karst scenery of bare limestone pavements and underground cave systems. Several mountain ranges rise above the plateau, the highest of these being the Blue Mountains in the east, topped by Blue Mountain Peak.

The climate is mainly tropical, with even temperatures all the year round. The mostly seasonal rains fall heavily on the northeastern slopes. These are still clad in the tropical rainforest that once covered most of the island, but the southern lowlands in the rainshadow of the mountains, support only savanna scrub: irrigation is necessary for agriculture in this arid port of the island. The wildlife includes the Steamertail hummingbird, Jamaica's national bird.

SOCIETY

Jamaica's indigenous Arawak peoples were wiped out by the Spanish settlers who followed Christopher Columbus (1451–1506), and African slaves were imported to work the land. The island was captured by Britain in 1655; it soon became an important base for buccaneers, who mounted attacks on Spanish ships. The Spanish, in the meantime, gave assistance to the Maroons – escaped slaves who had taken refuge in the Cockpit Country, and who harried the British for nearly two centuries. Jamaica became

an immensely profitable colony through its slave-worked sugar cane plantations, but this prosperity ended with the abolition of slavery in 1833. In 1866 Jamaica became a crown colony, and banana growing was introduced to help restore the island's fortunes.

Local self-government was introduced after World War II, leading to full independence in 1962. Jamaica is a constitutional monarchy within the Commonwealth. The sovereign is represented by the governor-general, and a two-chamber parliament on the British model is headed by a prime minister and cabinet. The two main parties are the moderate Jamaica Labour Party and the left-wing People's National Party.

The population is mostly English-speaking and of African descent, but there are several ethnic minorities, including Indians and Chinese. Life for many of the inhabitants is harsh, and poverty-stricken slums sit side by side with the wealthy tourist areas. Rastafarianism, the religious-political movement that regards Ethiopia, in Africa, as the spiritual homeland of black people, originated in the island.

ECONOMY

Agriculture has declined but remains an important sector. Sugar cane and bananas are still the main cash crops, along with coffee, cocoa and fruit; peppers and ginger are also grown. Staples are grown mostly at subsistence levels and for local sale. Forestry is underdeveloped, but re-afforestation programs re at work. Fisheries are much more significant, with modern fishing fleets.

The main mineral resource is bauxite,

Beyond the beach Few tourists venture to the waterfront areas of Kingston, once the hub of city life but now in decay since the large passenger liners and fruit ships have ceased to call.

and alumina processing is one of the main industries. Other varied activities include printing, textile manufacture and food processing, including rum distilling and sugar production. These supply a thriving export market, but tourism provides an even larger source of foreign income; nearly a million visitors a year are attracted by the beauty of the lush tropical island.

The transportation network is generally good, and health, welfare and housing are government priorities. Education is free and widely available at all levels.

NATIONAL DATA – JAMAICA				
Land area 10,991 sq km (4,244 sq mi)				
Climate		Temperatures		Annual
	Altitude m (ft)	January °C(°F)	July °C(°F)	precipitation mm (in)
Kingston	34 (112)	24 (76)	27 (81)	800 (31.5)
Major physical feature highest point: Blue Mountain Peak 2,256 m (7,402 ft)				
Population (2000 est.) 2,652,689				
Form of government multiparty constitutional monarchy with two legislative houses				
Armed forces army 3,000; Coast Guard 150; air force 170				
Capital city Kingston (644,000)				
Official language English				
Ethnic composition Black 76.3%; Afro-European 15.1%; Amerindian/Afro-Indian 3.4%; White 3.2%; others 2.0%				
Religious affiliations Protestant 55.9%; Roman Catholic 5.0%; nonreligious 17.7%; others 10.2%; not stated 11.2%				
Currency 1 Jamaican dollar (J$) = 100 cents				
Gross domestic product (1999) US $8.8 billion				
Gross domestic product per capita (1999) US $3,350				
Life expectancy at birth male 73.2 yr; female 78.1 yr				
Major resources sugar cane, tourism, bananas, rum, coffee, cocoa, other tropical fruit, bauxite				

Dominican Republic

T HE DOMINICAN REPUBLIC OCCUPIES THE eastern part of the Caribbean island of Hispaniola. It is twice as large as its western neighbor Haiti, and there are many marked contrasts between the two.

ENVIRONMENT

The landscape is mountainous but varied. At its heart lies the mighty Cordillera Central, which extends into Haiti as the Massif du Nord. The highest peak, Pico Duarte, is also the highest point in the Caribbean islands. There are several lesser ranges along the north coast, in the east and in the southwest bordering Haiti. These are interspersed by extensive lowlands, including the long Cibao Valley

NATIONAL DATA – DOMINICAN REPUBLIC				
Land area 48,443 sq km (18,704 sq mi)				
Climate		**Temperatures**		**Annual precipitation**
	Altitude m (ft)	**January** °C(°F)	**July** °C(°F)	mm (in)
Santo Domingo	17 (56)	24 (75)	27 (81)	1,400 (55.1)
Major physical feature highest point: Pico Duarte 3,175 m (10,417 ft)				
Population (2000 est.) 8,442,533				
Form of government multiparty republic with two legislative houses				
Armed forces army 15,000; navy 4,000; air force 5,500				
Largest cities Santo Domingo (capital – 1,609,699); Santiago (365,463); La Romana (140,204)				
Official language Spanish				
Ethnic composition Mulatto 73.0%; White 16.0%; Black 11.0%				
Religious affiliations Roman Catholic 91.9%				
Currency 1 Dominican Republic peso (RD$) = 100 centavos				
Gross domestic product (1999) US $43.7 billion				
Gross domestic product per capita (1999) US $5,400				
Life expectancy at birth male 67.9 yr; female 72.4 yr				
Major resources sugar cane, tobacco, cocoa, coffee, bauxite, salt, nickel, tourism				

in the north, and much of the south coast to the east of the capital, Santo Domingo.

The climate is mainly tropical with seasonal rains, but the mountainous terrain produces considerable variations in temperature and rainfall. The north and east have high rainfall, fertile soils and lush evergreen forests. However, low-lying areas in the south are dry to the point of desert, supporting only savanna scrub. Wildlife is relatively sparse apart from a great variety of migratory birds that pass through. Alligators and flamingoes live along the rivers.

SOCIETY

Hispaniola was first colonized by Spain, but in the 17th century the western third was ceded to France. The rest remained Spanish as Santo Domingo, but it later came under French control too. The French imported African slaves in great numbers, and established a profitable plantation economy. In 1821 Santo Domingo declared its independence as the Dominican Republic. However, it was immediately occupied by Haiti until Juan Pablo Duarte (1813–76) secured independence for the Dominican Republic in 1844. In the 1860s the country became Spanish again for a short time.

The republic has largely been ruled by dictators, with only brief periods of democratic rule. From 1916 to 1924 it was occupied by the United States, who did much to modernize the country. In 1930 Rafael Trujillo Molina (1891–1961) seized power, but his relentless suppression of

Tourism on the Dominican Republic is a growing industry, actively supported by the democratic government, and helped by Hispaniola's moderate tropical climate and golden beaches.

his opponents led to his assassination in 1961. In 1978, for the first time ever, the government changed hands in a democratic election. Democracy has since been maintained, but against a background of civil unrest.

The majority of the rapidly growing population are mestizos of mixed European and African descent, but there are several other ethnic groups. Most people speak Spanish and belong to the Roman Catholic church.

ECONOMY

The economy is still largely agricultural, although tourism and telecommunications led vigorous economic growth in the late 1990s. Exportable cash crops are grown on larger plantations; these include cocoa, coffee, tobacco and especially sugar cane. Staples such as rice and corn are produced mostly by low-output subsistence farming.

Mineral reserves are varied, but only rock salt, bauxite, nickel and some other metals are exploited in quantity. Industries are mostly light, ranging from sugar refining to textiles and fertilizers. Tourism is being promoted, but is not yet significant. The transportation network is good, and a social-security system offers reasonable benefits. However, health care is limited, and education, though free, is not available in isolated rural districts.

Saint Kitts-Nevis

FEDERATION OF SAINT KITTS-NEVIS

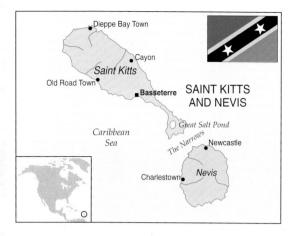

THE ISLANDS OF SAINT KITTS AND NEVIS FORM part of the western chain of the Leeward Islands in the eastern Caribbean.

ENVIRONMENT

The capital, Basseterre, is on Saint Kitts (Saint Christopher) – a mountainous volcanic island rising to Mount Misery. Nevis, to the south of a channel called The Narrows, is similarly volcanic and surrounded by coral reefs. The warm, humid climate is cooled by northeasterly trade winds, but there is a danger of hurricanes. The interior has lush vegetation, including tropical rainforest on some mountain slopes. The lower slopes have mostly been cleared for cultivation.

The volcanic island of Saint Kitts attracted early sugar cane planters with its verdant vegetation Tourism now supplements the island's sugar economy

SOCIETY

The British colony of Saint Kitts was founded by Sir Thomas Warner in 1623, but ownership was disputed by the French until 1783. In 1882 Saint Kitts and the neighboring islands of Nevis and Anguilla were united in a federal state. Anguilla became unhappy with the Saint Kitts administration, and declared unilateral independence in 1967. Saint Kitts-Nevis became fully independent in 1983. The British sovereign, represented by a governor-general, is head of state. The prime minister heads a 15-member parliament; most are elected, but a few are appointed. Nevis enjoys a degree of autonomy. Most of the population are black or are mixed-race descendants of former slaves. The official language is English, and the main religious groups are Anglican and Methodist Christians.

ECONOMY

The main cash crops are sugar cane on Saint Kitts, cotton and coconuts on Nevis. Other major exports include footwear, fabrics and electronic goods. Tourism is a growing source of revenue, thanks to the fine beaches. There are good roads and ferry connections, a deep-water harbor at Basseterre and an airport on each island. Education is free and compulsory, and literacy levels are high.

NATIONAL DATA – SAINT KITTS-NEVIS

Land area 269 sq km (104 sq mi)

Climate		Temperatures		Annual
	Altitude m (ft)	January °C(°F)	July °C(°F)	precipitation mm (in)
Basseterre	15 (49)	24 (75)	27 (81)	1,375 (54.1)

Major physical feature highest point: Mount Misery 1,156 m (3,793 ft)

Population (2000 est.) 38,819

Form of government multiparty constitutional monarchy with one legislative house

Armed forces none (paramilitary police 80)

Capital city Basseterre (12,605)

Official language English

Ethnic composition Black 90.5%; Mixed 5.0%; Indian 3.0%; White 1.5%

Religious affiliations Anglican 32.6%; Methodist 28.8%; other Protestants 21.3%; Roman Catholic 7.2%; others 10.1%

Currency 1 East Caribbean dollar (EC$) = 100 cents

Gross domestic product (1998) US $244 million

Gross domestic product per capita (1998) US $6,000

Life expectancy at birth male 64.9 yr; female 71.2 yr

Major resources sugar cane, coconuts, cotton, salt, fish, tourism

Antigua and Barbuda

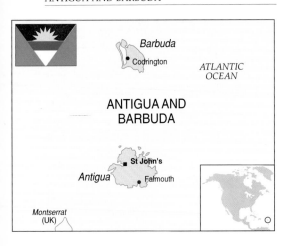

THE ISLAND STATE OF ANTIGUA AND BARBUDA is part of the Leeward islands group in the eastern Caribbean, and is of considerable strategic importance for the United States, which operates two military bases from the islands.

ENVIRONMENT

The low-lying island of Antigua has been mostly deforested, and includes an area of volcanic rock around Boggy Peak in the southwest. The coral island of Barbuda to the north is mostly flat and well wooded. The tiny islet of Redonda to the southwest is steep and totally uninhabited. The climate is warm and humid, but there is little fresh water, and the islands are subject to seasonal hurricanes.

SOCIETY

Barbuda was colonized by the British in 1628, and Antigua four years later. In 1685 the Codrington family leased Barbuda from the British, at a rent of one fat pig a year, but it reverted to the crown in the 19th century after the ending of slavery. In 1967 Antigua achieved internal self-government, but in 1979 demanded full independence. At the same time Barbuda sought secession from Antigua. The islands achieved their full independence together in 1981. The British sovereign, represented by a governor-general, is head of state. The two-chamber parliament consists of an appointed senate and an elected lower house. Most of the population live on Antigua. The official language is English, and the majority of the people are Anglican Christians.

ECONOMY

Tourism accounts for the majority of the islands' revenue; there are numerous white, sandy, palm-fringed beaches, a number of casinos, and some fine 18th-century architecture in the capital, St John's, which also has a splendid cathedral in the gothic style and a deep-water harbor. The roads are surfaced, and there are two airports. Good health-care and social-security schemes have been established. Basic education is free and compulsory, literacy levels are fairly high, and higher education is also available.

Whiling the time away (*above*) Now at leisure after a lifetime working in the canefields, an old man surveys the scene. The sugar cane industry, once the sole basis of Antigua's economy, has been closed down and is now supplanted by tourism.

A safe haven (*below*) Antigua was once a vital British naval base where Admiral Horatio Nelson (1758–1805) moored his fleet. Today it is still of strategic importance, and it supports two United States military bases.

NATIONAL DATA – ANTIGUA AND BARBUDA				
Land area 442 sq km (171 sq mi)				
Climate		**Temperatures**		**Annual**
	Altitude m (ft)	January °C(°F)	July °C(°F)	precipitation mm (in)
St John's	10 (33)	25 (77)	28 (82)	1,118 (44.0)
Major physical features highest point: Boggy Peak 405 m (1,329 ft); largest island: Antigua 280 sq km (108 sq mi)				
Population (2000 est.) 66,442				
Form of government multiparty constitutional monarchy with two legislative houses				
Armed forces 700				
Capital city St John's (36,000)				
Official language English				
Ethnic composition Black 94.4%; Mulatto 3.5%; White 1.3%; others 0.8%				
Religious affiliations Anglican 44.5%; other Protestants 41.6%; Roman Catholic 10.2%; Rastafarian 0.7%; others 3.0%				
Currency 1 East Caribbean dollar (EC$) = 100 cents				
Gross domestic product (1999) US $524 million				
Gross domestic product per capita (1999) US $8,200				
Life expectancy at birth male 71.0 yr; female 75.0 yr				
Major resources tourism				

Saint Vincent and the Grenadines

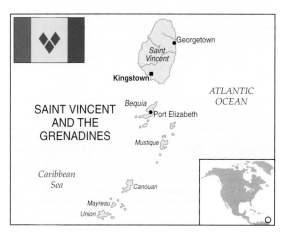

THE ISLAND STATE OF SAINT VINCENT AND the Grenadines forms part of the Windward Islands in the Lesser Antilles and comprises Saint Vincent and all but a few of the Grenadines.

ENVIRONMENT

Saint Vincent, the main island, is a thickly forested cluster of volcanic mountains. Soufrière, its highest peak, is still very much active. It caused severe damage to the island in 1891 and 1902, and resumed activity in 1979.

The Grenadines are a string of low-lying coral islands, which extend south of Saint Vincent toward Grenada. The climate is hot with seasonal rainfall and occasional destructive hurricanes.

SOCIETY

When Christopher Columbus (1451–1506) visited the islands on Saint Vincent's Day in 1498, he found them inhabited by the fierce Caribs, who successfully resisted European settlement until the 18th century. After a brief period in French hands, Saint Vincent came under British rule from 1783. African slaves were brought in to work the fertile plantations that were established on the rich volcanic soil. After the abolition of slavery, Indonesian and Portuguese laborers were also settled on the islands.

In 1958 Saint Vincent joined the Federation of the West Indies. In 1979 it became an independent constitutional monarchy headed by a governor-general representing the British sovereign. The prime minister is the leader of the majority party in the single-chamber assembly. English is the main language, but a French patois is also spoken on the islands.

ECONOMY

The economy of the islands rests largely on agriculture, mostly small-scale or subsistence farming on the lower slopes or terraces. Bananas are the chief cash crop and export, followed by arrowroot – used in the making of medicines, fine flour and computer paper.

The 1979 volcanic eruption, followed by a hurricane in 1980, devastated agriculture and discouraged tourism, but both have since recovered. Industry is confined to food processing.

NATIONAL DATA – SAINT VINCENT

Land area 389 sq km (150 sq mi)

Climate	Altitude m (ft)	Temperatures January °C(°F)	July °C(°F)	Annual precipitation mm (in)
Kingstown	1 (3)	26 (78)	28 (82)	1,524 (60.0)

Major physical features highest point: Soufrière 1,234 m (4,048 ft); largest island: Saint Vincent 347 sq km (134 sq mi)

Population (2000 est.) 115,461

Form of government multiparty constitutional monarchy with one legislative house

Armed forces none (paramilitary police 80)

Capital city Kingstown (27,000)

Official language English

Ethnic composition Black 74.0%; Mulatto 19.0%; White 3.0%; Black Carib 2.0%; Asian Indian 2.0%

Religious affiliations Anglican 36.0%; Methodist 20.4%; other Protestants 20.9%; Roman Catholic 19.3%; others 3.4%

Currency 1 East Caribbean dollar (EC$) = 100 cents

Gross domestic product (1999) US $309 million

Gross domestic product per capita (1999) US $2,600

Life expectancy at birth male 72.3 yr; female 75.4 yr

Major resources bananas, tourism, arrowroot

Barbados

BARBADOS

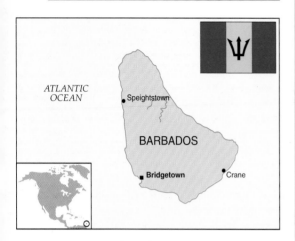

ATLANTIC
OCEAN

Speightstown

BARBADOS

Bridgetown   Crane

B ARBADOS IS AN ISLAND STATE IN THE Caribbean, lying outside the Lesser Antilles some distance from Venezuela.

ENVIRONMENT

The island is founded on coral deposits around a rocky core. The rolling terrain rises to a hilly region in the north and center. The west and south coasts have extensive sandy beaches. The climate is hot with seasonal rains and occasional hurricanes. Trees are plentiful, chiefly mahogany, palm and other tropical varieties, but there are no large forests, and not much wildlife apart from birds.

SOCIETY

Arawak peoples may once have lived on Barbados, but modern settlement was begun by British sugar planters in the 17th century. Present-day Barbadians are

Colonial and modern (*above*) British colonial architecture rubs shoulders with modern office blocks and hotels in Bridgetown, Barbados's capital, main port and tourist center.

descended from their slaves, liberated in the 1830s. Barbados is culturally the most British of the Caribbean states. From the 1930s onward, the island was given increasing self-government. It headed the short-lived West Indies Federation before becoming fully independent in 1966. The British sovereign, who is represented by a governor-general, remains the head of state, but power resides with the two-chamber parliament, which is constituted on British lines; it is headed by a prime minister and cabinet.

ECONOMY

Agriculture is dominated by sugar cane production, to which most of the flat land is devoted; despite a recent decline it remains by far the largest export. Sugar cane and its by-products, molasses and rum, are processed on the island. Diversification into other cash crops such as citrus fruits and cotton is officially encouraged in order to end the reliance on a single crop, as is fishing. Small petroleum and gas reserves are exploited. Light industries produce electrical components, clothing and many other items for export and for domestic use. Tourism, however, is now the single largest earner, visitors being attracted to the glittering white beaches and the coral reefs. Education is free and compulsory up to the age of 14, and available up to degree level. Social-security and health-care systems have also been introduced.

NATIONAL DATA – BARBADOS

Land area 430 sq km (166 sq mi)

Climate		Temperatures		Annual
	Altitude m (ft)	January °C(°F)	July °C(°F)	precipitation mm (in)
Bridgetown	55 (180)	24 (76)	27 (80)	1,275 (50.2)

Major physical feature highest point: Mount Hillaby 336 m (1,102 ft)

Population (2000 est.) 274,540

Form of government multiparty constitutional monarchy with two legislative houses

Armed forces paramilitary force 154

Capital city Bridgetown (7,000)

Official language English

Ethnic composition Black 91.9%; White 3.3%; Mulatto 2.6%; Indian 0.5%; others 1.7%

Religious affiliations Anglican 39.7%; other Protestants 25.6%; nonreligious 20.2%; Roman Catholic 4.4%; others 10.1%

Currency 1 Barbadian dollar (Bds $) = 100 cents

Gross domestic product (1998) US $2.9 billion

Gross domestic product per capita (1998) US $11,200

Life expectancy at birth male 72.2 yr; female 77.8 yr

Major resources sugar cane, citrus fruits, cotton, tourism

Grenada

GRENADA

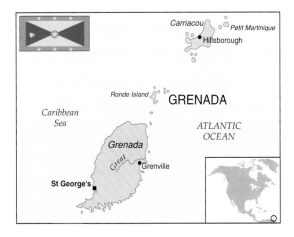

GRENADA IS AN ISLAND STATE IN THE LESSER Antilles, centered on the most southerly of the Windward Islands off the coast of Venezuela. The territory also includes the southernmost islands of the neighboring Grenadines group.

ENVIRONMENT

Grenada itself consists largely of a ridge of volcanic mountain peaks. Their slopes are thickly forested, thanks to the hot, humid climate and the fertile volcanic soils. The southern coasts have many bays and harbors, including that of the capital, Saint George's.

SOCIETY

Grenada's first inhabitants were the Arawak peoples, exterminated by the fierce Caribs whom Christopher Columbus (1451–1506) encountered in 1498. The island was settled by the French in 1650, but was seized by Britain in the 18th century. The people are mostly descended from former African slaves, and some still speak a French patois. Grenada became fully independent in 1974 with a parliamentary democracy based on the British system. In 1979 the New Jewel Movement, led by Maurice Bishop (1944–83), seized power in a left-wing coup. Bishop made some economic progress, as well as establishing links with Cuba, Libya and Algeria, but in 1983 he was deposed and murdered by rival Marxists. The United States, with some neighboring Caribbean states, launched a successful invasion. Constitutional government was restored, and the governor-general instituted free elections to the lower house of the two-chamber parliament. US troops finally withdrew in 1995.

ECONOMY

Grenada's economy depends almost entirely on agriculture and tourism. Agriculture is mostly small scale except for a few cooperatives. The main cash crops and exports are bananas, cocoa, and the spices such as nutmeg and mace that once earned Grenada the name Isle of Spice. There is little industry apart from various food-processing plants. Tourism, shattered by the 1979 coup, is gradually recovering. There is an effective healthcare program and free education facilities.

St George's, Grenada's capital, is attractively set on wooded hillsides surrounding a horseshoe bay. Traditional exports of spices, bananas and cocoa still leave the island from St George's port.

NATIONAL DATA – GRENADA			
Land area 345 sq km (133 sq mi)			
Climate		**Temperatures**	**Annual**
	Altitude m (ft)	January °C(°F)	July °C(°F)	precipitation mm (in)
St George's	1 (3)	25 (77)	27 (81)	1,560 (61.4)
Major physical feature highest point: Mount St Catherine 840 m (2,756 ft)			
Population (2000 est.) 89,018			
Form of government multiparty constitutional monarchy with two legislative houses			
Armed forces none (paramilitary police 80)			
Capital city St George's (35,742)			
Official language English			
Ethnic composition Black 84.0%; Mixed 12.0%; Asian Indian 3.0%; White 1.0%			
Religious affiliations Roman Catholic 64.4%; Anglican 20.7%; other Protestants 13.8%; others 1.1%			
Currency 1 East Caribbean dollar (EC$) = 100 cents			
Gross domestic product (1999) US $360 million			
Gross domestic product per capita (1999) US $3,700			
Life expectancy at birth male 69.0 yr; female 74.3 yr			
Major resources cocoa, bananas, nutmeg and mace, timber, tourism			

Trinidad and Tobago

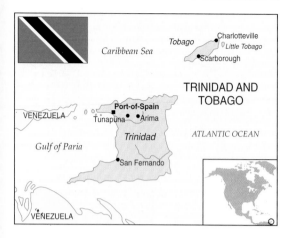

TRINIDAD AND TOBAGO IS MADE UP OF TWO islands lying between the Caribbean Sea and the Atlantic Ocean just off the coast of Venezuela.

ENVIRONMENT

Venezuela's coastal mountains effectively continue into Trinidad's Northern Range and Tobago's Main Ridge. The Northern Range rises steeply to the Cerro del Aripo, and its rivers create some spectacular waterfalls. Otherwise Trinidad is mostly rolling or flat, with many swampy areas along the coast. South of Tobago's Main Ridge is a coral plain that extends out to sea, creating some magnificent reefs. The climate is hot and humid, and much of Trinidad is still covered with thick rainforest. Both islands are rich in bird life, especially flamingoes and the scarlet ibis.

NATIONAL DATA – TRINIDAD AND TOBAGO				
Land area 5,128 sq km (1,980 sq mi)				
Climate		Temperatures		Annual
	Altitude m (ft)	January °C(°F)	July °C(°F)	precipitation mm (in)
Port-of-Spain	20 (66)	25 (77)	26 (79)	1,631 (64.2)
Major physical feature highest point: Mount Aripo 940 m (3,084 ft)				
Population (2000 est.) 1,175,523				
Form of government multiparty republic with two legislative houses				
Armed forces army 2,600; Coast Guard 600				
Capital city Port-of-Spain (58,000)				
Official language English				
Ethnic composition Black 43.0%; Asian Indian 40.0%; Mixed 14.0%; others 3.0%				
Religious affiliations Roman Catholic 32.2%; Protestant 27.6%; Hindu 24.3%; Muslim 5.9%; others 10.0%				
Currency 1 Trinidad and Tobago dollar (TT$) = 100 cents				
Gross domestic product (1999) US $9.41 billion				
Gross domestic product per capita (1999) US $8,500				
Life expectancy at birth male 68.2 yr; female 73.2 yr				
Major resources petroleum, natural gas, sugar cane, cocoa, coffee, citrus fruits, tourism				

SOCIETY

The original inhabitants were the Arawak peoples, exterminated on Tobago by the fierce Caribs. After colonization by Spain and France, both peoples were wiped out by disease and enslavement on tobacco and sugar plantations; they were replaced by African slaves. In the early 19th century both islands were ceded to Britain. With the ending of slavery laborers were brought in from Asia to work the plantations. Full independence was granted in 1962. In 1976 the islands became a Commonwealth republic, which survived an abortive coup led by Asian Trinidadians in 1980. The islands' ethnic mix of peoples has created a colorful local culture including carnival and calypso music. There is a large Hindu minority.

ECONOMY

The islands are among the most prosperous in the Caribbean. The economy depends heavily on the refining and export of the extensive petroleum reserves, but a fall in petroleum revenues has led to increased diversification in the industrial sector. Agriculture concentrates on cash crops for export – principally sugar cane, cocoa and coffee – with less emphasis on staple crops such as rice and vegetables. Tourism is an important source of revenue, and there are good education and health care facilities.

Tropical mix Trinidad is full of variety. Industrial in parts, it also has fertile agricultural land. In the towns, mosques and temples, English churches, the sounds of calypso and steel bands, all combine to form a vibrant cosmopolitan society.

Dependencies in the region

TURKS AND CAICOS ISLANDS
UNITED KINGDOM

The Turks and Caicos Islands are a British colony consisting of a string of about 30 small islands at the end of the Bahamas group, which they resemble in landscape and climate. Rainfall, however, is scantier except during hurricanes. The terrain is dry, and the vegetation is scrubby except in the coastal saltmarshes.

The inhabitants are descended from African slaves imported by the British in the 17th century to work saltpans. The islands have on several occasions been annexed both to the Bahamas and to Jamaica. In 1976 they were given self-government under the British crown, but their declared goal of full independence has so far been delayed indefinitely.

Salt production has become uneconomic, and agriculture is hindered by lack of water. Thus the island's economy rests largely on fishing, chiefly crayfish and conch, and on the development of tourism. Many offshore financial companies are also based here, taking advantage of the islands' status as a tax haven. Education and health care are government priorities, and are generally good.

BERMUDA
UNITED KINGDOM

The British colony of Bermuda occupies a string of coral islands in the North Atlantic. About 20 are inhabited, the largest being Great Bermuda. The climate is warm and humid, with moderate rainfall. The vegetation is luxuriant, with whispering pines and many flowering plants. Lizards are the only reptiles, and there are no native mammals.

In 1609 the crew of a shipwrecked English vessel landed in the islands, and in 1612 Bermuda became a colony of the British Virginia Company. It passed to the crown in 1684, but remained self-governing. In 1941 Bermuda leased air and naval stations to the United States. The 1968 constitution allowed greater self-government. The 40-member House of Assembly is directly elected, but the 11-member senate is chosen by the governor, who is appointed by the British crown. The majority of the people are descended from former African slaves, others from British or Portuguese settlers. The official language is English, but some Portuguese is spoken. Christianity is the dominant religion; the majority of people belong to one of the denominations of the Protestant churches.

There is little scope for much agriculture or for large-scale industry, and food and fuel must be imported. The colony relies almost entirely on the income from tourism, and from military and financial interests. The standard of living is high. There are no railroads, but there is a good road network, which links the islands by bridges and ferries. The main port at Hamilton is well served by international shipping lines, and the American airport base at Kindley Field serves both military and international traffic. Health care is readily available, and there is social security for all citizens. Education is free and compulsory, and literacy levels are high. Overseas scholarships are available for higher education.

CAYMAN ISLANDS
UNITED KINGDOM

The Cayman Islands are a British colony in the Caribbean to the northwest of Jamaica. Grand Cayman, Cayman Brac and Little Cayman are low-lying coral islands on a rocky base. The coasts are lined with magnificent beaches and reefs, and the tropical climate is pleasantly cooled by the sea.

Though visited by Christopher Columbus (1451–1506), the islands remained no more than a pirate lair until ceded to Britain with Jamaica in 1670. Later settlers from Jamaica lived mostly from turtle fishing. The Caymans became a separate colony after Jamaica's independence in 1962. They enjoy some local autonomy under a governor, but have yet to become fully independent.

A thriving British colony, Bermuda's picturesque towns are a magnet for tourists; lenient tax laws bolster the economy by attracting foreign investors.

There is little agriculture or industry, although some turtle farming is being developed. Tourism is one major earner, and offshore finance another, encouraged by liberal tax and confidentiality laws. The Caymans now house hundreds of financial companies. These help to create high living standards, and good health and education services.

PUERTO RICO
UNITED STATES

Puerto Rico, an island state in the West Indies, is a self–governing commonwealth in association with the United States.

Most of the main island is upland, rising from the narrow southern coastal plains to the Cordillera Central, a mountain range that runs along the island like a backbone; Cerro del Punta is the highest peak. To the north it flattens out into hill country, through which the island's main rivers flow down to the much wider northern coastal plain. The two adjoining islands to the east are similarly rugged.

The climate is mainly warm and humid, but rainfall is unevenly distributed. The north receives most of the island's rainfall, and is dotted with marshlands, small lakes and mangrove swamps. By contrast the south, in the rainshadow of the mountains, is too dry for farming without irrigation, and in the southwest there are several saltpans. The island was once covered in tropical

hardwood rainforest, but so much of this has been cleared that it now survives only in the Caribbean National Forest enclave. Wildlife consists mostly of small reptiles and birds.

When Christopher Columbus (1451–1506) reached Puerto Rico, the islands were already inhabited by the Arawaks and Caribs. Spanish settlers wiped out both these peoples, by disease and enslavement in gold mines and plantations. Puerto Rico, unlike nearby Hispaniola, remained Spanish throughout the 19th century. African slaves were introduced to work the plantations until slavery was abolished in the 19th century.

The island was granted self-government in 1897, only to be occupied and ceded to the United States in the Spanish-American war (1898); its people were given United States citizenship in 1919. Various independence movements developed, but disagreed on whether to become wholly independent or seek statehood within the United States. In spite of strong American influences, the culture has remained primarily Hispanic.

After World War II the office of governor was made elective, and in 1952 a commonwealth was established. However, a fierce debate still continues regarding possible independence or statehood. The island returns a nonvoting member to the United States House of Representatives, but elects its own governor, who appoints an executive cabinet.

El Morro (*above*) One of the two 16th-century forts on the clifftops of San Juan, Puerto Rico, this is an impressive reminder of the days of Spanish control.

Holiday bliss (*right*) The clear blue waters and sandy beaches of the United States Virgin Islands have brought a thriving tourist trade. The fine harbor at St Thomas, once frequented by pirates, is now the haunt of luxury cruisers.

Puerto Rico's close links with the United States have made it one of the most prosperous Caribbean countries. Since World War II investment policies have made industry more important than agriculture. The main cash crops are sugar cane, coffee and tobacco, along with dairy products and livestock, but large amounts of food have to be imported. There are few mineral resources, although copper and nickel deposits have been found. Industry is based on a wide range of products, from petrochemicals, plastics and pharmaceuticals to textiles, machinery and electronics. Considerable amounts are exported, chiefly to the United States, but there is also a high volume of imports. Tourism, however, has become a major earner.

Social-security and welfare benefits operate to United States standards, and health care is improving rapidly toward that goal. Education is a priority, freely available at all levels, up to and including university.

VIRGIN ISLANDS OF THE UNITED STATES
UNITED STATES

The United States Virgin Islands are an unincorporated territory of the United States, comprising Saint Croix, Saint John and Saint Thomas and some 50 smaller islets of the Virgin Islands group to the east of Puerto Rico. Their rugged landscapes are formed by the peaks of an undersea mountain range.

Christopher Columbus (1451–1506) named the islands after Saint Ursula's martyred virgins. They were settled by the Spanish and French before being acquired by Denmark in the 17th and 18th centuries. African slaves were introduced to work the sugar cane plantations. In 1917 the islands were bought by the United States. In 1981 a constitution, adopted by referendum, introduced self-government to the islands by an elected governor and senate.

were driven out by the Caribs, who were in turn wiped out by the Spanish. The islands were used as havens for piracy until they were annexed by Britain in the 17th century. They now have effective self-government through an elected council headed by an appointed governor.

Tourism is expanding to dominate the economy; the sheltered waters around the islands attract a great number of visitors who stay on yachts. Agriculture produces livestock for local use, and cash and food crops such as bananas and sugar cane. Fishing is also important, but manufacturing industry is very small. Despite water shortages, health care is excellent, as is primary education.

ANGUILLA
UNITED KINGDOM

Anguilla is the northernmost of the Leeward Islands in the eastern Caribbean. It consists of a long, thin coral island with a bare landscape of scrubland and occasional fruit plantations. The climate is warm and humid, and the island is subject to hurricanes.

Anguilla has been a British colony since 1650. For several years it was part of the federal state of St Kitts–Nevis–Anguilla, but since 1980 it has been a dependent territory of the United Kingdom. The governor is appointed by the crown, but internal affairs are managed by an elected assembly. Most Anguillans are descended from former African slaves. English is the chief language, and the main religions are Anglican and Methodist Christianity.

The chief exports are fish, salt and livestock. There are significant saltpeter deposits, and tourism is being developed, along with transportation and communications. Housing, health care and educational facilities are good.

MONTSERRAT
UNITED KINGDOM

The British colony of Montserrat is one of the Leeward Islands in the eastern Caribbean. Volcanic peaks, several of them active, dominate a mountainous landscape of pastureland and lush vegetation. The climate is warm and humid, with seasonal hurricanes.

Montserrat was colonized in the 17th century by Irish settlers from nearby Saint Kitts. It belonged to the Federation of the West Indies between 1958 and 1962, and hopes to gain full independence from the United Kingdom. The governor, who is appointed by the crown, is head of an

executive council and a partly elected legislative council. Most people are descendants of former African slaves. English is the chief language, and Christianity, with its various denominations, is the predominant religion.

The chief exports are vegetables and cotton, but tourism is a growing source of revenue. There are surfaced roads, a seaport at the capital, Plymouth, and an air link with neighboring Antigua. Sanitation is good and health care is improving. The island was devastated in June 1997 when the Soufriere Hills volcano erupted.

ARUBA
THE NETHERLANDS

The island of Aruba lies at the southwestern end of the Lesser Antilles off the Venezuelan coast. The terrain is mostly flat, but is generously scattered with volcanic boulders. The climate is warm and humid, but rainfall is generally poor, and vegetation is sparse apart from cacti and succulents.

Aruba became part of the Netherlands Antilles in 1634, but seceded in 1986, becoming an internally self-governing part of the Netherlands. The monarch is represented by a governor, but the 21 members of the States of Aruba are directly elected. Arubans are mainly of African, European and Asian descent, and most are Roman Catholic. Dutch is the official language, but Papiamento, a Spanish creole, is widely spoken.

Tourism is almost the sole source of revenue. Aruba has surfaced roads, deepwater harbors and an international airport. Most drinking water is distilled from seawater. Education is not compulsory, but literacy levels are high.

THE NETHERLANDS ANTILLES
THE NETHERLANDS

The Netherlands Antilles are made up of two island groups within the Lesser Antilles. The southern group includes Curaçao and Bonaire – and formerly also Aruba – off the Venezuelan coast. The northern group is part of the Leeward Islands, and comprises Sint Eustatius, Saba and the southern part of Sint Maarten, the rest of which is French. The southern islands are generally flat, but those in the north are mountainous and volcanic. The climate is warm and humid; Curaçao and Bonaire have poor rainfall, while the northern islands are subject to seasonal hurricanes. The vegetation is sparse apart from cacti and succulents.

Agriculture has shifted from sugar cane to food crops and livestock, mostly for domestic use. Manufacturing ranges from rum distilling to petroleum refining. Tourism has been developed since 1945, and now dominates the economy, with game fishing being one of the major attractions. Education and health care are widely available, reflecting the islands' relative prosperity.

BRITISH VIRGIN ISLANDS
UNITED KINGDOM

The British Virgin Islands are a British colony comprising Tortola, Anegada, Virgin Gorda, Jost Van Dyke and more than 30 islets of the Virgin Islands group in the Caribbean. Most are the peaks of a submerged mountain chain, and share a subtropical climate. The landscape is mainly hilly, with sandy beaches and coral reefs around the coasts. Anegada, however, is very flat.

The original inhabitants, the Arawaks,

In the 16th century Spanish settlers killed most of the original Amerindian inhabitants. The Dutch claimed these islands in the early 17th century. Curaçao and Bonaire were plantation colonies of the Dutch West India Company, and Sint Eustatius was the center of the local slave trade until the late 18th century. Bonaire was given a separate political status in 1868. In 1954 the islands became self-governing as an integral part of the Netherlands. The governor is appointed by the Dutch crown, but the 22 members of the States of the Netherlands Antilles are directly elected.

The people are mainly of African and European descent, and most are Roman Catholic. Dutch is the official language, but English is spoken in the north, and Papiamento – a Spanish-based creole language – on Bonaire and Curaçao.

Since the discovery of oil on Curaçao, petroleum and its derivatives have accounted for the vast majority of exports. Tourism and banking have also been successfully developed and are now an important source of revenue. Some fruit and vegetables are grown, including oranges for the famous Curaçao liqueur, but most food is imported.

Curaçao has an excellent road system, and there are international airports on Curaçao and on Sint Maarten. Most drinking water is distilled from seawater. Health care is good, and although education is not compulsory, literacy levels are relatively high.

Simple luxury (*above*) A modest beach-house in Guadeloupe is beautified by its idyllic location.

Mount Pelée (*right*), an active volcano that last erupted in 1929, dominates the lush tropical landscape of Martinique.

Running repairs (*below*) A fisherman checks his nets for damage. Martinique's fishing, farming and tourist economy is heavily dependent on subsidies from mainland France.

GUADELOUPE
FRANCE

The French overseas *département* of Guadeloupe consists of two groups of islands within the Lesser Antilles in the eastern Caribbean. The main islands are Basse-Terre and Grand-Terre, separated by a narrow channel. Nearby are Marie Galante, La Désirade and the Iles des Saintes. A separate northwestern group comprises Saint Barthélemy and Saint Martin, whose southern part belongs to the Netherlands.

Basse-Terre is a mountainous island, culminating in the still-active volcano of Soufrière. Grande-Terre is generally low-lying, but Saint Barthélemy and Saint Martin are both rugged. The climate is warm and humid, with seasonal rains and occasional hurricanes. The vegetation

but Creole is widely spoken on the island.

Income from agriculture, industry and tourism leaves a large deficit that is mostly made up by grants from France. The main islands have excellent roads, and ferries connect all the islands. There are ports at Basse-Terre, at Pointe-à-Pitre (near an international airport) and at Marigot on Saint Martin. Education, welfare and health care are the same as in mainland France.

MARTINIQUE
FRANCE

Martinique is a Caribbean island in the Lesser Antilles chain, situated between Dominica and Saint Lucia. Formerly a French colony, it is now an overseas *département* within France.

The island is mountainous and volcanic in origin, and is dominated by the immense and active Mount Pelée near its northernmost cape. The basin of the river Lézarde is the only significant lowland area. The hot, humid climate and the fertile volcanic soils have created lush vegetation, with tropical rainforests and mangrove swamps on the coasts.

When Christopher Columbus (1451–1506) discovered Martinique in 1493, he found it occupied by the Caribs who had exterminated the indigenous inhabitants, the Arawaks. In the 17th century the island was settled by French sugar cane growers, who imported large numbers of African slaves. These were not freed until 1848. The Creole dialect spoken by the islanders reflects their mixed African and European origins. Martinique became a French *département* after World War II. Since then, beset by economic problems, it has given birth to a vociferous independence movement, which has launched a number of terrorist campaigns in mainland France. However, the island's economic reliance on France makes genuine independence difficult to achieve.

Agriculture and tourism are the island's mainstays. The main cash crops include sugar cane, bananas and exotic flowers. Sweet potatoes and cassava, the chief food crops, are mostly grown at subsistence level. Forestry and fisheries represent largely undeveloped potential. Industry, mostly food processing, has been developed with French aid. Tourism from the United States and France is far more important, and the capital, Fort-de-France, has good air links with both countries. Education is widely available and standards are high. Welfare benefits operate on the same basis as in France.

is often lush, ranging from mangrove swamps near Pointe-à-Pitre on Grande-Terre to dense forests on Basse-Terre. On the smaller islands, however, cacti and dry forest are more usual.

In 1626 the French displaced small groups of Spanish settlers, and in 1674 the colony passed to the French crown. It fell into British hands several times, but was finally returned to France in 1816. In 1946 Guadeloupe became an administrative district of France. Despite increasing degrees of self-government, separatist violence has grown since the 1970s. The prefect is appointed by the French government, but the 36-member legislative council is elected, and Guadeloupe is represented in both chambers of the French parliament. Most inhabitants are the black or mixed-race descendants of slaves, and the majority are Roman Catholic. French is the official language,

Central America and the Caribbean

The heroes of communism paraded in Havana, Cuba

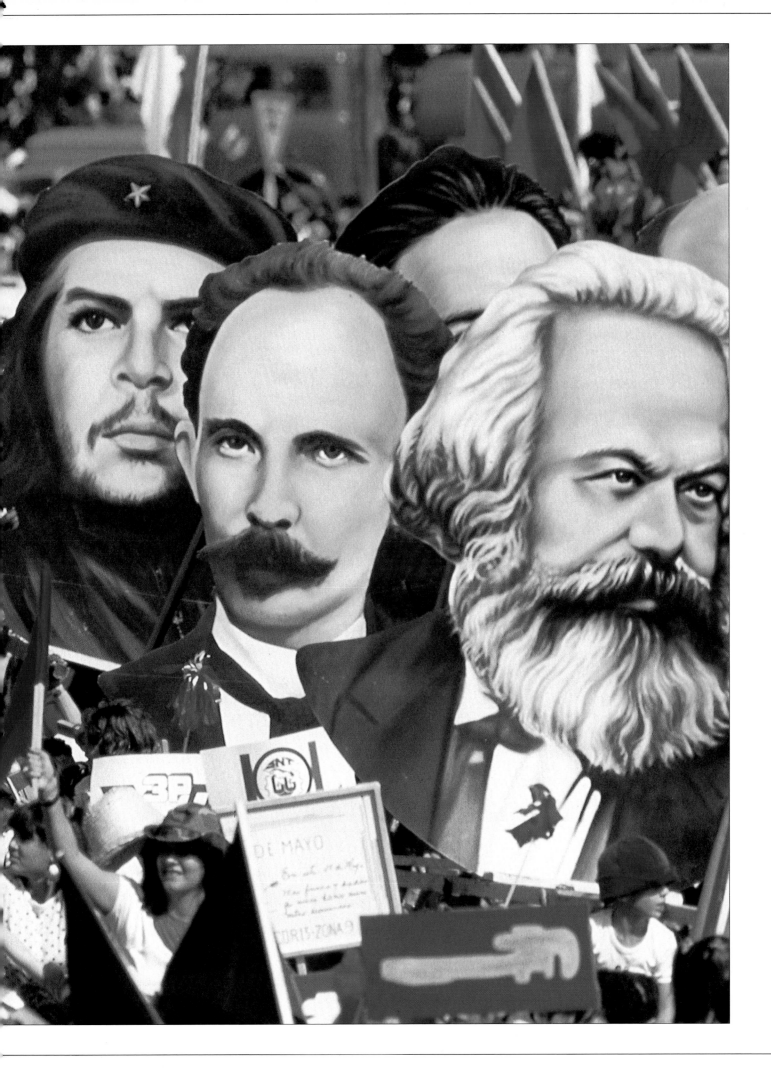

PHYSICAL GEOGRAPHY

MOUNTAINS, VOLCANOES AND ISLANDS · PATTERNS OF CLIMATE · EVOLVING LANDSCAPES

The funnel-shaped isthmus of Central America joins the continents of North and South America and separates the Pacific from the Atlantic Ocean. With the island chain of the Antilles or West Indies it encircles the tropical Caribbean Sea. Most of this mountainous land lies within the tropics. Tropical rainforest and torrential downpours are characteristic of the northeastern coasts and islands, contrasting with the hot deserts of the northwest. Climates are cooler in the high plateaus and mountains. A chain of volcanoes follows the mainland's western coasts on the Pacific Ocean's "Ring of Fire". The region lies on an unstable part of the Earth's crust, and is particularly subject to earthquakes, seismic sea waves (tsunami) and volcanic eruptions; it also suffers from landslides, hurricanes and storm surges.

COUNTRIES IN THE REGION

Antigua and Barbuda, Bahamas, Barbados, Belize, Bermuda, Costa Rica, Cuba, Dominica, Dominican Republic, El Salvador, Grenada, Guatemala, Haiti, Honduras, Jamaica, Mexico, Nicaragua, Panama, St Kitts–Nevis, St Lucia, St Vincent and the Grenadines, Trinidad and Tobago

LAND

Area 2,735,515 sq km (1,056,183 sq mi)
Highest point Citaltépetl, 5,699 m (18,700 ft)
Lowest point Lake Enriquillo, Dominican Republic, –44 m (–144 ft)
Major features volcanic mountain chain and Mexican plateau on isthmus, island chain of the West Indies

WATER

Longest river Conchos–Grande, 2,100 km (1,300 mi)
Largest basin Grande (part), 445,000 sq km (172,000 sq mi)
Highest average flow Colorado, 104 cu m/sec (3,700 cu ft/sec), at head of Gulf of California
Largest lake Nicaragua, 8,029 sq km (3,100 sq mi)

CLIMATE

| | Temperature °C (°F) | | Altitude |
	January	July	m (f)
Guayamas	18 (64)	31 (88)	4 (13)
Zacatecas	10 (50)	14 (57)	2,612 (8,567)
Mexico City	12 (54)	16 (61)	2,306 (7,564)
Havana	21 (70)	27 (81)	49 (161)
Bluefields	25 (77)	26 (79)	12 (39)
Seawell	25 (77)	27 (81)	56 (184)

| | Precipitation mm (in) | | |
	January	July	Year
Guayamas	8 (0.3)	47 (1.9)	252 (9.9)
Zacatecas	7 (0.3)	69 (2.7)	313 (12.3)
Mexico City	8 (0.3)	160 (6.3)	726 (28.6)
Havana	51 (2.0)	93 (3.7)	1,167 (45.9)
Bluefields	264 (10.4)	746 (29.4)	4,370 (172.0)
Seawell	68 (2.7)	141 (5.6)	1,273 (59.1)

Greatest recorded rainfall in 5 minutes: 305 mm (12 in) at Portobello, northern Panama

NATURAL HAZARDS

Earthquakes, landslides, volcanic eruptions, hurricanes

MOUNTAINS, VOLCANOES AND ISLANDS

Central America forms a land bridge, or isthmus, between North and South America, which became joined toward the end of the Pliocene epoch (5–2 million years ago). The isthmus and the Caribbean islands can be divided into nine areas based on their geological history and topography. These areas are defined by the effects of earth movements – folding and lifting up of rocks, earthquakes and the eruptions of volcanoes – and by quieter episodes when the land surface was eroded and sediments were laid down.

The Central American land bridge

The region is dominated by the Mexican plateau; it rises from an average 1,200 m (4,000 ft) in the north to 2,400 m (8,000 ft) in the south. The limestone mountains of the Sierra Madre Oriental in the east and the volcanic peaks of the Sierra Madre Occidental in the west form a high rim to the lower "hill-and-basin" relief of the plateau. Many of the rivers drain into interior basins; some of the westward-flowing rivers have cut deep canyons (*barrancas*), some of them rivaling the Grand Canyon in the United States in both size and splendor.

To the south the low, hot and dry basin of the river Balsas separates the Mexican plateau from the rugged crystalline rock terrain of the highlands of the Sierra Madre del Sur. This area has numerous peaks of 2,300–3,050 m (7,500–10,000 ft), and is heavily dissected by deep V-shaped valleys.

West of the Mexican plateau lie the desert landscapes of the Pacific coastal hills and the peninsula of Baja California or Lower California, a raised block of granite and volcanic rocks separated from Mexico proper by a rift valley drowned by the Gulf of California.

East of the Mexican plateau lies the coastal plain around the Bay of Campeche in the Gulf of Mexico. This is a geologically young area of marl, shale and sandstone marine sediments containing major oil and gas deposits, and more recent river-borne sediments. Barrier beaches enclosing the swamps and lagoons that fringe the coast reflect the softness of the rocks and the still-active process of sedimentation.

The oldest and geologically most complex part of the region encompasses Belize, Guatemala, Honduras and eastern Nicaragua on the isthmus, and also the

Map of physical zones The land bridge of Central America extends from the high Mexican plateau south to Panama, the gateway to South America. Both the mountainous mainland and the islands of the Caribbean are shaped by tectonic disturbance and climatic extremes.

Bermuda's coral-fringed islands are situated in the western Atlantic away to the north of the islands of the Caribbean. The offshore reefs are one of the most northerly coral formations in the world.

islands of the Greater Antilles in the Caribbean, which include Cuba, Jamaica, Hispaniola and Puerto Rico. In the Cretaceous period; 100 million years ago, this "Old Antillia" formed a single land-mass. It has since been broken up by numerous episodes of lifting, folding and erosion. Old Antillia is composed of a series of mountain ranges and depressions that run from east to west. In places the limestone and sandstone rocks have been completely eroded to expose the underlying granite. Where limestone still predominates, the combination of wet tropical conditions and high mountain relief has produced spectacular weathered terrain with deep enclosed hollows and tall limestone towers.

To the west and north of Old Antillia lie the Yucután peninsula and the Bahamas. Both are low-lying plains of limestone resting on crystalline rocks and have emerged relatively recently from the sea. Here the landscape is dominated by steep-sided hollows, and by underground streams and expanses of fluted and etched limestone pavement. Shorelines are marked by low, notched limestone cliffs, coral reefs and mangrove swamps.

The active volcanic belts of Central America and the Lesser Antilles to the east are the result of movements in the Earth's crust. The Cocos plate of the tropical Pacific has undercut the North American and Caribbean plates and the

Lake Atitlán in southern Guatemala fills a crater some 300 m (990 ft) deep. The mountains to the south are also volcanoes, a result of intense tectonic activity in the Central American isthmus.

Physical zones

- mountains/barren land
- forest
- grassland
- semidesert
- desert

▲ mountain peak (meters)

☒ climate station

475

Central American landmass to produce a line of volcanoes from western Guatemala to Panama. Volcanic deposits cover the older sedimentary rocks beneath.

The Lesser Antilles chain of volcanic islands was formed when the North American plate thrust under the Caribbean plate. The double arc of islands is the outcome of two distinct phases of volcanic activity. The low-lying eastern arc represents one phase, which lasted from 40 to 10 million years ago. These volcanoes were thoroughly eroded, then covered by limestones laid down during times of raised sea levels. In the second volcanic phase, which began about 7.5 million years ago, the arc of the volcanic belt moved westward and built new islands, such as St Christopher (Kitts) and Dominica, and added westerly extensions to older islands such as Guadeloupe, Martinique and St Lucia.

LIVING WITH NATURAL HAZARDS

There is hardly a town or city in western and southern Mexico, the Pacific side of Central America or the West Indies that has not been devastated by earthquake or by volcanic disaster at some time in its history. San Salvador, capital of El Salvador, has been partly or completely destroyed nine times since 1528.

The impact of earthquakes is often increased by the landslides, fires and, on the coastline, giant sea waves (tsunami) that they trigger. In 1692, when an earthquake hit Port Royal near present-day Kingston, Jamaica, two-thirds of the town slipped into the sea and what remained was inundated by a tsunami. Nearly all the 2,500 inhabitants perished.

In 1902 the eruption of Santa Maria in the Sierra Madre in Guatemala cost 6,000 lives. In the same year all but two of the 30,000 inhabitants of St Pierre in Martinique were killed by a glowing cloud of volcanic dust and poisonous gas that sped down from the erupting Mont Pelée to the north of the town. Only the day before, 130 km (90 mi) to the south, St Vincent's Soufrière had erupted, killing 2,000 people. In 1997 over half the population of Montserrat was evacuated after the violent eruption of the Soufrière Hills volcano.

Paradoxically, the unstable land attracts people to it: the benefits of cultivating the fertile volcanic soils outweigh the risk of damage from earthquake or eruption.

PATTERNS OF CLIMATE

The climates of Central America and the Caribbean are dominated by the northeast trade winds, which blow almost incessantly all year. In winter a zone of high pressure (anticyclone) lies over the Atlantic to the east, and the northeast trades are cool and mostly dry. Rainfall is low except over northeast-facing coasts and mountain ranges, where airflows are forced to rise, cool and release moisture.

In summer the belt of low atmospheric pressure over the Equator, with its rainy weather, advances north with the overhead sun and by July lies over Panama and Costa Rica. At the same time the Bermuda-Azores "high" weakens and retreats northward. Although the northeast trades still prevail the air is much less stable, and there are frequent rains as waves of convection currents and tropical cyclones track westward across the region. A few cyclones also develop off the Pacific coast.

The region's mountainous nature and latitudinal extent result in a wide range of climatic types. In general it is driest in northwest Mexico and wettest along northeast-facing coasts toward the Equator. In the extensive mountain and plateau areas of both Central America and the Caribbean the pattern of tropical climates is modified by altitude.

From rainforest to desert
In the tropical wet zone climates are hot and humid throughout the year, with an annual rainfall of at least 2,000 mm (80 in) and little or no dry season. Along the Atlantic coast of Central America from southern Mexico to Panama, and on the windward sides of the higher Caribbean islands, exposure to the northeast trades ensures substantial winter as well as summer rainfall. Most of the rain is concentrated in heavy falls of a few hours each day. Small areas such as the central mountains of Dominica, Guadeloupe and Martinique are "super-wet", with annual rainfalls of 5,000–9,000 mm (200–360 in), and never experience a dry month. The small annual range of temperature increases with latitude. In these hot, wet conditions tropical rainforest is the natural vegetation.

A tropical wet-dry climate characterizes areas in the rain shadow southwest of mountain ranges, including much of the Pacific side of Central America, and lower islands and peninsulas of the Caribbean. Temperatures are similar to those of the tropical wet zone, but there is a 4–7 month winter dry season. Annual rainfall us generally in the range 750–2,000 mm (30–80 in). Deciduous forests form the natural vegetation.

Much of the northern interior of Mexico is semiarid. Most of the 250–500 mm (10–20 in) of rain each year falls in just a few summer thunderstorms. Temperatures vary greatly with season: at Sabinas at the northern end of the Sierra Madre Oriental they range from 10°C (50°F) in January to 33°C (91°F) in July, with some frosts in winter. In the south, the Lesser Antilles islands of Curaçao, Bonaire and Aruba also have a semiarid climate. Their low rainfall is the result of cool temperatures above the sea surface where there is an upwelling of cold water. The natural vegetation of these semiarid area is low thorn woodland, but human activity has usually modified this to a grass and scrub landscape.

Parts of the extreme northwest and north of Mexico lie under the influence of a subtropical anticyclone throughout the year and have a hot desert climate. Only 75–250 mm (3–10 in) of rain falls each year. There is a comparatively wide average temperature range, for example from 18°C (64.4°F) in January to 31°C (87.8°F) in August at Guayamas in the desert of northwest Mexico. Maximum daily temperatures frequently reach 45–50°C (112–122°F) away from the cool and often foggy Pacific coast. The scanty vegetation is dominated by cacti and grasses.

Climate variations
Climates have been very different at times in the past. Studies of old lake levels have revealed that 18,000 years ago areas of northern Mexico that are now semiarid and desert were much wetter, while tropical Mexico was considerably drier. Even in the last hundred years climates have varied significantly. Records show that since 1959 rainfall in the eastern Caribbean has been only about three-quarters what it was in 1871–1901 and 1928–58.

Mount Gimie on St Lucia in the Lesser Antilles is an old and highly eroded volcanic mountain. Its sharp ridges and steep slopes, and the humid climate, ensure luxuriant tropical rainforest and a high rate of chemical weathering, making the slopes prone to landslides.

EVOLVING LANDSCAPES

The diversity of climate, relief and rocks in Central America and the Caribbean is reflected in a great variety of landscapes. The low-lying limestone coastlands of Yucatán and the Cayman Islands northwest of Jamaica are fringed by mosquito-ridden mangroves, while on the high plateau of northern Mexico the land is cold, bleak and dry. The rock desert of Baja California contrasts with the steamy, forest-clad mountains of Panama, Costa Rica, Nicaragua and Guatemala.

Landslides and weathering

Landslides are a major factor in landscape formation. The steep mountainous slopes, frequent earthquakes, the mainly humid tropical climate, the character of the soils and vegetation all contribute to landslides. In these warm, wet conditions weathering rapidly breaks down the rocks, forming layers of soil. Soil erosion by sheetwash (water moving over the surface) and rainsplash is restricted by the dense tropical forest. As a result deep soils build up. Plant nutrients are concentrated in the top layer of tropical soils, so rainforest trees typically have shallow

roots and the soil beneath is liable to slip. On the slopes intense tropical rainstorms can saturate the soil, which may then lose cohesion, triggering a landslide.

Another important process of erosion is chemical weathering. Areas of limestone and volcanic rock are particularly vulnerable, and the process also reflects the high rainfall and temperatures of most of the region. Weathering is caused by rocks being dissolved by rainwater that is acidic because of carbon dioxide absorbed from the atmosphere. In the very wet volcanic island of Dominica, in the Lesser Antilles, the rock surface is being eroded

by some 85–220 mm (3.3–8.7 in) every thousand years, one of the fastest rates of chemical erosion in the world. In places with active sulfur springs the rate rises to 775 mm (30.5 in) a thousand years.

The history of volcanic landscapes

The volcanic landscapes that cover much of the region vary greatly with the age of the volcano. The little-eroded cone or dome of a volcano that has erupted relatively recently, such as Soufrière on St Vincent in the Lesser Antilles or El Chichón in southeast Mexico, is shallowly incised by a radiating pattern of long hills and gullies. Older volcanoes, such as the rugged Mount St Catherine in Grenada and Mount Gimie in St Lucia, are deeply dissected, with knife-edge ridges and steep slopes vulnerable to landslides. The pattern of the drainage system is still basically radial, but more powerful streams have captured weaker flows. In long-eroded landscapes the original volcanoes can no longer be discerned. The drainage pattern has become branched and the slopes more gentle; north and central St Lucia provide an example of this type of landscape.

The impact of Europeans

People have had a considerable effect on the landscape of the region since the

Europeans arrived. Before the Spanish Conquest in the early 16th century the Indians practiced mainly slash-and-burn farming. With long fallow periods and little long-term disturbance, only minor damage was caused to the soils and natural forests of the area. In some areas the Spanish Conquest may actually have protected the forests – but only because the Indian population was destroyed. The 3–4 million Arawak Indians of Hispaniola (Haiti and the Dominican Republic) were reduced to 60,000 by 1510, and virtually eradicated by smallpox in 1518.

In the low-lying islands of the West Indies, such as Barbados and Antigua, the

natural seasonal forest was almost totally cleared for sugar planting from the 1640s onward. This had a serious impact, damaging the soil and disturbing plants and animals. The land surface was often rapidly eroded by heavy rain falling on the bare soil after clearance and later after cropping. Most of the sugar lands were so eroded and exhausted of soil nutrients by the time the sugar boom ended in the 19th century that the abandoned lands have reverted only to low scrub woodland rather than the tall forests of the pre-sugar era. In Cuba the same cycle was initiated when the forest was cleared for sugar planting in the late 19th century; today the impact of soil erosion is greatest in the southeast of the island.

Soil erosion and loss of natural habitats have accelerated dramatically in the 20th century. In southern Mexico population pressure, use of the plow, overcropping, and a shortening of the fallow period have all caused land degradation. Over wide areas of once-fertile volcanic soils sheet erosion has exposed underlying limey hardpan layers that are useless for cultivation. In the highlands north of the eastern end of the Sierra Madre del Sur disastrous gullying has transformed former cornfields and pasturelands into a bare, arid area of badlands that can no longer be used for agriculture. The coniferous highland forests of central north Mexico and the tropical rainforests of Central America farther south are today being cleared for agriculture and timber production. In the West Indies surviving rainforests on the higher islands have increasingly been cleared for banana and grapefruit cultivation as farming switches from the ruined and abandoned sugar-growing areas near the coasts.

Glowing with fire, the sides of the Soufriere Hills on Montserrat are smothered by lava and ash during a massive eruption in August 1997. A thick blanket of ash soon covered the area, wiping out the village of Plymouth and spreading all the way down to the sea – a dramatic long-term change to the tropical landscape.

Gray Whale Lagoon on the Baja California coast in Mexico. An offshore coastal bar has been created by ocean currents depositing sand and shingle. The lagoon has become stranded behind the bar, and sediments are slowly being built up in it. It will eventually become dry land.

Where hurricanes strike

The weaponry of a hurricane is fearsome – violent winds, very low pressure and extreme rainfall. High winds can destroy crops and light buildings, and severe hurricanes can defoliate and even flatten swathes of rainforest.

Tropical cyclones are classified by wind speed as storms (62–119 k/h, 39–72 mph) or hurricanes (winds upward of 120 k/h, 75 mph). In the west Pacific these are known as typhoons, in the Bay of Bengal east of India as cyclones. They are revolving systems of low atmospheric pressure accompanied by violent winds circulating in an anticlockwise direction (clockwise in similar latitudes in the southern hemisphere).

The combination of very low pressure and high winds can also generate storm waves of awesome power, which play a major part in coastal erosion and the building of barrier ridges and reef islands in the region. The accompanying floods in coastal areas are often the main cause of loss of life. Farther inland extremely high rainfall can lead to river floods and massive erosion of slopes, frequently triggering landslides.

Hurricanes in the Caribbean

Hurricane Mitch, which swept from Nicaragua to Mexico in October 1998, and Hurricane Gordon in 1994 in Haiti and other Caribbean islands had devastating effects on property and human life. This was so partly because most of the islands' mainly young populations had never witnessed a hurricane before. Where cyclones are frequent, human preparedness and building standards are better. Forest vegetation also adapts: it tends to be shorter, more "streamlined" and hence less susceptible to hurricane damage.

A hurricane normally brings exceptionally heavy rain, between 200 and 500 mm (8–20 in) in under twelve hours. In 1909 a hurricane moving slowly over the Blue Mountains of Jamaica deposited 3,428 mm (135 in) of rain in a week, including 728 mm (29 in) in one day!

In the Caribbean cyclones have traditionally been given girls' names, but since 1979 boys' names have been included too. On average seven cyclones (including four hurricanes) hit the Caribbean each year; within the region their frequency declines toward the south and west. They develop in the northeast trade winds in the tropical Atlantic and in the Caribbean Sea itself. Cyclones generally pass through the Caribbean in a west-northwest direction, but at latitudes of around 20–25°N they curve to the northeast. Over 90 percent develop between June and October, when the sea temperature is at its warmest, the air above it humid, and the atmosphere in the region least stable.

The tracks and frequencies of cyclones in the Caribbean have varied greatly over the past few hundred years. Over the Caribbean as a whole cyclones were comparatively frequent in 1871–1901 and 1928–58, whereas 1902–27 and the years since 1959 have been periods with fewer cyclones. The recent decline has been particularly dramatic, with less than half the expected number of cyclones in the Bahamas, Jamaica, Hispaniola and the northern Lesser Antilles.

Periods of very few cyclones, such as 1650–1760 and 1840–70, are associated with sea-surface temperatures some 1.5°C (2.7°F) below average. During the cyclone peak this century sea temperatures were 1°C (1.8°F) above normal. Some climatologists predict a significant increase in the frequency of cyclones if the expected global warming takes place as a result of the greenhouse effect. Some believe that the trend has already begun.

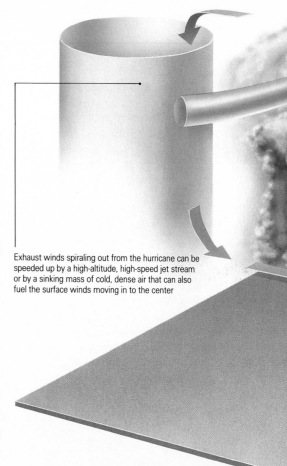

Exhaust winds spiraling out from the hurricane can be speeded up by a high-altitude, high-speed jet stream or by a sinking mass of cold, dense air that can also fuel the surface winds moving in to the center

Winds of up to 200km (125mi) per hour took this airplane and flung it into the trees when Hurricane Gilbert passed through Jamaica in 1988. Winds with Hurricane Mitch in 1998 were even stronger, reaching up to 290km (180mi) per hour, making Mitch the most powerful hurricane on record.

The streets of Tegucigalpa were under water after Hurricane Mitch dumped 102mm (4in) of rain per hour on Honduras in October 1998. Honduras was the worst affected country, with more than 5,600 dead and over a million people homeless. Floods and landslides wiped out half of the country's crops.

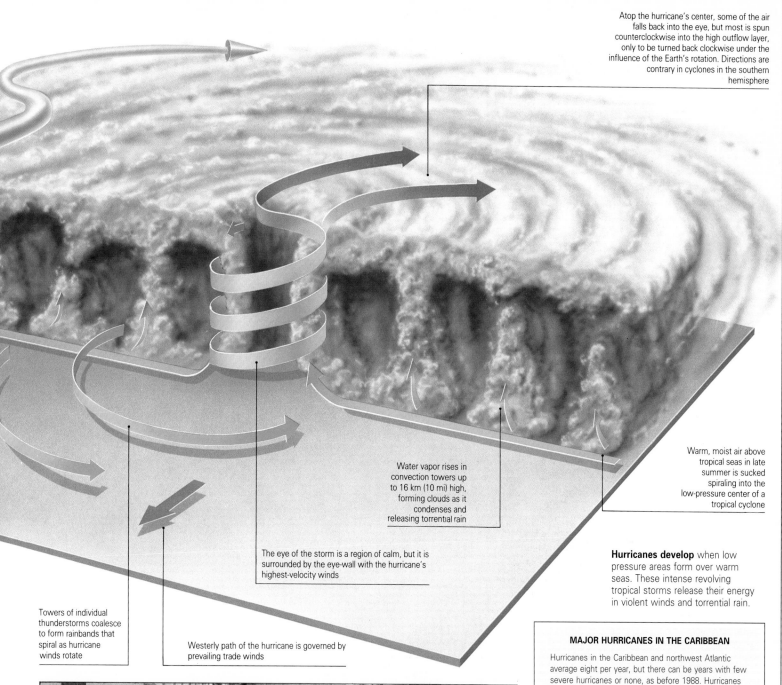

Atop the hurricane's center, some of the air falls back into the eye, but most is spun counterclockwise into the high outflow layer, only to be turned back clockwise under the influence of the Earth's rotation. Directions are contrary in cyclones in the southern hemisphere

Water vapor rises in convection towers up to 16 km (10 mi) high, forming clouds as it condenses and releasing torrential rain

Warm, moist air above tropical seas in late summer is sucked spiraling into the low-pressure center of a tropical cyclone

The eye of the storm is a region of calm, but it is surrounded by the eye-wall with the hurricane's highest-velocity winds

Towers of individual thunderstorms coalesce to form rainbands that spiral as hurricane winds rotate

Westerly path of the hurricane is governed by prevailing trade winds

Hurricanes develop when low pressure areas form over warm seas. These intense revolving tropical storms release their energy in violent winds and torrential rain.

MAJOR HURRICANES IN THE CARIBBEAN

Hurricanes in the Caribbean and northwest Atlantic average eight per year, but there can be years with few severe hurricanes or none, as before 1988. Hurricanes cause damage directly through high winds, sudden low pressure and torrrential rain, and indirectly through storm surges at sea and floods. The rainstorms can erode soils, start landslides and burst river banks.

Year	Location	Casualties
1976	Mexico	400 dead
1979	West Indies	over 1,200 dead, 500,000 homeless
1980	United States	272 dead
1982	Guatemala, El Salvador	over 1,000 dead
1988	Jamaica, Mexico	260 dead 1,000 homeless
1988	Nicaragua, Costa Rica to Venezuela	110 dead 300,000 homeless
1992	Bahamas, Florida, Louisiana	65 deaths, 250,000 homeless
1994	Caribbean Islands, Florida	over 1,000 dead
1998	Honduras, Nicaragua, Guatemala, Mexico	9,000 deaths

HABITATS AND THEIR CONSERVATION

THE RICHES OF NATURE · APPROACHES TO CONSERVATION · FORESTS UNDER THREAT

The habitats and wildlife of Central America and the Caribbean are among the Earth's richest. The mountains, plateaus, plains and islands encompass many different types of tropical forest, hot and cold deserts, mangrove swamps and coral reefs, which are home to plants and animals from both North and South America. Life on the two continents sometimes developed in isolation, but when the Central American land bridge surfaced during periods of low sea level, as happened some 3.5 million years ago, the region provided a unique mixing ground for many species. The isolation of populations of plants and animals on the islands of the Caribbean led to the evolution of hundreds of unique species. However, increasing rates of habitat degradation threatens the biodiversity of the region.

COUNTRIES IN THE REGION

Antigua and Barbuda, Bahamas, Barbados, Belize, Costa Rica, Cuba, Dominica, Dominican Republic, El Salvador, Grenada, Guatemala, Haiti, Honduras, Jamaica, Mexico, Nicaragua, Panama, St Kitts-Nevis, St Lucia, St Vincent and the Grenadines, Trinidad and Tobago

Major protected area	Hectares
Armando Bermúdez NP	76,600
Alto Golfode NP	934,756
Chiquibul NP	107,607
Corcovado NP	41,790
Darién NP BR WH	597,000
El Vizcaíno BR	2,546,790
Gandocá-Manzillo WR	70,000
Glovers Reef MR	30,800
Guanacaste NP	70,000
Juan Pablo Duarte NP	168,400
Inagua NP	74,330
Kuna Yala R	60,000
La Amistad R BR WH	584,590
La Michilia BR	42,000
Mapimi BR	103,000
Martinique RNaP	70,150
Montes-Azules BR	331,200
Patuca NP	220,000
Reserva de la Bíosfera La Encrucijada RS	302,706
Rio Plátano BR WH	500,000
Sand Sand Pond Sank WR	16,125
Sian Ka'an BR WH	528,147
Sierra Maestra NP	500,000
Sur Isla de la Juventud NP	80,000
Tikal NP WH	59,570
Whale Sanctuary of El Vizcaíno BR WH	370,000

BR = Biosphere Reserve; MR = Marine Reserve; Nm = National Monument; NP = National Park; RNaP = Regional Nature Park; R = Reserve; RS = Ramsar site; WR = Wildlife Refuge; WH = World Heritage site

---

THE RICHES OF NATURE

The landscape of Central America is so varied that it is possible to travel from mountainous terrain, tropical dry forest and swamp forest to rich coastal plains in the space of a single day. From the coast the land rises rapidly to high mountains. Volcanic peaks that soar to heights of 3,660 m (12,000 ft), tower above sub-alpine meadows and the deep emerald green forests, inhabited by a variety of animals, including monkeys, sloths, tapirs, toucans and snakes. Birds such as the rare and beautiful quetzal and distinctive scarlet macaw are still found here. Jaguars and pumas stalk their prey and brightly ringed coral snakes feed on birds and rodents.

The islands of the Caribbean, known as the Antilles or West Indies, also contain numerous ecosystems, from coral reefs to tropical upland forest, many with unique plant and animal species. The coral reefs provide habitats for marine species such as conchs, lobsters, sea anemones, and many kinds of reef fish; the mangrove forests and sea grass meadows support manatees and other plant-eaters, and also act as nurseries for the young of many reef-and ocean-dwelling fish. Sea turtles and shrimps migrate seasonally from one habitat to another.

The ecosystems on the islands themselves are just as diverse as those of the coast. There is a succession of forest types as the land rises from the coast to the mountains in the center of the larger islands. The evergreen woodland that fringes the coast gives way to dry lowland forest, then to moist rainforest, misty cloud forest, and finally to mountain thickets and "elfin forest", with strange, twisted dwarf trees. The proper management of the forests is vital to the prosperity of the island communities. They protect the watershed, ensuring that there is fresh water during the dry season, and also provide fuelwood and construction material; they shelter the islands from storms and hurricanes, and protect the coastal systems by checking the pace of soil erosion.

Exploiting the land

Tragically, this extraordinary region is falling victim to human disturbance. It is a process that has been going on for centuries – environmental destruction is

---

rooted deep in the history of the region. Before the Europeans arrived in Central America, the Aztec and Maya peoples, with populations that were in some areas greater than those of today, destroyed large tracts of forest. However, the agriculture of these indigenous peoples did not degrade the land: they cultivated Indian corn (maize), beans, squash and root crops, and supplemented these by hunting and fishing. The land was able to sustain their agriculture without becoming exhausted.

Systematic exploitation began in the 16th century, when the lure of vast mineral resources attracted the Spanish Conquistadors. The region's gold and

Riding the storm – a coral island off the coast of Belize. Coral reefs form a living barrier that protects the island against storm damage. Corals grow in warm, shallow seas where photosynthesis is high, providing energy for a large and complex food chain.

silver deposits were soon depleted, and the Spanish turned their attention to natural resources such as timber for export to the Old World. They began to cultivate native crops such as coffee, sugar and bananas for export, and later raised cattle on a large scale.

Fueled by rapid population growth and economic need, the overexploitation of natural resources that began with the Conquistadors has reached dangerous proportions. About 54 percent of original forest cover remains in Central America, and over 2 percent of the remaining unprotected forest is being destroyed every year. The coastal mangroves are being cleared to make way for urban development.

Reefs on almost all the Caribbean islands have severely deterioirated. The islands are increasingly popular resorts for tourists attracted by the warm climate, white sandy beaches, reefs and the exotic marine life, but their environments are threatened by sewage pollution, deforestation and agricultural run-off as land use has changed to supply tourist demands. These are just a few of the threats that must be overcome if the world is not to lose the beauty and genetic diversity of one of its biologically richest regions.

Cloud forest in Costa Rica At heights of between 900 and 1,500 m (2,500 and 5,000 ft) the forest is dim, damp and cold. There may be fewer than ten cloudless days a year, and trees are stunted and overgrown with lichens, mosses and other plants.

Map of biomes Central America joins two great landmasses. Its habitats range from cloud forest to hot desert and mangrove swamps. In the Caribbean are forested islands and coral reefs.

Biomes
- tropical humid forest
- tropical dry forest
- evergreen sclerophyll forest and scrubland
- warm desert and semidesert
- mountain and highland system
- island system
- lake system

- ◆ major protected area
- ○ Biosphere Reserve
- × World Heritage site

Gulf of Mexico

Bay of Campeche

Isthmus of Tehuantepec

del Sur

Gulf of Tehuantepec

Yucatán

Sian Ka'an

Calakmul

Tikal

Montes Azules

BELIZE

Half-Moon Caye

Belize Barrier Reef System

GUATEMALA

Sierra de las Minas

HONDURAS

Rio Plátano

Cape Gracias á Dios

Coco

La Tigra

EL SALVADOR

NICARAGUA

Lake Managua

Lake Nicaragua

Guanacaste

COSTA RICA

Cordillera Volcánica Central

Corcovado

Gandocá

Manzanillo

La Amistad

Kuna Yala

Darién

Barro Colorado

PANAMA

Great Abaco

Grand Bahama

Eleuthera

Andros

BAHAMAS

Long Island

Acklins Island

Turks and Caicos Islands (U.K.)

ATLANTIC OCEAN

Sierra del Rosario

CUBA

Great Inagua

Inagua

Hispaniola

Virgin Islands (U.S.A.)

Virgin Islands (U.K.)

Barbuda

ANTIGUA AND BARBUDA

Antigua

Luquillo

Guánica

DOMINICAN REPUBLIC

HAITI

Puerto Rico (U.S.A.)

Armando Bermudez

Guadeloupe (France)

DOMINICA

Morne Pitons

Martinique (France)

ST KITTS-NEVIS

Montserrat (U.K.)

ST LUCIA

BARBADOS

ST VINCENT AND THE GRENADINES

GRENADA

Isla de la Juventud

Cayman Islands (U.K.)

Sierra Maestra

G r e a t e r   A n t i l l e s

JAMAICA

L e s s e r   A n t i l l e s

Caribbean Sea

Netherlands Antilles (Neth.)

Aruba (Neth.)

Bonaire

Tobago

TRINIDAD AND TOBAGO

Asa Wright

Trinidad

483

APPROACHES TO CONSERVATION

In response to the worsening situation, the Central American and Caribbean countries have made considerable progress in conservation with 5.6 percent of land area protected in 1996. Puerto Rico, for example, has established the Caribbean National Forest encompassing 11,500 ha (28,000 acres) in the Sierra de Luquillo Mountains. Caribbean governments have for the most part concentrated on marine reserves, which they see as beneficial to the tourist industry upon which many of the islands depend. In 1993 Caribbean tourism generated 43 percent of combined GNP and one-third of export earnings. Approximately 100 million tourists visit annually and countries such as the Bahamas, are aware that their appeal is based almost exclusively on climate, environment and marine life.

Since 1970 well over a hundred marine reserves have been created throughout the Caribbean, though only a quarter of them are as yet reported to be properly managed. The management of underwater areas includes preventing over-exploitation, promoting nature-based tourism such as photography, underwater marine trails and scuba-diving, and protecting the marine environment from damage by urban development, dredgers, pleasure boats, souvenir hunters, inexperienced divers and land-based pollution. Despite the problems there have been many success stories, such as the marine reserve on the island of Bonaire in the Lesser Antilles, where tourism and conservation coexist to mutual advantage.

Conservation efforts in the region have been hampered by a lack of public awareness and limited mandate and have had little impact on agricultural and industrial activities; they are also difficult to monitor and enforce. In the Caribbean, however, most countries have begun to strengthen their environmental initiatives particularly in the areas of sustainable tourism, coastal and marine management and biodiversity conservation – all of which are vital to the tourist industry, and therefore, the economy.

Except for local efforts, systematic regional habitat conservation in Central America began only in 1974. Since then, each country has established protected areas. The Dominican Republic leads the

A typical peasant smallholding Many small farmers make a living on the edges of the forest. Their system of growing mixed crops, as well as raising a few cattle, makes few demands on the land, which is left fallow for periods so that secondary forest growth develops. These farmers also protect the water sources in the high forest.

Lush forest plants have sprung up where a stream runs through a lowland rainforest reserve. It creates an opening in the upper tree canopy so that light penetrates to the ground, stimulating growth. The understorey in the depths of the forest is much more open, but here the forest is impenetrable.

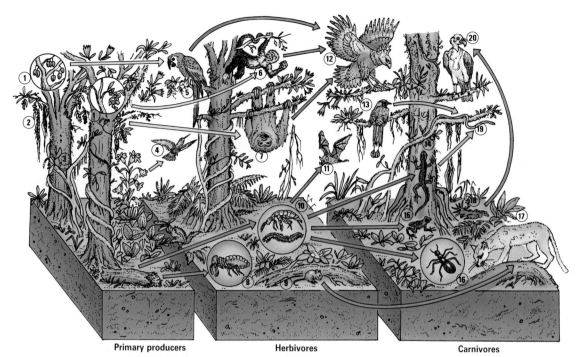

Components of the ecosystem
1 Fruits and seeds
2 Epiphytic plants
3 Liana
4 Hummingbird
5 Macaw
6 Squirrel monkey
7 Three-toed sloth
8 Termite
9 Mouse
10 Herbivorous insects
11 Bat
12 Harpy eagle
13 Insectivorous bird
14 Basilisk lizard
15 Poison arrow frog
16 Ants
17 Ocelot
18 Dead animal
19 Blunt-headed treesnake
20 King vulture

Energy flow
⇒ primary producer/primary consumer
⇒ primary/secondary consumer
⇒ secondary/tertiary consumer
⇒ dead material/consumer

A tropical forest ecosystem showing the interaction of organisms between the soil, forest floor, understorey and tree layers.

Primary producers   Herbivores   Carnivores

The desert peninsula of Baja California, which runs parallel to the northwestern coast of Mexico, has proved inhospitable to human settlement. This has been a major factor in its survival as a wilderness. Plants and animals have adapted to these dry and arid conditions. Cacti, typical plants of New World deserts, have developed their characteristically swollen stems and reduced leaves in order to ensure that water loss through transpiration is minimal.

field with 31 percent of its total land area designated as protected. Since 1970, when conservation laws were first developed, the number of legally designated protected areas in Central America as a whole has grown to 414, covering 5.6 percent of the land area. However, the quality of management in many of these areas varies considerably.

Managing the land

Lack of government funding and local protection remain major obstacles to effective management. One proposed solution is to entrust the management of an area to local people whose traditional use of the land does not overexploit its resources. In Mexico, for example, the Lacandón Indians cultivate forest farm plots (milpas). After clearing or burning the forest they plant root crops and a mixture of others such as corn, beans and squash. In a typical Lacandón field up to 80 crops are grown over a period of five to seven years. The land is then left fallow, and produces secondary forest growth that supports game animals.

Another solution is to reduce pressures on a reserve's resources by establishing projects that emphasize sustainable production. At the Gandocá-Manzanillo Wildlife Refuge in Costa Rica, farmers within and around the refuge receive help to diversify their crops. Over a hundred different species are cultivated. The cacao tree, of great commercial value for its seeds (cocoa beans), is the most widely grown. It is suited to the area; like the natural forest it does not expose the soil to erosion, and the crop is both easy to cultivate and profitable. Farmers here are participating in cooperative marketing schemes, and are working to secure rights of land ownership to help stabilize the peasant community.

In the absence of sufficient government finance, nongovernmental organizations have multiplied. They raise funds both internally, from membership dues and

THE NONSUCH ISLAND PROJECT

The reef system and mangrove zones of Bermuda are the most northerly in the Atlantic. They form a crescent-shaped chain of approximately 150 coral-fringed limestone islands. Bermuda faces considerable environmental problems. Its population of some 61,000 crowded into just 54 sq km (21 sq mi) puts increasing pressure on the land. The reefs are overfished to cater for the 600,000 annual visitors. The presence of so many tourists exacerbates the problems of sewage and garbage disposal, which pollutes the reefs and kills the reef-building coral polyps.

Bermuda has one of the most ambitious conservation experiments in the Caribbean. Since the Nonsuch Island project "Living Museum" was set up in 1963 more than 8,000 seedlings of rare native shrubs and trees have been planted. Once-endangered animals such as the endemic skink and Bermuda cicada are now thriving. The dwindling population of green turtles, which for centuries have returned to breed every 15 to 30 years, has been restocked.

Most attention has focused on the campaign to restore the island's only endemic bird, the cahow (a kind of petrel), which once lived here in its thousands. Hunted for food by settlers, these ground-nesting birds were also easy prey for introduced cats and rats. They were thought to be extinct, but in 1951 one breeding pair was discovered. Under careful management their numbers have slowly built up, and by the 1990s 45 nesting pairs had been identified. The Nonsuch Island project is so successful that it has become a model for island conservation.

Regreening the forest The agriculture practiced by the Maya before European conquerors destroyed their civilization sustained large populations but did not degrade the land. Trees grow densely around the ruins of a Maya settlement at Palenque in Mexico, showing how far the forest has been able to regenerate.

government grants, and externally from such organizations as the International Union for the Conservation of Nature and Natural Resources (IUCN), US-AID, the World Wide Fund for Nature (WWF) and Nature Conservancy International. It is not uncommon to find international funds being channeled through these private organizations, which have assumed responsibility for the management of some conservation areas.

A future for conservation?
Habitat conservation in Central America and the Caribbean has come a long way in the last 25 years, though many areas are still struggling to find a workable balance between exploitation and preservation. Despite the current economic, social and political problems, by 2000 many Central American countries were party to the major environmental conventions to protect habitats and species such as CITES, the Convention on Biological Diversity, the Protocol on Specially Protected Areas and Wildlife and the Ramsar Convention. Some countries, such as Mexico, Costa Rica, Honduras and Nicaragua have established national environmental policies

FORESTS UNDER THREAT

The achievements of the conservation movement are threatened everywhere in Central America. In areas of military conflict forests and crops have been destroyed by scorched-earth tactics; the population has been terrorized and dislocated, making it difficult to stabilize the way the land is used. Elsewhere, forests are cleared to make way for roads to consolidate government control over distant provinces, and this encourages destructive colonization by providing access to virgin areas. Between 1990 and 1995, Central America lost 6 percent of its forest.

Pressures on the land
Central America has a small landmass and a large – and rapidly growing – population, with relatively little industry. It is dependent on agriculture. Overwhelmed with foreign debts, governments try to improve their economic position both by industrial development and by the exploitation of natural resources – oil, gold and other minerals, timber, and water for hydroelectric power – as well as by producing cash crops for export. All these practices destroy the forest.

Half the population farms for its livelihood, but 80 percent of the farmers do not possess enough land to support their families. Most of the agricultural land is owned by a wealthy minority (in Guatemala 80 percent of the farmland is held by 2 percent of the population) that continues to expand large cattle ranches; already nearly 40 percent of land is under pasture.

The number of landless peasants has tripled since 1960 as the population has grown. This puts increasing pressure on remote, unprotected forested land for which ownership has not been established. Traditional peasant agriculture often cannot be sustained by the land, which is hilly and stony, with thin soils that do not retain plant nutrients and are easily eroded. After only a few years, when soil productivity declines, the peasants move

Deforestation in Haiti Once richly forested with pines and hardwoods, less than 1 percent of the forest now remains. Its disappearance has been hastened by slash-and-burn agricultural techniques. Once the vegetation is cleared, overcultivation exhausts the soil, leading to severe erosion and dereliction of the land.

REBUILDING THE FOREST

One of the most threatened types of forest in Central America is dry tropical forest. This unique forest has been reduced to only 2 percent of its former size, much of it in Costa Rica. The small patches of dry forest survive amid large expanses of degraded agricultural land and cattle ranches. In the 1980s, an ambitious project was launched to restore a large area of the forest creating the Guanacaste Conservation Area. The area sustains breeding populations of 150 mammal species (including rare tapirs and spotted cats), 300 bird species, over 6,000 species of butterflies and moths, 6,000 plant species and about 15,000 other species. It also includes migration routes from the dry forest to moist forest refuges used during the dry season by birds, mammals and millions of insects.

The abandoned agricultural land is dominated by African pasture grasses, which prevent forest seeds regenerating and are prone to severe fires. Under the management plan designed to bring back the trees, controlled grazing by livestock will help to keep down the grasses, and firebreaks protect the regenerating forest. Windblown seeds of forest trees reach the area unaided; large trees and hedgerows planted in the pastures attract birds, which bring the heavier seeds of forest fruit trees. Today, fires have been reduced by 90 percent and the African grasses have all but gone.

Efforts are also being made to ensure that the local people benefit by offering them employment as guards, managers and research assistants, by providing educational programs, and by encouraging tourism. The complete recovery of the forest is expected to take about 300 years, but significant progress will be made long before that.

on again. They lack the legal title that would allow them to take advantage of government improvement schemes, so they sell their holdings to ranchers, who thus acquire new pasture cheaply.

Honduras, with its weak economy and sizeable landless population, typifies the problems facing conservationists in Central America. The Río Plátano area has been given international conservation status as the region's first Biosphere Reserve and a World Heritage site. It contains every endangered species of mammal in Central America. Despite its enormous size – over 850,000 ha (2.1 million acres) – the entire reserve is under threat.

Invading peasant farmers, loggers and Miskito Indians who have fled across the border from war-torn Nicaragua practice shifting cultivation, logging and cattle ranching, activities that inflict severe erosion in the area. The wildlife is increasingly threatened both by habitat destruction and by hunting: animals command a high price on the international black market. A collection of private organizations has implemented a conservation initiative and eco-tourism is slowly developing. However, the degeneration continues as the government has neither the means nor the political will to establish real protection for the reserve.

Problems and solutions

The general economic crisis in the region limits efforts to conserve designated areas of forest. Parks and reserves are forced to operate on minimum budgets and are understaffed. The lack of financial support has taken its toll. Low salaries, minimal operating revenue, appalling living conditions in many parks and reserves and declining morale have all made it more difficult to tackle the growing problem of encroachment effectively. A further consideration is the resistance of the local population: to a land-hungry peasant the creation of a park in an area suitable for even short-term agriculture seems absurd. The associated problems can be equally serious. At La Tigra, Honduras' pilot national park, squatters are felling trees and destroying the watershed that supplies the capital, Tegucigalpa, with half its water (still recovering from the devastation caused by Hurricane Mitch in 1998). This situation is similar throughout the entire Caribbean, where tourism and local population pressures are degrading the island ecosystems.

Conservationists are working to preserve the Central American natural heritage. In 2000, 124 sites were classified as National Parks and 411 areas have protected status. However, the lesson of recent years is that conservation must prove itself economically productive if it is to survive. Eco-tourism, emphasizing the appeal of unexploited natural landscapes and providing wildlife experiences, is being actively promoted. Conservationists have also recognized the importance of acquiring trained staff, of long-term financing and of gaining the support of the local population. This rapidly expanding sector of the global tourism industry brings valuable income to developing countries and can, if properly managed, benefit the ecosystems and rural development of the region.

Kuna Yala Reserve

Throughout Central America the traditional way of life of indigenous peoples is threatened by the migration of landless peasants attracted by the prospect of unexploited cultivable land. Population pressure, together with economic incentives to develop the natural resources, has prompted successive governments to construct roads, which has increased the threat to Indian culture. In certain cases the indigenous people have resisted this process. In Panama the Kuna people have taken conservation into their own hands. They are applying traditional agricultural methods in their homeland in the territory (*comarca*) of the Kuna Yala Reserve, which occupies the archipelago of San Blas and the neighboring northeast coast of Panama.

Kuna Yala is inhabited by 30,000 Kuna Indians, who live on some of the 350 forested coral islands lying close to the narrow coastal plain that extends into the steep San Blas mountain range. For their livelihood the Indians fish, harvest coconuts, raise pigs and chickens and farm the coastal plains, in addition to hunting and gathering in the forest. The reserve was established in 1938 after a successful war against the government. Since then the

tribe has deliberately isolated itself from Panamanian society, but by early 1970 its independence was threatened by the construction of an all-weather road that brought peasant farmers, practicing their slash-and-burn agriculture, to the limits of the reserve.

At first the Kunas supported the construction of the road, believing that it would bring prosperity, but they soon became alarmed at the threat posed to their land and way of life. To demonstrate their rights to the area, and to conserve the forest, they initiated the Kuna wildlands project. The project aims to promote scientific research and natural history, to generate revenue by encouraging low-key tourism, and to preserve the integrity of the Kuna Yala Reserve by asserting ownership of the region. It began by demarcating the *comarca*'s boundary, installing patrol trails and stations and building a headquarters at Nusagandi.

The success of the project is a unique example of an indigenous people planning, implementing and managing a conservation area. The Kunas' harmonious relationship with the environment, and in particular with the forest, which serves as a supermarket, pharmacy and lumber-

yard, forms the basis of their prosperity and independence. Their home in the reserve is only 150 km (100 mi) from Panama City, and some of them have migrated to it, attracted by the prospect of employment. The value of Western education has been recognized – there are primary schools on all the major islands, and the best students are encouraged to continue their education, both in Panama City and by traveling abroad.

The Kunas are a confident people, aware that they can provide a model for their fellow Indians, and proud of the fact. While they maintain their traditional

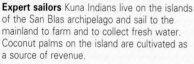

Expert sailors Kuna Indians live on the islands of the San Blas archipelago and sail to the mainland to farm and to collect fresh water. Coconut palms on the island are cultivated as a source of revenue.

Plantains being harvested Farming takes place along the banks of rivers. Two or three families farm each plot as a cooperative, growing fruit, corn and coffee for themselves and cacao as a commercial crop.

In harmony with their surroundings The way of life of the Kuna Indians preserves the natural processes of the forest and islands. Rivers provide a means of transport inland as well as a valuable source of fresh water; they are particularly respected.

farming, fishing and hunting they have also welcomed ecotourism which has now become a major source of income for them. They also accept technological advances such as electric generators and modern transportation methods, but reject materialism as a way of life. Private ownership is still an alien concept, and decisions that affect the future of the people are made collectively, according to tradition. The Kunas are succeeding in protecting their traditional lands, taking advantage of the modern world yet continuing to live in harmony with the unchanged wilderness of the reserve.

ANIMAL LIFE

MIGRANTS AND INVADERS · SPECIALIZING FOR SUCCESS · HABITAT LOSS AND CONSERVATION

Central America has been a center of evolution for many groups of animals for millions of years. In the last 5 million years, as the land bridge between South and North America formed, the region also became a mixing ground for species from both subcontinents. Animals that evolved early in South America, such as the marsupial opossums and the armadillos, ant-eaters and sloths, and had survived there in isolation from competition with the later-developing, more advanced mammals of the northern subcontinent, colonized Central America. Later, as the climate fluctuated during the recent ice ages, animals of both temperate and tropical habitats mingled in the region. New species also evolved in isolation on the many islands of the Caribbean and off the Pacific coast, adding to the region's diversity of animal life.

COUNTRIES IN THE REGION

Antigua and Barbuda, Bahamas, Barbados, Belize, Costa Rica, Cuba, Dominica, Dominican Republic, El Salvador, Grenada, Guatemala, Haiti, Honduras, Jamaica, Mexico, Nicaragua, Panama, St Kitts-Nevis, St Lucia, St Vincent and the Grenadines, Trinidad and Tobago

ENDEMISM AND DIVERSITY

Diversity Low (for example Caribbean island mammals) to very high (most groups in Central America)
Endemism High to very high

SPECIES

	Total	Threatened	†Extinct
Mammals	550	46	10
Birds	*1,300	80	7
Others	unknown	210	13

† species extinct since 1600
* breeding and regular non-breeding species

NOTABLE THREATENED ENDEMIC SPECIES

Mammals Haitian solenodon *(Solenodon paradoxus)*, Central American squirrel monkey *(Saimiri oerstedi)*, Volcano rabbit *(Romerolagus diazi)*, Jamaican hutia *(Geocapromys brownii)*, Gulf of California porpoise *(Phocoena sinus)*
Birds St Vincent amazon *(Amazona guildingii)*, Highland guan *(Penelopina nigra)*, Resplendent quetzal *(Pharomachrus mocinno)*, Ocellated turkey *(Agriocharis ocellata)*, Cahow *(Procellaria cahow)*
Others Kemp's ridley turtle *(Lepidochelys kempii)*, Jamaican ground iguana *(Cyclura collei)*, Golden toad *(Bufo periglenes)*

NOTABLE THREATENED NON-ENDEMIC SPECIES

Mammals Geoffroy's spider monkey *(Ateles geoffroyi)*, Giant anteater *(Myrmecophaga tridactyla)*, Ocelot *(Felis pardalis)*, Central American tapir *(Tapirus bairdii)*, Caribbean manatee Trichechus manatus)
Birds Orange-breasted falcon *(Falco deiroleucus)*, Solitary eagle *(Harpyhaliaetus solitarius)*
Others American crocodile *(Crocodylus acutus)*, Logger-head turtle *(Caretta caretta)*, Green turtle *(Chelonia mydas)*

DOMESTICATED ANIMALS (originating in region)

turkey *(Meleagris gallopavo)*, Muscovy duck *(Cairina moschata)*

MIGRANTS AND INVADERS

The varied inhabitants of the Central American tropical rainforests include not only monkeys, wild cats, deer, bears and peccaries, but also invaders from South America such as armadillos, sloths, ant-eaters and opossums, species of rodents such as the pacas and agoutis, and tree-climbing porcupines, which have pre-hensile tails used for gripping.

The first immigrants were generally grazers, as savanna covered much of the region. As the climate warmed and tropical forests spread, many animals evolved new features to suit the warm, moist conditions, and jungle animals invaded from the south. Other species of animals that thrive in temperate habitats, such as the White-tailed deer and Mountain lion or puma, remained to add to the diversity of the wildlife.

Over 200 bird species migrate to Central America from both South America and northern North America to escape the winter – the Sandhill crane, geese, ducks, shorebirds, flycatchers, swallows and a host of smaller birds. In spring they leave for richer feeding grounds to breed. This ensures that enough food remains for the resident birds to rear their young.

Abundant specialist rainforest animals (*above*) The Red-eyed tree frog is highly adapted for its arboreal life: it has suction pads on its toes and a flattened body for extra grip on smooth leaves.

Helping one another (*left*) As a hummingbird sips nectar from a passionflower, the flower's stamens brush pollen onto its head, to be rubbed off on the stigma of the next flower visited, thus performing the vital task of pollination. Many such interrelationships have evolved in the tropical forest.

Biodiversity

Rainforests, with their complex physical structure and their abundant food in the form of leaves, flowers, fruits, dead wood and the myriad insects that feed on them, provide opportunities for many different lifestyles. So great is the variety that there often seem to be two kinds of animal for every biological niche: raccoons and coatis in open forest, deer and tapirs in swampy areas, rattlesnakes and bushmasters in dense forest. Sloths, monkeys, toucans, quetzals and parrots live in the treetops; jaguars and ocelots prowl the forest floor; deer browse in the undergrowth; peccaries snuffle among the dead leaves; and frogs and toads croak in the pools. Fer de lances, pit vipers with a powerful venom, lie in wait for small mammals among the buttress roots of huge forest trees. Tarantulas hide under the rotting logs that are food for termites and wood-boring beetles.

With the large number of immigrant species to the region, competition for resources has been fierce, and new species have arisen to take advantage of the smallest opportunity. Nowhere is this more obvious than among the birds – the Central American jungles boast no fewer than 50 species of hummingbird, out of a world total of 315, of which 35 are found in Costa Rica. There are 72 of the Americas' 100 or so species of flycatcher and 45 species of tanager (small, sparrow-like songbirds), each differing slightly in their feeding and nesting behavior.

From the desert to the sea

Not all Central America is green and lush. There are also deserts in the north and northwest of the region. These are the hunting grounds of nocturnal spiders and scorpions, rattlesnakes and the Elf owl, and the daytime haunts of the Gila monster (a poisonous lizard), kangaroo mice and the Gopher tortoise. In the desert pools several endemic species of fish have evolved in isolation.

The region's two coastlines have their own distinct mix of inhabitants. The wealth of food in the upwelling waters off the Pacific coast attracts Fin, Humpback and Sperm whales, while the Gray whale migrates over 8,000 km (5,000 mi) from the Arctic to the sheltered lagoons of Baja California to give birth and mate. Colonies of Sea lions, the Northern elephant seal and the rare Guadalupe fur seal inhabit the rocky beaches, the males battling for territory and possession of the females. Offshore islands are the home of millions of gulls and terns, boobies, pelicans and tropicbirds. A number of interesting species are unique to these islands – a rattlesnake without a rattle, kangaroo rats that never drink, a fish-eating bat and a Black jackrabbit.

The mangrove swamps of the Caribbean coast shelter ibises, herons, egrets and storks, which pluck fish from the shallows, as well as larger predators, the alligators and crocodiles. Docile manatees graze the beds of sea grass, and sea turtles visit the beaches to lay their eggs. The coral reefs around the islands are home to a wide variety of tropical fish, mollusks and other marine invertebrates.

SPECIALIZING FOR SUCCESS

One of the main results of competition in the tropical forests has been the evolution of many animals with highly specialized feeding habits. Several different species of monkey manage to coexist by living at different levels in the trees and feeding on different foods. The tyrant flycatchers – with 376 species the largest family of birds in the New World – have evolved numerous hunting methods, such as perch-feeding, hovering and even chasing their prey on foot. Some change their diet according to the season, and may include fruit at certain times of the year. As a result of these varied diets there is a wide range of variation in body size and bill shape.

The bats are equally diverse, with over 100 Central American species. Fruit- and nectar-feeding bats are common in the rainforests, where flowers and fruits can be found all year round. Nectar-feeders hover in front of flowers to lap up nectar with their long, rough tongues. There are many insect-eating bats. Fast-flying free-tailed bats forage above the forest canopy, while other bats with large ears and shorter wings are able to fly in and out of the trees, where they scoop up insects from leaves and branches. Some of the larger insect-eaters have taken to eating small lizards as well as insects, and one bat specializes in capturing frogs by homing in on their mating calls. Other species of carnivorous bat prey on small mammals, birds and fish.

The Common vampire bat is famous for its method of feeding on the blood of animals. It attacks deer, tapirs, peccaries and domestic livestock, using its hindlegs and thumbs to shuffle along the ground in search of sleeping animals. Its teeth are so sharp that its victims seldom realize they have been bitten. An anticoagulant in its saliva keeps the blood flowing until it has drunk its fill. As they are carriers of rabies and many other infections, all three species of vampire bat pose very serious problems for farmers.

A number of tropical animals have evolved adaptations to cope with life high among the trees. For example, groups of animals as different from each other as monkeys, anteaters, opossums, mice and even porcupines have all developed prehensile tails that act as a fifth limb for climbing in the canopy.

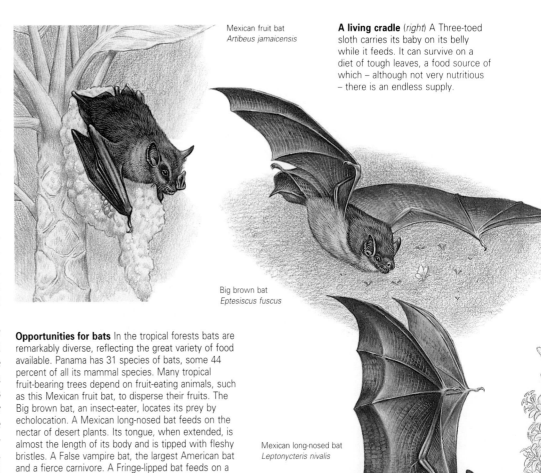

Mexican fruit bat
Artibeus jamaicensis

A living cradle (*right*) A Three-toed sloth carries its baby on its belly while it feeds. It can survive on a diet of tough leaves, a food source of which – although not very nutritious – there is an endless supply.

Big brown bat
Eptesiscus fuscus

Opportunities for bats In the tropical forests bats are remarkably diverse, reflecting the great variety of food available. Panama has 31 species of bats, some 44 percent of all its mammal species. Many tropical fruit-bearing trees depend on fruit-eating animals, such as this Mexican fruit bat, to disperse their fruits. The Big brown bat, an insect-eater, locates its prey by echolocation. A Mexican long-nosed bat feeds on the nectar of desert plants. Its tongue, when extended, is almost the length of its body and is tipped with fleshy bristles. A False vampire bat, the largest American bat and a fierce carnivore. A Fringe-lipped bat feeds on a variety of prey ranging from insects to lizards, but prefers frogs. The Mustache bat has skin flaps on its lips and chin instead of on the nose. A Fishing bulldog bat uses its claws to catch its prey.

Mexican long-nosed bat
Leptonycteris nivalis

Forest amphibians

Moist rainforests are ideal places for frogs and toads, but contain few permanent ponds or streams in which they can lay their eggs. Tropical frogs overcome this in a number of ways. Most poison-arrow frogs carry their tadpoles to water on their backs. The tadpoles of nest-building frogs spend their lives in foam nests, and some tiny tree frogs lay their eggs in the little pools in the centers of bromeliads, plants that grow along the branches of forest trees. Leaf frogs lay their eggs on leaves overhanging streams, out of reach of aquatic predators, and repeatedly urinate over them to keep them moist. On hatching the tadpoles fall into the water below.

Some species have a life cycle in which the tadpole stage has been eliminated; development is completed inside the egg, which hatches to release a fully formed froglet. In some species the eggs may be laid straight on the ground, but the so-called marsupial frogs carry their eggs around in a pouch under the skin of their backs until the young frogs have hatched.

Fringe-lipped bat
Trachops cirrhosus

Sloths are the commonest large mammals in the Central American rainforests, though they are seldom seen. Their lazy existence is a fascinating adaptation to a life spent feeding on the forest's least nutritious foliage – a diet for which they encounter very little competition. Like ruminant mammals such as cattle or deer, sloths have continuously growing teeth, a slow digestive system and a many-chambered stomach that houses bacteria to help them digest plant cellulose.

Sloths move extremely sluggishly, and sleep for up to 19 hours a day. Their slow habits conserve energy, thus minimizing food requirements. Unlike most mammals, the sloth has a body temperature that fluctuates markedly, dropping at night and in wet weather, so reducing the need to generate heat. Its thick fur, together with a complex arrangement of blood vessels rather similar to those of marine mammals, also helps to conserve heat.

The sloth's long hair is a camouflage mixture of black, yellow and white. Algae live in grooves in the hairs, turning yellow in periods of drought and green in damp weather, further enhancing the camouflage.

The animals spend most of their time hanging upside down. This posture misleads predators looking out for the typical upright outline of a four-footed animal on a branch. The sloth descends to the ground only to defecate, about every six days. Its powerful grip persists even in death; the long, curved claws remain firmly clasped around the branch until its body rots. This deters many local people from hunting it.

False vampire bat
Vampyrum spectrum

Fishing bulldog bat
Noctilio leporinus

Mustache bat
Pteronotus parnelli

HABITAT LOSS AND CONSERVATION

Like many tropical regions, Central America has a rapidly increasing human population. The need to plant crops and rear livestock inevitably destroys natural habitats. However, protected areas have been established, and more are planned. Some are specifically designed to protect particular species, such as the jaguar in Belize and the quetzal (a bird with iridescent plumage) in Guatemala.

Most of the Caribbean islands are fringed by mangrove swamps and coral reefs rich in marine life. Belize on the mainland has the second largest coral reef in the world. Reefs are under threat from sewage pollution, coral mining, overfishing and tourism damage.

Although Caribbean governments have brought in conservation legislation and created marine nature reserves, the rapid growth of tourism, especially of diving and watersports, has brought new threats to the reefs. Shell- and coral-collecting for souvenirs damages fragile corals that may have taken hundreds of years to grow. Manatees (herbivorous sea mammals) are injured by boat propellers as they graze in the shallow sea grass beds. Tourism has created fewer problems on the Pacific coast of Baja California.

Conservation efforts have been made to protect the many sea turtles – Loggerhead, Hawksbill, Green, Ridley and Leatherback – that visit the beaches of the Caribbean. Local people help to guard beaches against egg collectors; the eggs are removed to safe incubators, and the hatchlings later returned to the sea. This achieves a much higher survival rate than for those young turtles that are allowed to hatch in the wild.

Many Central American species are threatened by the trade in animals and animal skins. Although it is banned by most countries in the region, the illegal export of the pelts of ocelot, margay and other small cats continues. The exotic pet trade damages not only wild birds such as parrots, but also the Indigo snake and the Red-kneed tarantula. Particularly at risk are the colorful parrots of the genus Amazona, some species of which are confined to individual Caribbean islands. Fourteen species are already extinct.

Farming the forest

The loss of their forest habitats threatens hundreds of species. In Costa Rica, an attempt is being made to save the iguanas and their habitat by developing a form of ranching. The meat of iguanas – fast-growing tree lizards up to 2 m (6.5 ft) long – is valued for eating. A single hectare (2.5 acres) of cleared land provides poor grazing for cattle, yielding only 12.5 kg (27.5 lb) of beef. As forest it can yield over

The West Indian manatee (*above*) is up to 4.6 m (14.7 ft) long, and can weigh 1,600 kg (3,500 lb). Manatees are the only fully aquatic freshwater herbivores in the world. With their docile temperament, slow-moving pace, delicious-tasting flesh, and slow breeding rate, they are an endangered species.

A school of French grunts (*left*) cruises over a West Indian coral reef. Grunts are so named because of their ability to make grunts and drumlike noises by vibrating powerful muscles on either side of the swimbladder. These noises are loud enough to be heard out of the water, especially in the breeding season, when huge groups of fish drum furiously together.

A solitary hunter (*right*) A margay stalks the forest floor in Belize. Together with the larger, even more sought-after ocelot, the margay has been hunted almost to extinction for its beautiful pelt. About the size of a domestic cat, the margay is equally at home on the ground and climbing among the trees.

BERMUDA'S EMBATTLED CAHOW

The cahow, Bermuda's endemic petrel, was only recently rescued from the brink of extinction. It was first discovered by sailors in 1603; early European settlers took a heavy toll of the birds, hunting them for food, and introducing pigs and cats that, together with the rats that came ashore from their ships, preyed on the hatchlings. The cahows survived only on small outlying rocky islands. In 1609 a plague of rats caused a famine in Bermuda, and the hunt for the birds spread to these islands. For more than 300 years the birds were believed to be extinct.

However, in 1951 about 18 breeding pairs were found. The cahows faced competition for nest sites from tropicbirds, which killed their young and took over their burrows during the day while the cahows were at sea. Conservationists poisoned the rats and erected baffles at the nest entrances to keep out the larger tropicbirds. The breeding rate of the cahows improved – for a short time. The number of surviving young then declined markedly; the adults were taking in DDT and other pesticides while feeding in the North Atlantic. The North American pesticide ban of the early 1970s came just in time, and the cahows are now recovering with 45 breeding pairs recorded in 1994. Nevertheless, rats and feral cats still prevent them from thriving.

225 kg (495 lb) of iguana meat. Encouraging farmers to keep patches of forest on their land to rear iguanas benefits many other species. The iguana population is now recovering and 80,000 have also been released into the wild.

Some animals have gained from the presence of people. The Marine toad has invaded sugarcane plantations to feast on the insect pests there. The Cattle egret, originally from Africa, feeds well on the insects disturbed by livestock.

Chains of distress

Disturbance to one part of an ecosystem can set in train a series of consequences that may affect humans as well as wildlife. For example, Guatemala's beautiful Lake Atitlán is the only home of the Giant pie-billed grebe. This flightless waterbird has a sturdy head and bill, and legs set so far back on its body that it has great difficulty in walking. It nests in the reed beds on the lake's shores, and probably evolved to take advantage of the crabs that were once abundant near the shore. Today, its main food source is small fish.

In 1958 Large-mouth bass and three other species of exotic fish were introduced to the lake for sport fishing. The bass flourished, outcompeting the grebes for fish and crabs, and eating the young birds; the population rapidly declined. Some 50,000 Indian people live around the shore of the lake. They depend on fishing, and their livelihood suffered as the bass took over. The crabs retreated into deeper water, and the local fishing collapsed. As the bass multiplied their numbers also stabilized, and the grebes recovered. But by then city people were building vacation houses on the lake shores, cutting the reeds to clear beaches and build boathouses. The wash from their motorboats and waterskiing activities damaged the nesting sites and greatly disturbed the birds, and their sewage began to pollute the lake.

Conservationists blocked a scheme to dam the lake for hydroelectric power. But they could not protect the lake from the effects of an earthquake in 1976 that led to the water level falling by more than 3 m (10 ft). More reed beds were lost, and the grebe population has fallen to fewer than 50 birds. Renewed conservation is put under threat by the region's political instability. Not only the grebe but a whole ecosystem and the livelihood of 50,000 indigenous people are at risk.

Ants – the teeming armies

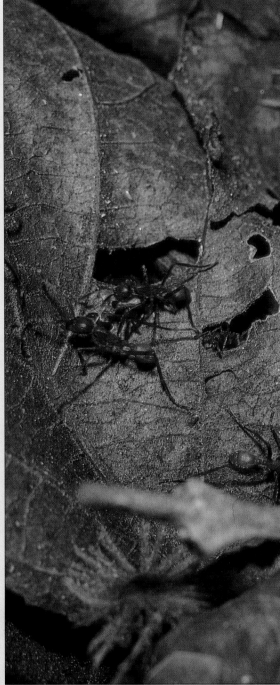

There are several thousand species of ant worldwide, and perhaps 10 million billion individual ants alive at any one time. Throughout Central America, as in all other tropical regions of the world, ants are found everywhere and in vast numbers. They are social insects, living in large colonies. One or more very large queens form the heart of the colony, spending almost their entire lives laying eggs. Queens are produced as a result of special feeding of the larvae from fertilized eggs. The rest of the colony is made up chiefly of nonreproducing worker females with specific roles.

Worker ants have clearly defined tasks – brood rearing, tending the queen, foraging – usually allocated by age. In some species there are distinct castes of workers; soldier army ants are much larger than other workers, and have massive heads with powerful jaws. Leafcutter ants have extra small workers; they ride on the leaves being carried by larger workers and fend off parasitic insects.

Colonies vary in size from a few thousand to several million ants. The nests may take the form of networks of underground chambers, vast mud-plastered balls suspended from branches by tiny hollow thorns. The behavior of the colony is controlled by chemical signals (pheromones) given off by the queen. Each ant

Honeydew lovers (*above*) Aphids and other sap-sucking insects ooze a sugary solution, honeydew, that many ants like to eat. The ants stimulate the insects to produce the honeydew by stroking them with their antennae. In return, the sap-suckers are defended against predators and may be herded down to the ant nest for protection at night.

Army ant soldiers (*right*) guard the marching column on its daily search for prey. When the ants need to cross a gap, they form a living bridge, linking claws to form a chain, and allowing other ants to walk over them. They breed in a 35-day cycle; while the larvae are growing they move to a new bivouac site every night, but while the pupae are maturing they remain in the same place until the new workers emerge.

Living larders (*below*) Honeypot ants have a caste, the "gasters", that are fed with nectar and honeydew, which they store in hugely distended crops. Never leaving the nest, the gasters serve as living larders for the colony.

acquires the distinctive smell of its own colony, and may attack ants from other colonies. Ants also communicate by touch, using their antennae, and workers often lay chemical trails to guide others to an abundant food source. Ants have a second stomach or crop in which they store food that can be regurgitated to feed other ants of the brood.

Farmers, gardeners and soldiers

Many ants are herbivores. Some of the commonest ants in the tropical forest are the leafcutters, which bite off pieces of leaf and take them back to their underground nest. Chewed and coated with digestive juices, they serve as food for a fungus found only in ant nests. It pro-

duces spherical fruiting bodies, which the ants eat and feed to their larvae.

The leafcutters have evolved foraging strategies that ensure they do not deplete their food supply. They vary their route frequently, and never forage very close to the colony. Experiments have shown that leafcutters favor a varied diet. When offered a choice of food, they prefer one particular kind of leaf for a time, but will eventually tire of it and switch to another species. This gives the first species time to recover. They are also careful to space out their nests, never siting them too close to another colony of the same species.

Other ants also keep food in their nests. Ants of desert areas have a rather unpredictable source of food. Harvester ants

collect seeds and grass cuttings to store in the nest for times of scarcity.

Army ants do not build permanent nests but bivouac on the trail. With the queen and brood in the center, army ant columns may be up to 20 m (66 ft) wide and contain some 200,000 individuals. They fan out over the forest floor, devouring any creature not quick enough to make an escape.

Some ant species have formed intimate associations with plants. Many forest plants have hollow stems or leaf nodes that house colonies of ants. The plants produce food bodies and nectaries for them on stems or leaves; in return the ants defend the plants against hungry insects and larger herbivores.

Attack and counterattack

Wherever so many predators and prey live in close proximity, some bizarre defenses evolve. In Central American rainforests many plants accumulate poisons in their leaves to deter caterpillars and other plant-eating animals; some animals manage to accumulate these chemicals in their bodies and use them for their own defense. Flower bugs and *Heliconius* butterflies ingest the poisons from certain passionflower vines.

Heliconius butterflies and their caterpillars may have overcome the poisons of the passionflower, but that is not the end of the story. The female butterflies are very choosy about which passionflower leaves they lay their eggs on – they will not lay on any leaf already occupied by an egg. The passionflower develops tiny outgrowths on its leaves that mimic the eggs of the butterflies, so reducing the predation.

Poisonous insects are usually clearly identified with bright warning patterns of black and red, orange or yellow. After one unpleasant meal, a predator learns to avoid these color combinations. Other insects have taken advantage of this, evolving a similar appearance, even though they are quite palatable. As long as there are more poisonous "models" than "mimics", so that most encounters with these forms are unpleasant, the mimics gain protection. Similar strategies have evolved among harmless and poisonous snakes.

Warning colors The bright colors of these Mexican grasshoppers signal that they have poisonous flesh. When in flight their bright red underwings reinforce the warning.

PLANT LIFE

DESERT THORNS AND PALM-FRINGED ISLANDS · PLANTS AND POLLINATORS · A STOREHOUSE OF FOOD AND FLOWERS

From subtropical forest to desert scrub and cloudcapped islands, the plant life of Central America and the Caribbean islands is extremely diverse. In the luxuriant forest grow many species of bromeliads, ferns and orchids; some are ground-dwelling, while others are epiphytic, growing on the bark of trees. Numerous species of cacti thrive in the desert areas of Mexico and Cuba. Most major groups of plants such as orchids, palms and grasses grow throughout the region, but mainland Central America and the islands of the Caribbean have many different species. The least tropical plants of the Greater Antilles are related to those of North America; those of the Lesser Antilles have relatives in South America. The islands support about 200 endemic genera, most with only a few species.

COUNTRIES IN THE REGION

Antigua and Barbuda, Bahamas, Barbados, Belize, Costa Rica, Cuba, Dominica, Dominican Republic, El Salvador, Grenada, Guatemala, Haiti, Honduras, Jamaica, Mexico, Nicaragua, Panama, St Kitts-Nevis, St Lucia, St Vincent and the Grenadines, Trinidad and Tobago

DIVERSITY

	Number of species	Endemism
Central America (mainland)	30,000	very high
Caribbean islands	12,000	high

PLANTS IN DANGER

	Threatened	Endangered	Extinct
Mexico	1,593	234	11
Costa Rica	527	103	2

Examples *Ariocarpus agavoides; Auerodendron glaucescens; Carpodiptera mirabilis; Eupatorium chalceorithales; Freziera forerorum; Guzmania condensata; Ipomoea villifera; Lincania retifolia; Lycaste suaveolens; Streblacanthus parviflorus*

USEFUL AND DANGEROUS NATIVE PLANTS

Crop plants *Gossypium species* (cotton); *Ipomoea batatus* (sweet potato); *Persea americana* (avocado); *Psidium guajava* (guava); *Theobroma cacao* (cocoa); *Vanilla planifolia* (vanilla); *Zea mays* (maize)
Garden plants *Echeveria setosa; Fuchsia fulgens; Lobelia fulgens; Mammillaria elegans; Plumeria rubra* (frangipani); *Sedum allantoides*
Poisonous plants *Abrus precatorius; Comocladia dodonaea* (Christmas bush); *Croton betulinus* (broom bush); *Daubentonia purica* (purple sesbane); *Euphorbia pulcherrima* (poinsettia); *Jatropha curcas* (physic nut); *Lophophora williamsii*

MAJOR BOTANIC GARDENS

Royal Botanic Gardens, Kingston (1,000 taxa); University National Autonoma of Mexico (3,000 taxa); Jardin Botánico Cecon, Guatemala; Lankester Botanic Garden, Costa Rica

DESERT THORNS AND PALM-FRINGED ISLANDS

The Central American mainland, from Mexico to Panama, is home to more than 300 endemic genera. Some, such as the dahlias (*Dahlia*), and the tuberous agave-relatives (*Polianthes*) have a limited natural range, while others, such as the true agaves (*Agave*) extend into the Caribbean and the southwestern United States.

Mexico contains a great diversity of cacti; these grow from the dry central plateau at 2,000 m (6,500 ft) down to the lowland deserts. Armed legumes such as mesquite (*Prosopis juliflora*), and species of *Acacia* and *Pithecellobium* make up a scrubby thorn forest. Higher up there are mixed forests of pine and oak; they are dominated by Aztec pine (*Pinus teocote*) and *Pinus patula*.

Toward the Isthmus of Tehuantepec in the south of Mexico the climate becomes more humid, particularly on the wetter Atlantic coast. The area supports several well-known plant families, including the legumes (Leguminosae), laurels (Lauraceae) and peppers (Piperaceae). The main genera of the peppers are *Piper*, with several hundred species of shrubs and small trees in the humid forests, and *Peperomia* with many small herbs growing on shaded rocks and trees.

Lowland deciduous forest, characterized by the red birch (*Bursera simaruba*), is widespread throughout the region. Where the rainfall is low but humidity nevertheless high, mahogany (*Swietenia macrophylla*) and other small- to medium-sized trees form seasonal evergreen

woodland. In dry areas, and where the soil is thin and poor, grasses and sedges predominate, but some woody plants are found, including chaparro (*Curatella americana*) and fat pork (*Chrysobalanus icaco*). Mangrove forests form along estuarine coasts; species include red mangrove (*Rhizophora mangle*), white mangrove (*Laguncularia racemosa*) and black mangrove (*Avicennia germinans*).

The Caribbean islands

The plant life on the islands is largely determined by the seasonal climate, with local variations in topography, soil and the underlying rock creating diverse ecological niches. In Cuba, for example, the locally endemic pino-hembra (*Pinus tropicalis*) colonizes the ridges of thin sandy soil on the Alturas de Pizzaras; in adjacent valleys with deeper sandy soil hardwood forest grows, dominated by

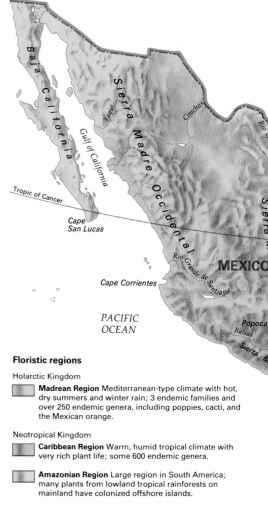

Floristic regions

Holarctic Kingdom

Madrean Region Mediterranean-type climate with hot, dry summers and winter rain; 3 endemic families and over 250 endemic genera, including poppies, cacti, and the Mexican orange.

Neotropical Kingdom

Caribbean Region Warm, humid tropical climate with very rich plant life; some 600 endemic genera.

Amazonian Region Large region in South America; many plants from lowland tropical rainforests on mainland have colonized offshore islands.

Tropical convolvulus The genus *Ipomoea* includes the perennial climbing morning glory, which scrambles up trees and over bushes in many parts of the region.

encina (*Quercus virginiana*). At the northern end of these heights, pure stands of Caribbean pine (*Pinus caribaea*) indicate magnesium-rich serpentine rock.

The smallest islands provide only a sandy or rocky shore, where the ubiquitous beach morning glory (*Ipomoea pes-caprae*) grows. Pedro Cays to the south of Jamaica has a strand woodland, dominated by buttonwood (*Conocarpus erectus*). Some low islands have a small element of endemism, particularly among cacti and agaves. Of the 539 species found on the Cayman Islands, for example, 21 are endemic, including the orchid *Schomburgkia thomsoniana*.

The larger islands, which have greater topographic diversity and higher rainfall, support more specialized plants: the cool, humid upland areas of Jamaica, Cuba and Hispaniola have a unique montane vegetation. On Hispaniola, at heights of between 2,650 and 3,000 m (8,700–9,850 ft), species of *Ilex*, *Lyonia* and *Garrya* grow in open woodland characterized by pino de guaba (*Pinus occidentalis*). The larger islands also support some plants found on the mainland. These include palms, the kapok tree (*Ceiba pentandra*), dogwood (*Piscidia piscipula*) and, in drier areas, scrubby legumes.

Desert scrub in northern Mexico Silvery brittlebush (*Encelia farinosa*) and spiny teddybear cholla (*Opuntia*) grow in arid regions, though *Opuntia* species are widespread. These jointed cacti may be treelike, creeping or with flattened segments.

Map of floristic regions Northern Central America, with its arid climate, high plateaus and mountains has plants very different from those of tropical zones to the south.

501

PLANTS AND POLLINATORS

In the forests of Central America the reproductive activity in plants is concentrated in the period when the fruits mature, between the end of the main dry season and the onset of the rains.

The flowering pattern of trees and shrubs usually conforms to seasonal changes, and in deciduous species may coincide with the cycle of leaf-fall or the flush of new leaves. Not all deciduous plants shed their leaves every year – whether they do or not depends on the length and severity of the dry season. However, in species of the tree *Tabebuia*, leaf-fall takes place every year and corresponds with flowering. In other species, the leaves fall when the fruits mature; this is particularly true of plants whose fruits are exposed, once the leaves have fallen, to the animals that feed on them and subsequently disperse the seeds. In others, such as the high climbers of the families Bignoniaceae and Malpighiaceae, leaf-fall coincides with the dispersal of seeds by the strong winds that blow at this time.

Some species coordinate their flowering with the start of the rainy season. All the individuals open their flowers the same number of days after sufficient rain has fallen; these include the shrub *Hybanthus prunifolius* in Panama, a species of *Miconia* in Costa Rica, and cultivated coffee (*Coffea arabica*). The strategy is clearly coordinated with the availability

Shocking pink blooms (*above*) *Echinocereus pentalophus*, in common with other cacti, has become superbly well adapted to living in the hot, dry conditions of the desert zones. It has no leaves, but has developed a ridged stem that can expand to store water, and it also loses water very slowly.

Covered by flowers (*left*) The flowers almost obscure the rest of this prickly pear in their effort to attract a pollinator. Opuntias are very successful; even a tiny piece of stem can take root and grow into a new plant.

Tubular flowers of *Columnea* (*right*) Blossoms like these are typical of those pollinated by birds. This trailing epiphyte of the family Gesneriaceae inhabits the cloud forests of Costa Rica in the south of the region.

PINES AT THEIR SOUTHERN LIMIT

On the fringes of any vegetation zone it is common to find widespread and versatile plants growing alongside species at the extremes of their natural range. *Pinus* is a genus of more than seventy species that range throughout the northern hemisphere. It reaches its most southerly limit in central Nicaragua, the Bahamas, Cuba and Hispaniola. Pino de guapa (*Pinus occidentalis*), known in Cuba as pino de la maestra, grows in a few small areas at high altitude in the eastern mountains of Cuba and in similar habitats on Hispaniola. It predominates in open conditions, or where soils are shallow. However, as the humus becomes enriched the pines are succeeded by hardwoods that flourish in the more favor-

able soil conditions. As the hardwoods reach maturity and die, the pines return again, and so the cyclic succession continues.

The wide range of sites and soils on Cuba has encouraged many endemic species to evolve into new species by diversifying from tropical plants that have reached their northern limit. This subtropical "interzone" consequently supports the anomaly of pines growing together with tree ferns on both Cuba and Hispaniola. However, the pines have retained their ability to grow in pure stands or in association with only a few other species in these areas, in contrast to the more usual multiplicity of different species that compete for dominance in most tropical forests.

of appropriate pollinators. It results in mass fruiting, which ensures that some new seedlings will survive predation and mature into new plants. The fruits of *Miconia*, in particular, attract large numbers of birds that disperse the seeds.

Insect and bird pollinators

Although wind is important for the dispersal of some fruits and seeds, animals are generally more instrumental in the transfer of pollen from plant to plant. Some plants extend their flowering season by opening only a few flowers a day in what has been called a "traplining" pattern. It enables pollinating animals to visit a great many individual blossoms over a long period, spreads the burden of pollinators and reduces the competition for their services. Not all

plant species flower every year, which may protect their seeds from being eaten regularly by predators. Many tropical forest plants, such as orchids (Orchidaceae) and milkweeds (Asclepiadaceae) have sticky, spiny or clumped pollen, specially adapted to cling to the insects and birds that feed from the plant; the pollen is then deposited on the next flower that the animal visits. Some of the plant–animal relationships are quite haphazard, but where cross-pollination is essential, the plant is best served by an exclusive pollinator.

At least 3,000 species of orchids that grow in the New World tropical zones are pollinated by bees. Most of these orchids are epiphytes, growing on the bark of trees. They include the *Gongora* orchids, which are visited exclusively by the bright metallic blue or green male *Euglossa* bees. The flowers are extremely fragrant, yet they attract no other types of bees or other insects. It has been established that certain chemicals in the fragrance of the plant attract only one kind of bee, isolating closely related plants and avoiding the possibility of interbreeding between them. Other specialized flowers include *Aristolochia*, which has the appearance and odor of rotting meat, and attracts only carrion flies.

Hummingbirds and certain plants are thought to have coadapted; the depth of the tubular petals on some flowers are the same length as the bills of certain hummingbird species. In addition, the colors of the flowers, usually red or orange, attract the birds. However, some interdependent relationships between plants and animals are not as exclusive as they at first appear. The streamertails, or doctor birds, of Jamaica, for example, usually visit bell-shaped or tubular flowers such as *Gesneria* or *Lobelia*, but in arid places they use their long beaks to feed from the open, daisylike flowers of cacti such as prickly pear (*Opuntia*) and *Melocactus*. They are probably the only birds that can feed on *Melocactus* without being impaled on the needlelike spines that surround the flowers.

A number of alien or introduced plants are pollinated by native insects, and illegitimate crosses with different species of the same genus result in natural hybrids. For example, ginger lilies (*Hedychium*), introduced to Jamaica from Asia, have formed hybrids in the areas where they grow together.

A STOREHOUSE OF FOOD AND FLOWERS

Central America and the Caribbean are the home of many crop plants that now form staple foods around the world. In addition, several native species are used in industry, such as henequen (*Agave fourcroydes*), which provides fiber, and maguey (*Agave atrovirens*), a source of alcohol. Others have become popular garden plants, as well as providing substances with medicinal properties used as drugs today.

Edible tubers and fruits

The drier upland areas of Mexico and its southerly neighbors are the home of many useful plants that have long provided the staple foods of the indigenous peoples. Sweet potatoes (*Ipomoea batatas*), grain crops of the family Amaranthaceae, pulses and other legumes, gourds and squashes (*Cucubita*), potatoes (*Solanum*) and maize (*Zea mays*) all originated from, and have been developed in, this region. Other members of the family Solanaceae, including tomatillos (*Physalis*), sweet peppers and chilli peppers (*Capsicum*), are now widely grown and add zest to the local cuisine.

In contrast, the rainforests of the lowland isthmus areas (from Panama to Nicaragua) and the larger islands have produced trees and forest climbers with edible fruits. The best known and most economically important of these are the cacao bean, from *Theobroma cacao*, and the avocado (*Persea americana*). Less familiar are the brown fruits of the mammee sapote (*Pouteria sopota*), a distinctive evergreen tree with large leaves clustered at the ends of the twigs. Canistel belongs to the same genus and is similar, but with smooth, yellow-skinned fruits that resemble mangoes. Star apple (*Chrysophyllum cainito*) probably originated in the West Indies, but is widely cultivated and naturalized on the mainland. The robust climber chayote (*Sechium edule*), which is described as "a squash with prickles" by the Maya, is unusual in that the large seed germinates within the flesh of the fruit.

Some plants are not native to the region but now grow as freely as indigenous species. Pawpaw (*Carica papaya*), for example, is now a weed tree in the forests of Central America. Its milky sap is widely used for medicinal purposes and as a source of the enzyme papaine, used commercially to tenderize meat. This property has long been appreciated by the indigenous people, who use the leaves to make their meat more palatable.

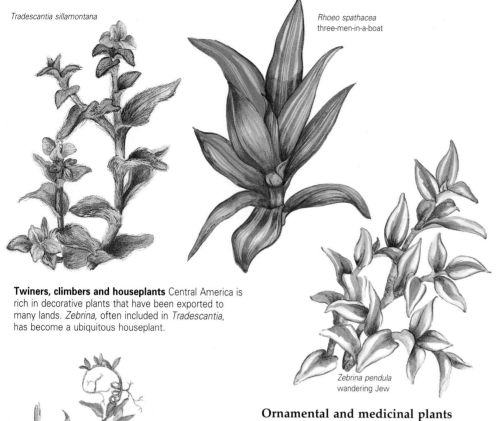

Tradescantia sillamontana

Rhoeo spathacea
three-men-in-a-boat

Zebrina pendula
wandering Jew

Cobaea scandens
cup-and-saucer vine

Solandra guttata
goldcup chalice vine

Solanum wendlandii
Costa Rican nightshade

Twiners, climbers and houseplants Central America is rich in decorative plants that have been exported to many lands. *Zebrina*, often included in *Tradescantia*, has become a ubiquitous houseplant.

Ornamental and medicinal plants

Mexico is particularly rich in ornamental plants, including dahlias, Mexican aster (*Cosmos*), *Zinnia*, marigolds (*Tagetes*), tree daisy (*Montanoa*), *Viguiera* and sunflower (*Helianthus*). Most are also aromatic, and some have medicinal properties, such as the margarita del mar or bay tansy (*Ambrosia hispida*). This annual, lowgrowing herb has numerous creeping branches and small lobed leaflets, with minute yellow-green flowers clustered in small heads. It occurs naturally on coastal dunes, and is used to control fever.

Some medicinal plants have a milky sap that has caustic properties. The sap of many euphorbias, for example, is used to treat warts. One example is nochebuena, or poinsettia (*Euphorbia pulcherrima*), a shrub that grows about 4 m (13.5 ft) high and produces spectacular red floral bracts in the dry season. A popular Christmas pot plant in Europe and garden plant in the tropics, it grows in deciduous tropical forests and some oakwoods of the Pacific side of Mexico.

Other plants with milky sap include flor de mayo or frangipani (*Plumeria*). *Plumeria obtusa* and *P. rubra* are open-branched shrubs or trees with large leaves and very fragrant white or red flowers. They grow wild in rocky thickets in warm areas, and are popular garden plants in the tropics. They are used medicinally against intestinal parasites and for skin and respiratory disorders.

Mexican breadfruit, known too as pinanona or monstera (*Monstera deliciosa*), also has a milky sap with irritant properties. This evergreen climber grows wild in forests in several parts of Mexico, but is probably better known as one of the most common houseplants worldwide. It can reach up to 15 m (50 ft) in height, and has large, deeply cut and perforated leaves. The long roots are used for weaving baskets and the fruit is edible.

One of the most famous and longest known medicinal plants is guayacan, or lignum vitae (*Guaiacum officinale* or *G. sanctum*). The gnarled tree grows to 4–8 m (13.5–26 ft). Its blue flowers are the national flower of Jamaica, and it produces orange-yellow fruit. An extract of the wood is used as a stimulant and to induce perspiration, the resin is used as a purgative, and other parts of the plant have been taken to treat rheumatism, skin ailments and venereal diseases.

PRICKLY CUSTOMERS

It is a popular misconception that cacti grow only in the desert – in fact they are found in forests too. Some cacti, such as *Epiphyllum hookeri*, live in the forests as epiphytes clinging to other plants and drawing moisture from the air. Others are climbers, invading the crowns of trees or scrambling over rocks, putting out roots as they go. These include *Hylocereus undatus*, with its triangular stems, and *Cephalocereus swartzii*, with slender ribbed stems. Many of these cacti have huge, solitary, fragrant, nocturnal flowers, which have earned them names such as *reina de la noche* (queen of the night).

Typical cacti are barrel-shaped or columnar, with succulent, leafless, ridged, spiny stems. In the arid thickets of northern Mexico grows the largest cactus, *Pachycereus pringlei*, a massive columnar plant reaching 20 m (66 ft). Species of prickly pear also grow in thickets and thorn scrub, adopting creeping, shrubby or treelike habits. A spineless version is the smooth pear (*Nopalea cochinellifera*), which is often the host of the cochineal bug, the source of carmine dye. West Indian gooseberry (*Pereskia aculeata*) is also a fruit-bearing cactus, but unlike most cacti it has leaves at maturity.

The story of cocoa

For nearly 300 years after its discovery by Columbus in 1498, Trinidad was a sparsely inhabited Spanish colony. Initially the colonists spent their time growing tobacco for export to Europe and attempting to subjugate the indigenous Arawaks. Toward the end of the 17th century, missions of Capuchin friars set about employing the Arawaks as agricultural laborers, giving them protection from other Spanish settlers in return. They added maize and cotton to their crops, but put even greater emphasis on cacao trees; soon large plantations were supplying all of Spain's needs.

It is said that the Spaniards found cacao growing wild in Trinidad when they arrived, but this conflicts with other reports that they introduced the tree from Central America in 1625. The cacao they grew was of the Criollo variety, which has white or pale violet cotyledons (fleshy seed leaves). The chocolate flavor, which in this variety has no astringency, develops only after the seeds have been fermented and dried. Once processed, the beans produce highly flavored cocoa.

A world crop

In 1727 disease struck Trinidad's cacao crops, causing the young pods to wither on the trees. The economy collapsed completely and many settlers departed. The disease, referred to as "blast", was probably the condition now known as Cherelle Wilt, an exaggerated state of

natural fruit-thinning. It was attributed by priests to the wickedness of the planters, and by the planters to "death winds" from the north or to drought. The response was a state of apathy that for the next fifty years reduced the social and economic life of Trinidad to a state of complete inactivity.

In about 1757 the Dutch introduced another variety, known as Amazonian Forastero, or Amelonado, probably from Venezuela. The plantations were soon reestablished, and the new variety was subsequently crossed with the white-beaned Criollo to create the Trinitario hybrids; the best selections of these have the vigor of Forastero combined with the quality of Criollo.

Long before this time, Spanish explorers had taken Amelonado cacao first to Brazil and then to the Spanish island of Fernando Póo, now called Bioko, off the coast of Equatorial Guinea in West Africa. There they established plantations worked by labor imported from eastern Nigeria and other parts of the Guinea coast. In 1879 one of these workers, Tetteh Quarshie, took cacao to what was then called the Gold Coast, farther west along the Gulf of Guinea. The forest soil, seasonal climate and peasant culture were

Cacao relatives (*below*) Cacao belongs to a genus of some 30 species of small trees that are found in the rainforests of both Central and South America. Other species are cultivated locally either for cocoa or for their edible fruits.

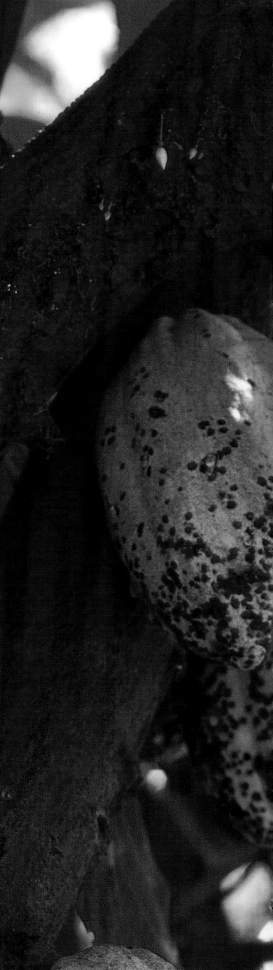

Dominica

COMMONWEALTH OF DOMINICA

THE ISLAND OF DOMINICA IS AN INDEPENDENT republic in the eastern Caribbean, situated in the Leeward Island chain between Guadeloupe and Martinique.

ENVIRONMENT

Dominica has a backbone of steep mountains, rising to Morne Diablotin. Vents and hot springs are a reminder of their volcanic origins. The climate is warm and humid, with a rainy season from June to October, when there is a risk of hurricanes. Rainfall is much higher in the mountains. The island is covered with lush tropical vegetation that supports abundant wildlife. The Morne Trois Pitons National Park is a wildlife preserve and an important tourist attraction.

SOCIETY

For many years the British and the French fought for possession of Dominica, but the British eventually took over in 1783. The island was made a separate colony in 1771, but did not become self-governing until 1967; full independence followed in 1978. Soon afterward Dominica was devastated by a series of hurricanes. Despite two failed coup attempts, the 1980s were mainly a period of rebuilding. The president is head of state, and appoints a prime minister from the majority party. The president is appointed by parliament, which has a majority of elected members. The people are mostly the descendants of former African slaves, though several hundred Caribs (descendants of the original inhabitants) also live on the island. The official language is English, but a French patois is spoken, and there is a Roman Catholic majority.

ECONOMY

The chief cash crops are bananas, citrus fruits and coconuts, while cocoa, bay leaves and vanilla also produce revenue. Other major exports include galvanized sheets and coconut products. Tourism is an ever-increasing source of further revenue. Food, fuels and manufactured goods have to be imported. The roads are good, and the capital, Roseau, has a port

Untamed beauty Dominica's mountainous interior is covered with dense rainforest. The clouds that shroud its peaks send cascades of water into the valleys below Some parts are still unexplored.

and two airfields nearby. Medical services are adequate, but disease continues to be a problem. Education is free.

NATIONAL DATA – DOMINICA				
Land area 750 sq km (290 sq mi)				
Climate	Altitude m (ft)	Temperatures January °C(°F)	July °C(°F)	Annual precipitation mm (in)
Roseau	16 (60)	24 (76)	27 (81)	1,956 (77.0)
Major physical feature highest point: Morne Diablotin 1,447 m (4,747 ft)				
Population (2000 est.) 71,540				
Form of government multiparty republic with one legislative house				
Armed forces none (paramilitary police 300)				
Capital city Roseau (21,000)				
Official language English				
Ethnic composition Black 91.2%; Mixed 6.6%; Amerindian 1.5%; White 0.5%; others 0.2%				
Religious affiliations Roman Catholic 76.9%; Protestant 15.5%; others 7.6%				
Currency 1 East Caribbean dollar (EC$) = 100 cents				
Gross domestic product (1998) US $225 million				
Gross domestic product per capita (1998) US $3,400				
Life expectancy at birth male 75.2 yr; female 81.0 yr				
Major resources bananas, citrus fruit, coconuts, cocoa, bay leaves, vegetables, vanilla, tourism				

Saint Lucia

SAINT LUCIA

S AINT LUCIA IS A SMALL ISLAND STATE IN THE eastern Caribbean – part of the Lesser Antilles chain that stretches from Puerto Rico to Venezuela.

ENVIRONMENT

The island's rugged landscape was created by volcanic activity. The mountains at its heart rise to Mount Gimie, its highest point. Near the west coast is the volcano Qualibou, which was last active in 1766. It still vents gases, and is responsible for the boiling sulfurous springs that gave the neighboring town of Soufriere its name. The climate is hot and humid, and the volcanic soils are fertile. The mountain slopes are wooded, but the lush rainforest that formerly covered the island has been cleared, depriving wildlife of most of its habitat.

NATIONAL DATA – SAINT LUCIA

Land area   617 sq km (238 sq mi)

Climate	Altitude m (ft)	Temperatures January °C(°F)	July °C(°F)	Annual precipitation mm (in)
Castries	3 (10)	25 (77)	28 (82)	1,500 (59.1)

Major physical feature   highest point: Mount Gimie 959 m (3,145 ft)

Population   (2000 est.) 156,260

Form of government   multiparty constitutional monarchy with two legislative houses

Armed forces   none (paramilitary police 300)

Capital city   Castries (54,000)

Official language   English

Ethnic composition   Black 87.0%; Mixed 9.1%; Indian 2.6%; White 1.3%

Religious affiliations   Roman Catholic 90.0%; Protestant 7.0%; others 3.0%

Currency   1 East Caribbean dollar (EC$) = 100 cents

Gross domestic product   (1998) US $656 million

Gross domestic product per capita   (1998) US $4,300

Life expectancy at birth   male 68.1 yr; female 75.7 yr

Major resources   timber, bananas, mineral springs, pumice, tourism

SOCIETY

The indigenous Arawak peoples were driven from St. Lucia by the Caribs, who were themselves killed off by the diseases introduced by 17th-century French settlers. The island changed hands frequently between Britain and France, but was finally ceded to Britain in 1814. The population is mainly descended from African slaves; their French patois and Roman Catholic faith reflect the island's checkered history. Saint Lucia became self-governing in 1967 and independent in 1979. The British sovereign remains head of state, represented by a governor-general, but power lies with the prime minister and cabinet, responsible to an elected two-chamber parliament.

ECONOMY

Saint Lucia's economy depends chiefly on tourism and agriculture. Sugar cane has been replaced as the main cash crop by bananas, which provide some two-thirds of exports. Food crops such as cassava and sweet potatoes are produced by subsistence farmers, and much food has to be imported. Industry is developing, aided by the use of geothermal power, and tourism is a vital and ever-increasing source of foreign revenue. Primary education is free and compulsory.

The Pitons, twin peaks rising dramatically from the sea to a height of over 750 m (2.560 ft) on the southwest coast of Saint Lucia. Exposed by erosion, they are formed from the lava plugs of volcanoes that erupted many thousands of years ago.

Cacao flowers (*above*) Cacao is a small evergreen tree with large thin leaves. The complex flowers have petal-like appendages, and are borne on the old wood of the trunk and the lower parts of the main branches.

Cacao pods (*left*) As the pods ripen they change from green to orange-yellow or red according to variety. They are large and heavy, and need the strength of the trunk or big branches to support their weight. The beans are rich in a fat known as cocoa butter, which is used in making chocolate.

ideal for its growth. In a few years the Gold Coast became the world's largest producer of cacao and, later, the center for scientific research on this plant. Most of the cacao trees in present-day Ghana are still of the same Amelonado variety.

Two-stage growth

The cacao sapling grows in two phases. First, upright shoots (called chupons) with spiral leaves develop; the terminal buds on these shoots produce three to five horizontal fan-branches (called jorquettes) with leaves in two rows. The leaves develop in series; the new leaves hang down and are often reddish at first. Eventually, with the change of season, chupon development resumes and the lower fan-branches wither and fall off, leaving a straight trunk.

The method of pollination of the small, scentless and nectarless flowers is unknown, but small midges probably perform this essential function. It is clear, though, that no one kind of insect is entirely responsible for pollination, in view of the success of this plant in a wide range of tropical areas.

AGRICULTURE

THE LEGACY OF COLONIALISM · SUBSISTENCE AND SURPLUS · BREAKING WITH THE PAST

Central America and the Caribbean incorporate a range of tropical farming systems based mainly on savanna and rainforest environments. Root crops were probably being grown here 6,000 years ago; and the ancient civilizations of the Aztecs in Mexico and the Maya on the borders of Mexico, Guatemala, Belize and Honduras had cultivated the land for at least 2,000 years before the arrival of the first Spanish colonists at the beginning of the 16th century. Although some indigenous farming has remained largely unchanged, European colonization has had a long lasting influence, particularly through the introduction of plantation farming. There is largescale commercial production of cash crops such as sugar, bananas and coffee, and cattle ranching provides meat mainly for the United States market.

COUNTRIES IN THE REGION

Antigua and Barbuda, Bahamas, Barbados, Belize, Costa Rica, Cuba, Dominica, Dominican Republic, El Salvador, Grenada, Guatemala, Haiti, Honduras, Jamaica, Mexico, Nicaragua, Panama, St Kitts-Nevis, St Lucia, St Vincent and the Grenadines, Trinidad and Tobago

LAND: Total area 2,735,515 sq km (1,056,183 sq mi)

Cropland	Pasture	Forest/woodland
14%	36 %	28%

FARMERS	Highest	Middle	Lowest
Agriculture as % of GDP	34 (Panama)	17 (Costa Rica)	2 (Trin & Tob)
% of workforce	66 (Honduras)	30 (El Salvador)	1.8 (Panama)

MAJOR CROPS: Agricultural poducts Fruits and vegetables; livestock; sugarcane; cotton; coca; tobacco; fish; shrimp; rice; corn; sorghum; spices

Total cropland (000 ha)	27,300 (Mexico)	2,746 (Nicaragua)	89 (Belize
Cropland (ha) per 1000 people	587 (Nicaragua)	241 (Panama)	96 (Trin. & Tob.)
Irrigated land as % of cropland	25% (Costa Rica)	12% (Jamaica)	3% (Bel./Nicar.)
Number of tractors	172,000 (Mexico)	78,000 (Cuba)	136 (Haiti)
Average cereal crop yields (kg/ha)	3,851 (Dom Rep)	2,164 (Panama)	969 (Haiti)
Cereal production (000 tonnes)	28,839 (Mexico)	1,152 (Guatemala)	3 (Jamaica)
Change since 1986/88	27%	–17%	–39%

LIVESTOCK & FISHERIES			
Meat production (000 tonnes)	3,911 (Mexico)	1,152 (Guatemala)	10 (Belize)
Change since 1986/88	44%	105%	79%
Marine fish catch (000 tonnes)	1,037 (Mexico)	145 (Panama)	0.1 (Belize)
Change since 1986/88	2%	–15%	–73%

FOOD SECURITY			
Food aid as % of total imports	15 (Nicaragua)	5 (Guatemala)	0 (Bel, CR, Mex.)
Daily kcal/person	3,097	2,480	1,869

THE LEGACY OF COLONIALISM

The traditional communal agriculture of the indigenous peoples of the Central American isthmus was completely transformed by the first Spanish settlers who established largescale production on haciendas – large family-owned estates based on the Spanish system of aristocratic landownership. The hacienda used cheap landless labor to produce crops for the new urban markets that colonization created in Central America. Although it is an inefficient system of production, relying on large amounts of land and labor, it still survives as the basic form of land organization in much of the region.

By contrast, the northern Europeans – chiefly the British and French – who colonized the scattered islands of the Caribbean and a small area of the coastal lowlands of Central America, introduced the plantation as the basic unit of organization; later it was extended into Cuba, Puerto Rico and the Dominican Republic following their break with Spain at the end of the 19th century. The plantation system was based on the largescale production of a single crop, usually sugar cane or bananas, for export, making use of the capital, technology and managerial skills of the colonial power. Like the hacienda, the plantation requires extensive land, but production tends to be more intensive and therefore more efficient. Although most plantations were originally family-owned, many have been taken over by large multinational corporations such as the United Fruit Company, Fyffes and Del Monte. This reduces the financial returns received by the producing countries.

New kinds of livestock

The indigenous people of the region had few domesticated animals until the Spanish colonists introduced horses and pigs. Horses were to become valuable draft animals, and pigs joined chickens as the staple livestock of subsistence farmers. Cattle, sheep and goats were all introduced early on, and the new livestock transformed the rural economy as well as the Indians' diet. Commercial stock raising was first established in the highland basins that are found in much of Central America, in lowland savanna areas, interior valleys and the dry steppelands of northern Mexico.

The close proximity of the huge United States market has encouraged American investment in ranching, even in the tropical rainforest areas. Rich, diverse forest has been replaced by poor grassland, but ranching is nevertheless profitable because of the higher price of beef in the United States. Similarly, American and other foreign capital has been invested in a range of other agricultural and food processing ventures based on cheap land and cheap, plentiful labor. Fruit – especially bananas – coffee, sugar and tobacco are the main crops produced in this way.

The region encompasses a wide range of tropical environments and weather systems, from the Caribbean islands and the Central American isthmus, where there is rainfall all year round, to the semidesert of northern Mexico. This means virtually all the tropical crops are

grown. Many of the colonial plantations were established in areas where rich rainforests flourished; these forests were originally exploited for their valuable hardwoods, such as mahogany. Subsequent poor management by the European colonists has degraded the tropical soils, which are rich in laterite deposits containing iron and other oxides. In normal circumstances these would be leached away downward through the soil, but the removal of the tree cover and consequent

Fishing and tourism in Martinique (*above*) The tourist boom has benefited many Caribbean islanders. Fishermen now earn a large part of their living by supplying fresh fish to the tourist trade.

Hillside farming (*left*) Intricate terracing in Guatemala helps to conserve moisture as well as making economic use of every available piece of land. Vegetation is lush after the seasonal rains.

Map of agricultural zones The moist, warm climate allows a range of tropical crops to be cultivated. Rough pastures in drier areas support cattle ranching.

erosion of the soil into deep gullies exposes the laterites, making the soil more and more infertile and unproductive. This is a major problem for agriculture in some parts of the region – notably on the island of Haiti, for example.

Traditional farming

Some groups of people still use traditional agricultural practices. The indigenous Indian populations in Central America – descendants of the Aztecs, Maya and other Indian tribes, many now of mixed blood – farm today in much the same way as their ancestors. Using hand tools, they cultivate maize, beans and squash as their

Agricultural zones

- arable
- fruit and vegetables
- rough grazing
- woods and forest
- nonagricultural land

▲ mountain peak (meters)

staple crops, and also rear pigs and poultry as livestock.

The Black Caribs – rare survivors of the original Indian population of the Caribbean – have retained a distinctive farming system in scattered areas on the Atlantic coastline of Central America, to which they were exiled by the British in 1797. They grow starchy root crops, chiefly cassava, sweet potato, arrowroot and peanuts, but rely heavily on fishing and hunting, with women often performing most of the husbandry.

Subsistence farming is practiced by the Afro-Americans of the Caribbean and parts of the Atlantic seaboard from Belize to Panama. These people are descendants of African slaves brought to the region by colonial powers as cheap labor for plantations, mines and forestry. By 1640 large sugar plantations that used black slave labor had been established in Barbados, and soon spread throughout the Caribbean; by 1800 Africans outnumbered Europeans by five to one. The eventual abolition of slavery from 1833 to 1865 created a new class of smallholding or subsistence farmers, as well as labor shortages on the plantations. These were filled by importing laborers from the Dutch East Indies and India.

Coffee country Young coffee plants are kept well watered in a nursery until they are transferred to the plantation. They take six to eight years to bear a full crop of berries, which grow at the same time as the plant is flowering.

THE LEGACY OF COLONIALISM

The creation of haciendas and plantations concentrated large amounts of the best available land into the hands of relatively few owners, so preventing the development of a class of independent small farmers and a more balanced rural economy. This inequality in the distribution of land is still a severe problem in rural areas, with too many people trying to work too little marginal land – if they possess any land at all. Today the vast majority of people working in agriculture in Central America and the Caribbean are either landless laborers or are subsistence or semi-subsistence farmers eking out a living on small plots of land.

Subsistence farmers grow the traditional crops of maize, rice or beans, supplemented in different areas with other cereals such as sorghum, a variety of vegetables including squashes, potatoes and other root crops, and tropical fruits. Of all the subsistence crops, maize is the most widely grown – in Mexico it occupies over a third of agricultural land – and recent production has been increased as the result of improved seed varieties. In some parts of Cuba, Mexico and Panama, where there is high rainfall or where irrigation has been introduced, rice is the staple grain.

Subsistence farming is most prevalent in the rainforest areas of Central America where small clearings (milpas) are created in the jungle by felling and burning. The remaining tree trunks are removed by draft animals before the crops are sown. Without the addition of either fertilizer or manure, *milpas* are exhausted within three to four years, and in sparsely populated areas such as Belize, parts of northern Guatemala and southeast Mexico, they are frequently abandoned, being left to regain their fertility while cultivation moves to neighboring plots. Elsewhere population pressure has required a more permanent form of semi-commercial cultivation using fertilizers, systematic periods of fallow, and cash sales. The continued practice of subsistence farming reveals the widespread rural poverty in the region, but there is little malnutrition as the diet is usually well balanced.

Farming for export

Commercial agriculture was initially associated with sugar production, and later extended to include other crops. Although sugar remains the principal export crop in many of the Caribbean island economies, particularly those of Cuba and Jamaica, major export production in the region now also includes bananas, cotton, citrus, and coffee.

The cultivation of bananas has had a dramatic history of rapid expansion and decline due to market volatility and crop disease. The main period of expansion came after the establishment of the United Fruit Company in 1899, which developed large tracts of sparsely settled land in the hot, rainy Caribbean lowlands of Costa Rica, Panama, Honduras and Guatemala for banana plantations. However, a high incidence of disease in the years before World War II shifted production to the Pacific lowlands. Today, with the development of more disease-resistant varieties, there has been a return to the Atlantic coast, especially in Honduras and Costa Rica where bananas are a major export. They are also widely grown in the West Indies, particularly in Jamaica, Dominica and St Lucia, and the French territories of Guadeloupe and Martinique. Bananas have recently replaced sugar cane in some countries, and their production has moved from the plantation sector to smallholders who sell the fruit to corporate buyers.

Coffee farms (*fincas*) were established as early as the 1830s in the central highlands of Costa Rica and by the 1860s coffee

growing had spread rapidly to the neighboring countries of El Salvador, Guatemala and Nicaragua. In these countries the fincas are situated on fertile volcanic ground and coffee is a major export crop, though its production in El Salvador and Nicaragua was drastically affected by the civil wars of the 1970s and 1980s, which had a disastrous effect on the countries' economies. Panama and Honduras also export coffee, but on a smaller scale.

Commercial production of coffee in Mexico began in the late 19th century and remained smallscale until the 1950s, when the amount of land devoted to its cultivation doubled. It is now more widely grown than sugar cane and is the country's third most valuable export. Today, Central American coffee contributes about 10 per cent of the world's total crop.

Cotton was a boom crop in Nicaragua, El Salvador and Guatemala in the 1960s, being grown by largescale landowners on the drier Pacific lowlands and employing large numbers of landless peasants to pick the crop. The civil strife in all three countries, and poor prices on the world market, severely disrupted production of what

Colonial-style cattle ranching Central American livestock haciendas are based on the Spanish model of aristocratic landownership of vast tracts of land. Despite the poor pasture, ranching is profitable because beef commands a high price.

had become their main export crop. Irrigated production in northern Mexico has now made Mexico the region's leading producer of cotton.

Commercial cattle raising

Livestock production in Central America is limited by the hot, wet, tropical climate throughout much of the region, which does not provide good pastureland. Subsistence farmers raise a third of Mexico's livestock. Sheep farming in the highlands provides the basis for woollen mills and textile manufacturing, while cattle are much more important in the tropical lowlands and especially in the drier, semiarid areas of northern Mexico. Here the sparse pastures are only able to maintain low densities of cattle, resulting in huge livestock haciendas extending over hundreds of thousands of hectares. Commercial cattle farming developed in the 1950s with the aid of US-backed agencies. Beef was (and remains) in huge demand in the United States, and the industry expanded, providing export dollars to the region. Cattle ranching has been widely blamed for the deforestation of the tropical rainforest and the eviction of subsistence farmers from their land.

LIQUOR FROM AN AGAVE

In dry, rocky areas of central Mexico, fields of a spiky, gray-green plant, the maguey agave, are grown. The fermented juice, known locally as *agua miel*, or "honey water", is used to make pulque and tequila, the national drinks of Mexico. Fully grown, the maguey plant reaches a height of 3 m (10 ft), but it is harvested before maturity, when it is about six to eight years old. The juice is collected by cutting the flower bud from the plant's pineapple-like base, leaving a cavity. After several months the sap that has accumulated in the cavity is drawn off; the plant refills and the sap is drawn off again – one plant may provide up to 9 liters (15 pints) of sap before it dies. The sap, which contains up to 10 percent sugars, is fermented in vats for several days, and is widely drunk as pulque – a cloudy, whitish beer that is an important source of carbohydrates and proteins for many of Mexico's poorer people.

Tequila, a clear or sometimes golden liquor, is distilled from pulque. It takes its name from the town in the central highlands that has been the center of the drink's production since the 17th century, or even earlier, when the art of distillation was introduced to the region by the Spanish. Mexicans drink it undiluted with salt and a slice of lime; it forms the basis of the Margarita cocktail, traditionally served in a salt-rimmed glass, which has become a universally popular drink, following the growth of the tourist industry.

BREAKING WITH THE PAST

Few parts of the region are completely unaffected by modern commercial farming methods. Despite formidable physical barriers, such as the mountains of the Sierra Madre in southeast Mexico, even remote rural communities have started to farm for the market economy, abandoning ancient cultivation techniques and communal land tenure. Even so, there is a vast gulf between these semi-commercial farmers and the large ranches and plantations. Although small farmers are in the majority – in Central America three-quarters of all land holdings are less than 20 ha (50 acres) – they occupy only 5 percent of the agricultural area.

Land reform programs

Unequal distribution of land, resulting in rural poverty, and low productivity due to the system of land tenure and technological backwardness, is a fundamental weakness in the agricultural economies of the area. It has been a major factor in fueling the political unrest that has been endemic in the region for most of this century. A few governments, following popular revolution, have attempted to remove land from the few, and redistribute it among the landless. Most success has been achieved in Mexico and Cuba and to some degree in Nicaragua. The World Bank has established a land-related lending program in Central America which supports better land distribution and the strengthening of property rights with the aim of promoting investment and reducing poverty.

Mexico's history of land reform goes back to the beginning of the 20th century, when over 40 percent of the land was occupied by only 8,000 haciendas; some 96 percent of rural families owned no land at all, and many people were obliged to work as virtual serfs on the large estates. After the 1910 revolution, however, the traditional communal landowning system of the Indian tribes was adopted on a large scale. This started a process of land reform with land being gradually taken from the haciendas and redistributed to the former estate workers under a system of land tenure that is known as *ejido*; the *ejidores* – workers – cultivate the land either in family farms or as a collective.

Today nearly half of Mexico's cultivated land has been redistributed in this way, with the greatest reorganization in the center and south of the country. However, approximately 30 percent of Mexico's rural families still own no land, and most Mexican governments have neglected the *ejidos*, giving them little financial or technical assistance. The quality of the land that has been redistributed is generally poor, and many *ejidores* as a consequence remain impoverished. Most of the land that has been improved in quality, particularly by irrigation, has benefited the private sector. Nevertheless, the collective *ejidos*, which are in the majority, tend to operate more commercially than the family farms.

Single-crop economies

Another major problem affecting the region is the reliance of its economies on a single crop. This is largely the result of its colonial past, because traditionally the plantations were established in order to feed the rapidly growing urban populations of the colonizing powers.

Most plantations in the Caribbean are

Going to market (*above*) Central America's many subsistence farmers – who are mostly of Indian origin – produce only small surpluses of their crops. They sell these at weekly village markets, which may be some distance from the farm.

A principal plantation crop (*right*) Many banana plantations are owned by American, British and French companies, but more and more smallholders, such as this farmer on the Caribbean island of Tobago, produce the fruit and sell it to corporate buyers.

owned by foreign corporations: British in the West Indies; United States' in Puerto Rico, the Dominican Republic and Haiti; and French in Guadeloupe and Martinique. Their control of the plantations derives from ownership either of the land or of the processing, transportation marketing facilities.

Revenue derived from sugar exports remains the mainstay of many economies in the region. There are three main disadvantages to such dependency on a single crop: it encourages a high degree of foreign ownership; it leads to over-dependence on one main source of export revenue, as Jamaica found to its cost in 1988 when Hurricane Gilbert destroyed

A famous export Tobacco was one of the first crops that European colonists exported from the New World in the 16th century. Each plant produces about twenty large leaves that are harvested and then cured by air, fire or flue drying. The curing process dries out the sap, and also induces chemical changes in the leaves that enhance the flavor and aroma of the tobacco.

almost the entire crop; and the imposition of quota agreements to protect sugar producers in the United States and Western Europe restricts access to these crucial markets.

Some partial solutions to these problems have been found. In Antigua and Trinidad, as well as Cuba, nationalization of the plantations has limited foreign ownership. Efforts have been made to find new markets. The falling price of world sugar during the 1980s quickened the search for alternative crops, such as bananas in Dominica, and has substantially reduced the reliance on sugar in most West Indian economies. In the Leeward and Windward Islands both citrus fruits and market garden crops have become important exports. In much of the Caribbean tourism has replaced sugar as the most important creator of revenue.

Similar diversification on the Central American mainland has encouraged greater commercial production of a wide range of fruits and vegetables. Sugar peas (snow peas or mangetout peas), for example, are grown for export in the Guatemalan highlands, and oranges for the production of frozen juice concentrate for the United States' market in Mexico's Gulf lowlands.

CUBA'S SOCIALIST AGRICULTURE

One of the first actions of the socialist-revolutionary government in Cuba in 1959 was to take control of the sugar cane processing industry, the island's principal source of revenue, bringing an end to foreign (chiefly American) ownership of the plantations and sugar mills. Although the government took over ownership of landholdings of 65 ha (160 acres) or more, the remainder – belonging to 80 percent of farmers – were left in private hands. There were subsequent spasmodic attempts to reduce the numbers of these small landholders through so-called "microplans", which encouraged both early retirement and land transfers to the state in order to ensure the "fulfillment of socialist principles". State control was less rigidly enforced than it was by the communist regimes of China or the former Soviet Union, though state farms and collectives often held the best land.

Farming on about a quarter of the surviving private smallholdings is for subsistence purposes only, but the practice of growing small amounts of fruit and vegetables for sale is widespread. Traditionally tobacco for production of the world-famous Havana cigars was grown in these smallholdings. After the revolution output fell as a result of the loss of Western markets, particularly the United States trade embargo. More emphasis has been placed upon growing food crops and sugar cane, and little attempt has been made to extend the area under tobacco. The government has maintained the economy's dependence on sugar exports, but has replaced the United States' market with Russia, Canada and Spain.

The story of cane sugar

Sugar cane (*Saccharum officinarum*) is a giant, thick, perennial grass of the plant family Graminae. Raw sugar is derived from the sweet sap in its stem, which can grow up to 4.5 m (15 ft) tall and 2.5–5 cm (1–2 in) in diameter. The plant needs a minimum of 1,250 mm (49 in) of rain annually, and a short dry season to aid maturation. It is grown in most of the world's tropical regions; it can be planted and harvested by hand, so was suited to areas where labor was plentiful.

The cultivation of sugar cane probably originated in the South Pacific and spread from there to India and then to the Arabian countries and Europe. Christopher Columbus (1451–1506) is believed to have brought sugar cane to the New World on his second voyage west across the Atlantic in 1493, though it is possible that it had already been introduced to the Arawak and Carib peoples of the Caribbean by a route across the Pacific.

By the 17th century sugar plantations had been established throughout the West Indies. Islands such as Jamaica and Barbados were developed by British colonizers primarily for their ability to produce sugar for the home market, and were part of the notorious "Atlantic triangle" that linked Britain, West Africa and the West Indies in trading slaves and sugar. Ships sailed from British ports to collect slaves from West Africa to work on the sugar plantations. They then returned to their home port laden with cargoes of refined sugar, rum and molasses.

Barbados was the first island to experience the "sugar revolution" brought about by the use of slave labor on plantations. So many slaves were introduced that by the early 19th century the population density had reached 585 people per square kilometer (700 people per square mile), and Barbados had become known as a "city with sugar cane growing in the suburbs". Some 240 plantations, each of about 80 ha (200 acres) accounted for four-fifths of all land on the island.

The colonial plantations were adversely affected in the 19th century by slave uprisings and the eventual emancipation of the slaves, which made labor more expensive, as well as by soil exhaustion, competition from Cuba and the other Hispanic islands, and by the growth of the European sugar beet industry and loss of monopoly access to the British market. However, the modernization of plantations, made possible by more capital and land, more efficient management and more sophisticated technology, ensured the survival of a substantial sugar economy in the Caribbean.

Refining the sugar

Modern refineries serve large areas of plantation land and are easily accessible to bulk raw sugar carriers, minimizing transportation costs. Sugar is removed from the canes in one of two ways – by milling or by a diffusion process, which was originally developed to extract sugar from beet. In the first process, rapidly revolving cane knives cut the cane into chips, and the juice is then extracted by crushing and shredding the cane in large metal rollers that squeeze it from the fiber. In the diffusion process the sugar is separated from the finely cut stalks by dissolving it in hot water.

In the next stage of processing the extracted juice is clarified to remove the non-sugar components. Evaporation then removes the water, and the raw syrup is boiled until crystallization takes place and a mixture called massecuite forms. The raw sugar crystals are separated from the massecuite by centrifugal machines; molasses, which is distilled to make rum or used as feed for farm animals, is crystallized out of the remaining juice. Nothing is wasted: the cane residue, left over in the processing, is used to fire the boilers in the processing plants.

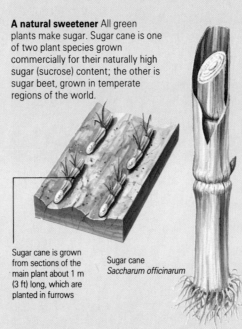

A natural sweetener All green plants make sugar. Sugar cane is one of two plant species grown commercially for their naturally high sugar (sucrose) content; the other is sugar beet, grown in temperate regions of the world.

Sugar cane is grown from sections of the main plant about 1 m (3 ft) long, which are planted in furrows

Sugar cane
Saccharum officinarum

The harvest Sugar cane is harvested – mostly still by hand – when sugar content and moisture are greatest. The stems are stripped of leaves before being sent for immediate processing.

INDUSTRY

Central America has sufficient resources to support an independent industrial sector. However, most governments lack capital to invest in training and technology, relying heavily on the United States for funding and as a market for exports. The region exports oil (particularly from Mexico), natural gas, precious metals and other minerals. It also processes sugar, fruit, crude oil and metallic ores. Its cheapest resource is the labor force. Employees earn a fraction of equivalent wages in Western Europe or the United States. Low wages and large populations have encouraged labor-intensive manufacturing, but industrial expansion is constrained because the market for manufactured goods is fragmented by political boundaries. A thriving tourist industry has also developed, notably on the Caribbean islands.

COUNTRIES IN THE REGION

Antigua and Barbuda, Bahamas, Barbados, Belize, Costa Rica, Cuba, Dominica, Dominican Republic, El Salvador, Grenada, Guatemala, Haiti, Honduras, Jamaica, Mexico, Nicaragua, Panama, St Kitts-Nevis, St Lucia, St Vincent and the Grenadines, Trinidad and Tobago

INDUSTRIAL OUTPUT (US $ billion)

Total	Mining	Manufacturing	Average annual change since 1960
105	n/a	80	n/a

INDUSTRIAL WORKERS (Mexico)
(figures in brackets are percentages of total labor force)

Total	Mining	Manufacturing	Construction
n/a	n/a	6.03m (16.1%)	1.95m (5.2%)

MAJOR PRODUCTS (figures in brackets are percentages of total world production)

Energy and minerals	Mexico (1996)	Jamaica (1996)	Honduras (1993)
Oil* (mill barrels)	2.9 (4.9%)		
Bauxite (thou tonnes)	n/a	10.8	
Antimony (thou tonnes)	1.8 (1.5%)		
Silver (thou tonnes)	2,536.1.1		24 tonnes
Sulfur (thou tonnes)	921.3		
Fluorspar (thou tonnes)	n/a		
Gypsum (thou tonnes)	3,758.9	208,017	
Lead (thou tonnes)	167.1		4.9
Copper (thou tonnes)	328		
Zinc (thou tonnes)	348.3		26.5

*crude petroleum

Manufactures

Gas (thou tonnes)	16,795	852.8m liters	
Cement (tonnes)	28,168	523,000	999.6
Steel (tonnes)	5,867		
Passenger cars	782,743		
Fertilizer (tonnes)		57,500	

OIL-RICH MEXICO

Petroleum is the region's most important natural resource and its major source of energy. Reserves are concentrated in Mexico, where oil was first discovered in the early 20th century. By 1920 the country was second only to the United States as a world producer. In 1938, however, output was slowed when the government controversially nationalized the oilfields, provoking an international embargo. In the early 1970s huge new reserves of oil were discovered in the Bay of Campeche and in the southeast of the country. Exploitation of these oilfields has transformed the Mexican economy and placed the country among the world's leading five oil producers. In the early 1990s, it was estimated that Mexico had more than five percent of the world's oil reserves, as well as substantial supplies of natural gas. Trinidad is the only other country in the region to have significant oil and gas resources. Mexico also has a modest coal-mining industry in the Sabinas basin north of Monterrey.

Hydroelectric power is becoming increasingly important in Central America. The mountains and heavy rainfall in parts of the region have been harnessed to generate significant amounts of hydro-electricity, which in some countries now meets up to a third of national needs. In addition, geothermal heat is being tapped in volcanic areas of Mexico, Nicaragua and El Salvador. These power stations are efficient even when they are very small and are well suited to serving rural areas. Mexico has experimented with nuclear power but found it too expensive to produce. In Cuba and other sugar-growing parts of the region bagasse – the dry, pulpy residue left after the extraction of juice from the sugar cane – is used to make fuel, providing a further local source of power. Another plant, sisal, has also been harnessed for industrial use, especially in the Yucatán in Mexico. Its fibrous parts are used for making cord and rope.

Precious metals and minerals

Gold, zinc, silver and nickel are mined and processed in many areas of Central America. Long before the European invasion the local population was using gold for ornamental purposes, and the search for the precious metal was one of the main forces behind subsequent Spanish exploration. Since then many veins have been exhausted, and as long ago as the 16th century silver overtook gold in importance. The Dominican Republic is now the only country in the region with significant gold production. Mexico remains the world's leading source of silver, with fresh sources continuing to be discovered. The Reál de Angeles silver mine in the central province of Zacatecas, opened in 1983, is the world's largest.

During the 20th century Mexico has become an important producer of other metals too. Copper succeeded silver in importance in the 1900s, lead replaced copper in the 1930s and was itself over-

Resources and industry

◆ industrial center
○ port
• other town
— major road
— major railroad

mineral resources and fossil fuels
• iron and other ferroalloy metal ores
• other metal ores
▪ nonmetallic minerals

▢ bauxite
▢ gold
▢ natural gas
▢ nickel
▢ oil
▢ silver

Map of principal resources and industrial zones
(above) Most of the resources in the area are in Mexico, the world's leading producer of silver and a member of OPEC (Organization of the Petroleum Exporting Countries). Jamaica, Haiti and the Dominican Republic have large reserves of bauxite, and Cuba is rich in both gold and nickel.

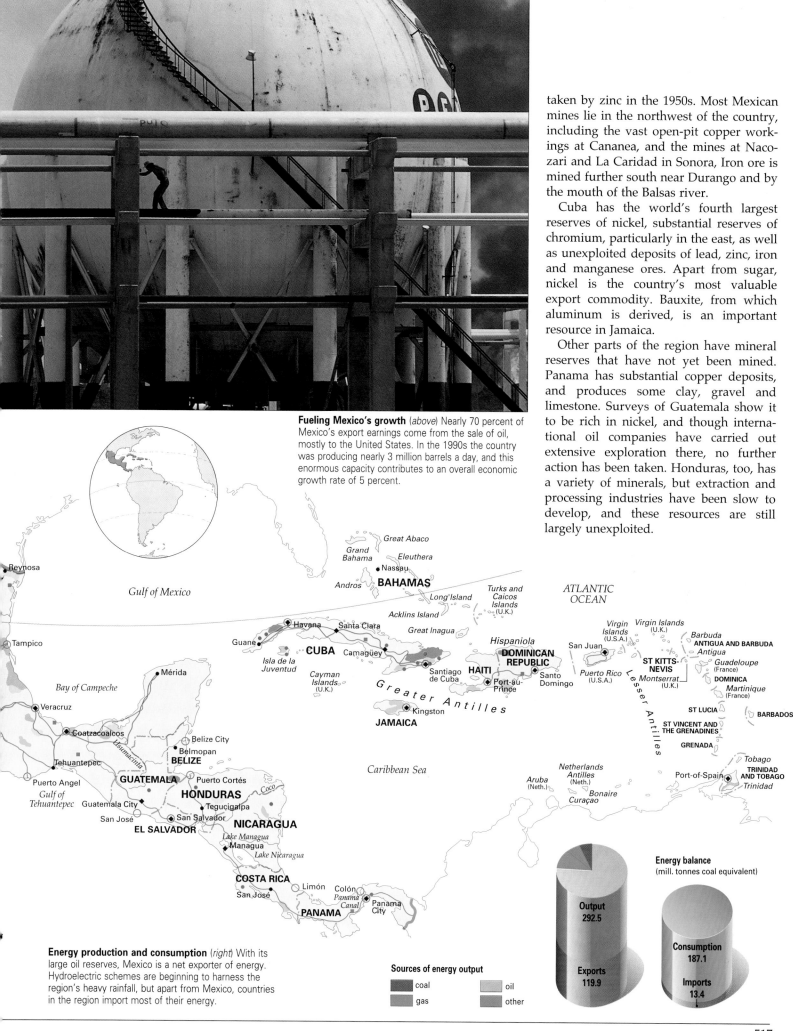

taken by zinc in the 1950s. Most Mexican mines lie in the northwest of the country, including the vast open-pit copper workings at Cananea, and the mines at Nacozari and La Caridad in Sonora, Iron ore is mined further south near Durango and by the mouth of the Balsas river.

Cuba has the world's fourth largest reserves of nickel, substantial reserves of chromium, particularly in the east, as well as unexploited deposits of lead, zinc, iron and manganese ores. Apart from sugar, nickel is the country's most valuable export commodity. Bauxite, from which aluminum is derived, is an important resource in Jamaica.

Other parts of the region have mineral reserves that have not yet been mined. Panama has substantial copper deposits, and produces some clay, gravel and limestone. Surveys of Guatemala show it to be rich in nickel, and though international oil companies have carried out extensive exploration there, no further action has been taken. Honduras, too, has a variety of minerals, but extraction and processing industries have been slow to develop, and these resources are still largely unexploited.

Fueling Mexico's growth (*above*) Nearly 70 percent of Mexico's export earnings come from the sale of oil, mostly to the United States. In the 1990s the country was producing nearly 3 million barrels a day, and this enormous capacity contributes to an overall economic growth rate of 5 percent.

Energy production and consumption (*right*) With its large oil reserves, Mexico is a net exporter of energy. Hydroelectric schemes are beginning to harness the region's heavy rainfall, but apart from Mexico, countries in the region import most of their energy.

Sources of energy output

- coal
- gas
- oil
- other

Energy balance
(mill. tonnes coal equivalent)

Output 292.5
Exports 119.9

Consumption 187.1
Imports 13.4

TRADITION MEETS THE MODERN WORLD

Almost everywhere throughout Central America traditional handicrafts exist side by side with modern, capital-intensive manufacturing industries. These traditional craft workshops produce goods mostly for local consumption, drawing on the region's resources and requiring no imported technology. Many of the building materials for ordinary homes are made locally by small family concerns, which can respond to the ebb and flow of demand more readily than sophisticated, largescale manufacturers.

In some places, production has grown to supply areas outside the immediate locality. In highland Guatemala, for example, Amerindian villages specialize in household products made to a local design. One might make a particular type of pottery, another specialize in a style of furniture or a particular textile weave, and each village trades its speciality in the regional markets. Other smallscale manufacturing such as tilemaking, tanning, candlemaking and carpentry are usually carried out by farmers in their homes. Sometimes regional specializations become national ones. León, in central Mexico, has become the country's footwear capital through combining local handicraft skills with the marketing and organizational methods of modern industry. Much of the leatherwork in León is subcontracted to smaller operators, reducing overheads and risk, as well as allowing rapid responses to changes in style. This system is effective, too, in garment manufacturing. In the region as a whole, about half the manufacturers employ no more than five workers.

Processing and progress

The region also supports largescale industries processing raw materials, whether for export or as the first stage in a longer manufacturing chain. Particularly important is the refining of oil, metallic ores and agricultural produce, as well as the manufacture of iron and steel, petrochemicals and sulfuric acid. These industries, which are well developed in Belize, Costa Rica, Panama and Mexico, are capital-intensive, rely heavily on imported expertise, make only modest demands on unskilled labor, and generate relatively little employment.

WEALTHY NEIGHBORS

According to the United States' trade policy, goods made from American components but assembled in Mexico can be exported to the United States without paying duty (except on the value added to the article by the assembly process). This gives a huge boost to Mexican industry. Wages are so much lower in Mexico – in the early 1990s they were only one-tenth of those in the United States – that many American companies have found it worthwhile to set up subsidiary production just across the border. The Mexican government has encouraged this trend by doing all it can to make the newcomers welcome: it has removed restrictions on employment and property ownership by foreigners by liberalizing planning laws.

By the early 1990s no fewer than half a million Mexicans – four times as many as ten years earlier – were working at "in-bond" factories (*maquiladoras*), assembling imported parts for the United States market. The most important products are electrical and electronic accessories, closely followed by automobile components and vehicles for export. The towns in the border zone – Tijuana, Ciudad Juárez, Neuvo Laredo, Reynosa, Matamoros – now employ one in eight of all Mexicans working in manufacturing and generate substantial export earnings.

Assembling in new industrial areas (*above*) To lure industry away from its traditional base around Mexico City, the government began the *maquiladora* program with the United States, offering companies incentives to export parts and import finished goods.

Economy up in smoke (*below*) Hand-rolled Cuban cigars, highly prized around the world, have been a mainstay of the island's economy. Tobacco is grown in the fertile northwest and central areas, and cigars are made in small factories and homes.

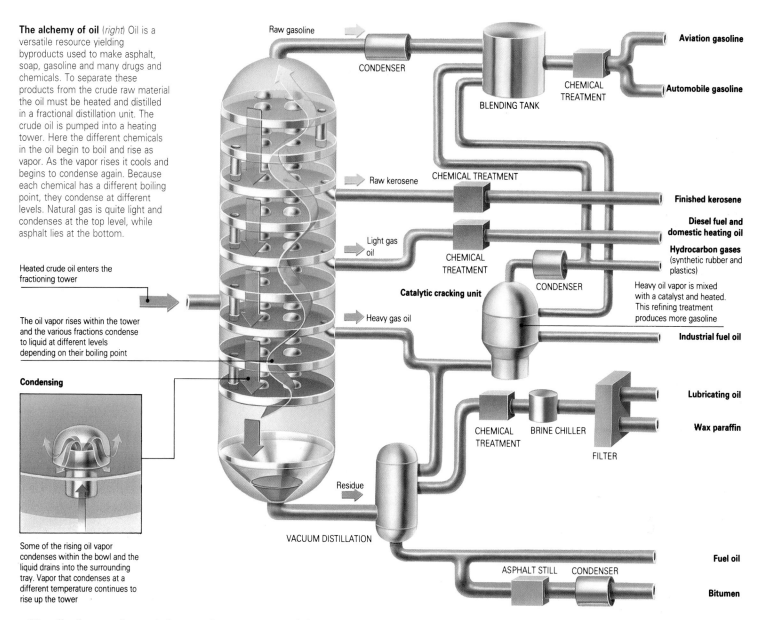

The alchemy of oil (*right*) Oil is a versatile resource yielding byproducts used to make asphalt, soap, gasoline and many drugs and chemicals. To separate these products from the crude raw material the oil must be heated and distilled in a fractional distillation unit. The crude oil is pumped into a heating tower. Here the different chemicals in the oil begin to boil and rise as vapor. As the vapor rises it cools and begins to condense again. Because each chemical has a different boiling point, they condense at different levels. Natural gas is quite light and condenses at the top level, while asphalt lies at the bottom.

Heated crude oil enters the fractioning tower

The oil vapor rises within the tower and the various fractions condense to liquid at different levels depending on their boiling point

Condensing

Some of the rising oil vapor condenses within the bowl and the liquid drains into the surrounding tray. Vapor that condenses at a different temperature continues to rise up the tower

Raw gasoline

CONDENSER

BLENDING TANK

CHEMICAL TREATMENT

Aviation gasoline

Automobile gasoline

Raw kerosene

CHEMICAL TREATMENT

Finished kerosene

Light gas oil

CHEMICAL TREATMENT

Diesel fuel and domestic heating oil

Hydrocarbon gases (synthetic rubber and plastics)

Catalytic cracking unit

CONDENSER

Heavy oil vapor is mixed with a catalyst and heated. This refining treatment produces more gasoline

Heavy gas oil

Industrial fuel oil

CHEMICAL TREATMENT

BRINE CHILLER

FILTER

Lubricating oil

Wax paraffin

Residue

VACUUM DISTILLATION

ASPHALT STILL

CONDENSER

Fuel oil

Bitumen

Usually they are located close to the raw materials they use. Refineries are often built near the mines. In Mexico an iron and steel complex has been established at the Pacific port of Lazaro Cardenas, near the large iron-ore deposits at Las Truchas and Pena Colorado and the cheap hydroelectric power produced at the nearby Infiernillo and La Villita dams. Also in Mexico, vast petrochemical complexes have been built at Cactus and La Cangrejera in the southeast, close to the country's newly discovered oilfields. These manufacture a whole range of organic chemicals, including detergents, acrylic resins, polyester fibers and emulsifying agents, as well as the raw materials for fertilizers. Oil refining, by contrast, is often located close to the industrial plant where it is needed, as tankers and crude-oil pipelines offer cheap bulk transporta-

tion of the unrefined product. This is particularly true of Mexico, where refining capacity has increased dramatically in recent years, and by 2000 the majority of the country's oil production was being processed near industrial sites.

The flourishing food industry

Food processing is a significant activity in many Central American countries. In the tropical parts of the region, preparing and roasting coffee beans is a valuable export industry. Cigarettes and alcohol are produced in most countries, as are textiles, canned food and soft drinks. Belize and Guatemala possess a large number of sawmills for their lumber trade, while Costa Rica is an exporter of paper products to neighboring countries. Tires are made in Guatemala, and both Costa Rica and Panama exploit their dense forests to

produce items of furniture.

Cotton gins, beef slaughterhouses, fruit canneries and other factories process the region's growing range of agricultural produce. Sugar mills have been industrial features of the rural landscape in much of the region since the 17th century. Today their numbers are reduced but individual mills are larger and serve wider plantations. Cuba, in particular, has an extensive processing capacity. It is still the world's leading sugar exporter though in the years following the socialist revolution in 1959, the industry was heavily dependent on export to the former Soviet bloc, which paid artificially high prices. The major political upheavals in the former Soviet Union in the early 1990s forced Cuba to find other markets for its sugar crop and the industry took a further knock in 1998 following an unprecedented poor harvest.

VAST WORKFORCE, LITTLE WORK

European exploitation of the region's natural resources had a devastating effect on the peoples of Central America. The Spanish conquerors were anxious to lay claim to the region's rich deposits of gold and silver, and to gain these they drove many Amerindian people from their traditional way of life to work in the mines. Output increased rapidly, and by the late 18th century Mexico alone was producing more than half of the world's silver. However, the wealth created by the mining industry was shared by only a small number of Mexicans, most of them descendants of the Spanish. By far the larger portion was exported, providing two-thirds of Spain's revenue. The mining workforce of Amerindians and Mestizos (part Spanish, part Amerindian) remained very poor.

Poverty is still a serious problem among the industrial workforce today. Even during the 1960s and 1970s, when Mexican industrial output increased fourfold, workers' living standards were very low. Recession in the early 1980s made poverty among the workforce very much worse. At the root of the difficulty was the region's rapid population increase. In the period between 1950 and 2000 the inhabitants more than tripled in number, from 53 million to about 167 million. This pushed down industrial wages, and also encouraged inefficient overemployment. The demographic trends also led to the emergence of a young workforce whose expectations cannot be fulfilled in their own countries. Significant numbers of Mexicans, Guatemalans, Salvadoreans and others cross illegally into the United States every year in search of better paid jobs, often in the service industries. The exploitation of people as a resource is probably the most remarkable industrial feature of the region. The border between Mexico and the United States draws a line between an abundance of cheap labor and a vast market in which to sell it.

Government intervention

The ruling parties in the region have had a significant influence during the 20th century over how and where their country's industry has developed. In Mexico throughout the 1960s and 1970s manufacturing growth was disproportionately concentrated in the capital. As a result, Mexico City, which in 1990 had a population of 16 million, may soon be the world's largest urban center, housing half the country's industry. Partly this is due to the capital's location at the hub of Mexico's transportation system, but government policy has also been important. Administrations exempted factories in Mexico City from the country's otherwise strict antipollution laws. This was done in an attempt to find employment for the city's swelling population, but it only encouraged more people to join them.

In Cuba the pattern has been very different. There the socialist government has deliberately promoted smaller cities, using capital investment to create jobs away from Havana, to prevent urban growth being concentrated in the capital. The policy has had some success. The governments of other Caribbean islands, too, have exerted strict control over where industries establish themselves – an important consideration in countries where land is scarce.

Recently even Mexico has begun to adopt this approach. Alarming pollution and congestion in the capital have finally led to a complete change of policy, and further industrialization is now discouraged, with growth being promoted instead in other cities, particularly the coastal ports.

The trade policies of the region's governments have also had important effects on industry. During the 1960s and 1970s protectionist policies were adopted in an attempt to encourage increased manufacturing in fields such as cigarette

Modern pirates of the Caribbean (*above*) Tourism is the leading industry in most islands of the Caribbean. Much of the attraction stems from the area's maritime history and its scenic beauty.

Made in the USSR (*below*) Cuba and the former Soviet Union had close trade and economic links dating from the 1960s. Over 75 percent of Cuba's exports, mostly sugar, were to Eastern Bloc countries. In return, the Soviet Union supplied equipment, money and cheap oil.

During the 1990s a series of free trade agreements between various countries in the region contributed to slow overall economic growth. The most notable of these was the 1994 North American Free Trade Agreement (NAFTA) which linked Mexico to the United States and Canada. Despite vociferous opposition in all three countries, the agreement has encouraged investment in Mexico and has boosted employment and export levels. By the end of the 1990s the US government was convinced enough of the benefits of trade liberalization to seek swift moves towards the expansion of NAFTA. The first likely partner to the new Free Trade of the Americas (FTAA) is Chile.

Budding trade unions

In those countries where the trade unions have managed to gain a position of power, they have had an important influence in shaping the region's industry. This was true of Honduras, where in 1954 the trade union movement won agreement to a labor code that is regarded as one of the most all-encompassing in Central America. The code regulates the relationship between management and the labor force, attempting to protect both workers and businessmen. In other countries unions have played a less positive role, and during the 1960s and 1970s many countries suffered disruptive and economically damaging strikes.

It is in Mexico that unions have become most important. The mighty oil union, for example, holds great power over its members' jobs, and such control makes the strike weapon particularly effective. It also exerts influence directly over the government: chiefs of the oil union have long held office through the former ruling Institutional Revolutionary Party (PRI), which was in power from 1929 to 2000. From the 1970s the oil union gained substantial revenues from members' wages, from contracts awarded to outside companies, and – until prevented by legislation in 1984 – also from subcontracting half of all drilling arrangements. Naturally this generated a significant reserve of wealth, and in some cases this did benefit union members. Workers employed at the Pajaritos petrochemical complex had an entire town – Nanchital – built by their union, complete with paved streets, hospital and church. However, significant sums of money nevertheless disappear through simple and widespread corruption.

ANCIENT CITIES, SILVER SEAS

The Caribbean Islands are in a prime position to benefit from tourism. As well as a hot, sunny climate and fine beaches, they are conveniently close to the huge market of the United States. On the whole, they have made the most of this potential. In the Bahamas tourism now accounts for 60 percent of national income and 70 percent of the population are employed in the industry. In Barbados and the Dominican Republic tourism has now replaced the sugar industry as the most important source of foreign exchange.

The mainland countries have often had greater difficulty in developing tourism; many of them are struggling to overcome reputations for political instability. Mexico, however, has a large tourist industry, helped by easy access to the United States. Remains of the Mayan civilization and other pre-Spanish relics have proved an important attraction for visitors, notably sites such as Teotihuacán near Mexico City and the jungle city of Tikal in Guatemala. Belize has exploited its remarkable coral reefs, which are among the most spectacular in the world. In addition the region's exotic plants and animals have proved popular attractions, and both Guatemala and Costa Rica have established national parks to safeguard their natural heritage.

making and rice processing. The policies were effective in some ways, but many countries have since begun encouraging agriculture rather than industrialization. Another area of experiment was in extending the market for industrial goods. Although the population of the region is large, the lack of wealth in many countries has meant that the buying power per capita is very little. In the early 1960s the West Indian Federation (later the Caribbean Community, CARICOM) and the Central American Common Market (CACOM) were formed to widen domestic markets, but these were not wholly successful. Commercial ties have always been stronger with third parties – especially the United States – than within the region.

Aluminum – mining and refining

Mining bauxite, the ore from which aluminum is obtained, plays an important role in the region's economy, most notably in Jamaica, which is one of the world's leading producers. Aluminum, a light, strong and malleable metal, became industrially important in the 20th century. Jamaican production dates from 1942 when bauxite was first discovered on the island, The international company Alcan was the first to set up operations, and mining began in 1952. Alcan went on to pioneer the refining of alumina (a purified form of the ore) in Jamaica, and by 1960 bauxite and alumina had become the country's leading export commodities. A second company, Alcoa, started operations in 1968.

Despite this promising start, Jamaican bauxite production soon ran into difficulties. From the early days of the industry, the island's government showed a tendency to intervene in operations, particularly when it encouraged domestic refining by placing a levy on bauxite exports. In 1974 state intervention was extended, with disastrous consequences. The government under Michael Manley (1972–80), which is committed to "demo-cratic socialism", decided to take a controlling interest in the bauxite industry, an action that caused aluminum companies to divert investment to other suppliers, notably in Australia. Matters worsened when the recession of the 1980s reduced world demand for aluminum. The Jamaican industry virtually collapsed as output fell and refineries closed.

Matters began to improve, however, when a program backed by the International Monetary Fund was implemented to counter the country's economic crisis. Under this program, state involvement in mining was reduced and private investment revived. The effort proved effective and by the beginning of the 1990s state-owned companies were responsible for only a quarter of bauxite production on

Refinery works (*right*) In Jamaica, bauxite is only refined into alumina. Turning it into aluminum requires huge amounts of electricity, so refineries have to be located near sources of cheap power. Jamaica has poor energy resources and exports raw alumina.

Ore to alumina (*below*) Aluminum-bearing bauxite ore is moved by conveyor belt through refining processes. First the ore is ground, mixed and filtered in a chemical solution that separates out impurities. When the solution dries out, it leaves powdered alumina.

Jamaica. Mines and refineries were reopened and new joint ventures were negotiated between the government and various companies.

The refining process in Jamaica

The first stage in the conversion of bauxite to aluminum is the creation of a pure aluminum oxide, known as alumina. This reduces the material's bulk by half – tripling its value in the process – and is done as close to the mine as is practical. Control of transportation costs is a major

factor in profitable bauxite extraction. The next stage of the process – the reduction of alumina to aluminum metal – is highly energy intensive, and refining ideally takes place close to cheap sources of electricity.

Jamaica enjoys easy bauxite extraction and transportation. The deposits lie close to the surface, while mines are located near coastal ports, allowing easy access to the North American market. The only disadvantage is that some of Jamaica's tourist resorts have suffered from their proximity to the industry. In terms of processing, however, the country is at a disadvantage, especially compared to South America. Brazil and Venezuela have recently begun to exploit bauxite reserves in the Amazon Basin, making use of the huge hydroelectric power supplies that are located nearby. In Jamaica, by contrast, energy has to be imported at high cost, making the final stage of processing – from alumina to aluminum – uneconomic.

As a result, the country exports no aluminum. This is a disadvantage, as refined aluminum is worth four times as much as alumina. Nevertheless the bauxite industry remains of great importance to Jamaica's economy, and is set to continue that way. In 1997 Jamaica produced 12 million tonnes of bauxite ore and was the third largest producer behind Australia and Guinea. Although production brings some wealth to the island, it creates few jobs. Bauxite mining and processing are both labor intensive, and together they employ only 7,000 people in a country rife with unemployment.

ECONOMY

THE TRADING LINK WITH EUROPE · FRAGILE INSTABILITY · POVERTY AND PREJUDICE

Drawn into the international economy as colonies of European powers, Central America and the Caribbean islands have traditionally been producers of raw materials (silver, coffee, bananas, sugar, bauxite and oil) for Western markets. Apart from Mexico, where manufacturing and the oil industry are thriving, the economies of the region remain undeveloped. Most are linked closely to the fortunes of a single export sector and are dangerously dependent on their largest trading partner, the United States. Since the 1960s, economic cooperation has been promoted through several organizations, notably the Caribbean Community (CARICOM). The implementation of the North American Free Trade Agreement (NAFTA) in 1994 has doubled trade between Mexico and the US and Canada.

COUNTRIES IN THE REGION

Antigua and Barbuda, Bahamas, Barbados, Belize, Costa Rica, Cuba, Dominica, Dominican Republic, El Salvador, Grenada, Guatemala, Haiti, Honduras, Jamaica, Mexico, Nicaragua, Panama, St Kitts-Nevis, St Lucia, St Vincent and the Grenadines, Trinidad and Tobago

ECONOMIC INDICATORS: 1996/97

	*UMIE Mexico	*UMIE Jamaica	*LMIE Honduras
GDP (US$ billions)	404.2	5.3	4.5
GNP per capita (US$)	8,120	3,470	2,200
Annual rate of growth of GDP, 1990–1995	1.1%	2.9%	3.5%
Manufacturing as % of GDP (1994)	18.7%	17.3%	17.1%
Merchandise exports (US$ billions)	110.4	1.38	n/a
Merchandise imports (US$ billions)	114.8	3.132	n/a
% of GNP received as development aid	0.1%	1.4%	9.2%
Total external debt	154 bn	4.2 bn	4.1 bn
Debt as % of GDP (1995)	38.4%	98%	103%

WELFARE INDICATORS (mid 1990s)

Infant mortality rate (per 1,000 live births)			
1965	82	49	128
1995–2000	31	22	35
Population per physician	625	6,420	266
Teacher–pupil ratio (primary school)	1 : 28	1 : 31	1 : 36
No. of telephone lines per 1,000 pop.	96	140.3	36.8
Health expenditure as % GDP	4.2%	4.9%	5.6%
Adult literacy	89.6%	85%	72.7%

Note: The Gross Domestic Product (GDP) is the total value of all goods and services domestically produced. The Gross National Product (GNP) is the GDP plus net income from abroad.

* UMIE (Upper Middle Income Economy) – GNP per capita between $3,031 and .$9,360 in 1997. LMIE (Lower Middle Income Economy) – between $761 and $3,030. LIE (Low Income Economy) – below $760.

THE TRADING LINK WITH EUROPE

The 33 countries of the region first encountered international trading when European explorers and merchants established colonies after Columbus's voyage to the region in 1492. During the colonial period, trading in each country was dominated by its European mother country. Spain held sway over the mainland while Britain, France and Spain each controlled several Caribbean islands. During the late 17th century, the British established a trading network linking Europe (supplying manufactured goods), Africa (slaves), the colonies in the Caribbean (sugar), North America (wood and provisions) and the Spanish Main. Throughout Central America, production depended on forced labor. Central American Indians worked for the Spanish government in return for "protection" (*encomienda*), and black Africans were imported throughout European and American territories to work as slaves.

Independence and free trade

Following the withdrawal of Spanish colonial power in 1821 and the emancipation of British slaves beginning in 1834, free trade was established in the region. The British immediately began to trade with the countries of the mainland, where the United States became their chief rival. The building of the railroads made it possible to open up land in the interior to grow coffee and bananas, newly introduced as cash crops. Several American corporations took advantage of the improved infrastructure to establish their own banana plantations, while the coffee growers of El Salvador set up locally controlled rural ventures. In the Caribbean, sugar plantations flourished in Cuba and the Dominican Republic, and the crops fetched good prices on the open market. After Spain's defeat in the Spanish–American War of 1898 the United States' involvement in sugar growing and processing in the former Spanish islands of Cuba and Puerto Rico grew substantially. In contrast, sugar plantations in the former British and French Caribbean territories declined or stagnated after 1900 and the loss of trade was only partly offset by banana exporting (particularly in Jamaica), controlled by an emerging class of peasant farmers, the descendants of

former slaves. The economy continued to develop along these lines until the Great Depression of 1929, when the progress made in previous years was swept away and recession set in during the 1930s.

The agriculture-based economies of the Caribbean have suffered from France's and then Britain's membership of the European Union (EU). Various supply agreements have been set up to try to maintain the region's trade in bananas sugar and rum (distilled from fermented sugar cane). However, the Caribbean is a high-cost producer, making their exports uncompetitive in a market that is shrinking anyway as Western nations reduce their sugar consumption. The countries of Central America have diversified away from bananas and coffee into cotton,

sorghum (used for cattle fodder and processed into a sweet syrup) and cattle farming. However, these largescale enterprises benefit the large multinational corporations, with little being passed on to the impoverished rural population.

The need to diversify

In recent years several parts of the region have followed policies of diversification into modern manufacturing and service industries. This has proved most successful in Mexico and the surrounding countries where American firms are prominent. Various tax incentives have also

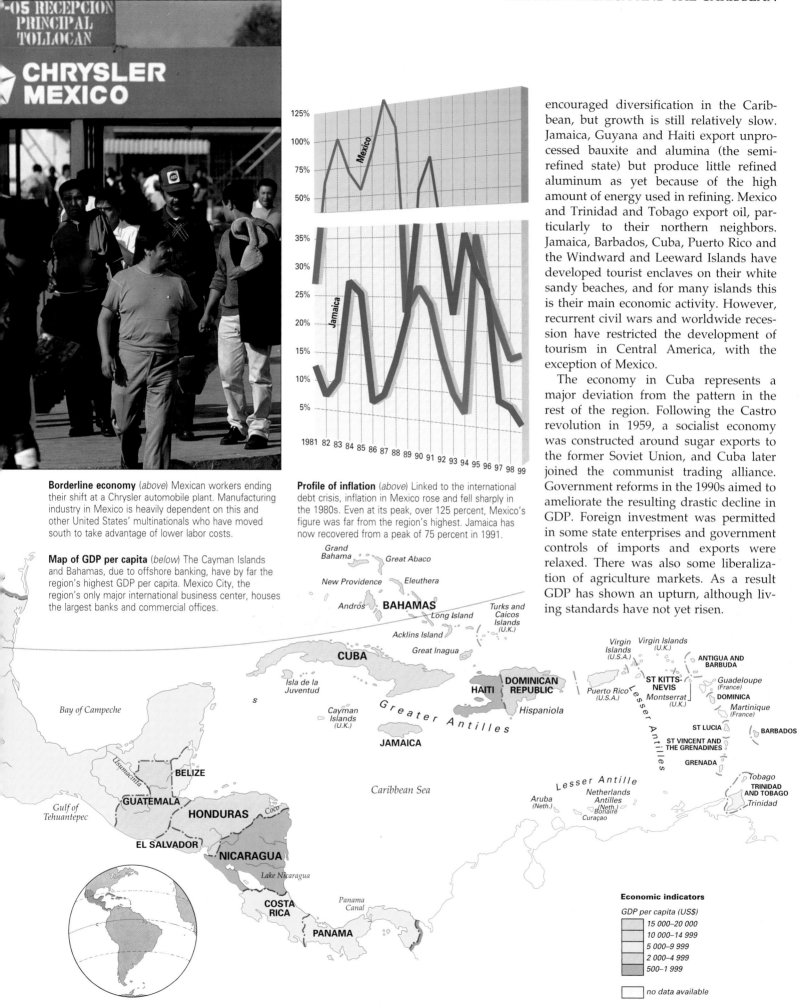

encouraged diversification in the Caribbean, but growth is still relatively slow. Jamaica, Guyana and Haiti export unprocessed bauxite and alumina (the semi-refined state) but produce little refined aluminum as yet because of the high amount of energy used in refining. Mexico and Trinidad and Tobago export oil, particularly to their northern neighbors. Jamaica, Barbados, Cuba, Puerto Rico and the Windward and Leeward Islands have developed tourist enclaves on their white sandy beaches, and for many islands this is their main economic activity. However, recurrent civil wars and worldwide recession have restricted the development of tourism in Central America, with the exception of Mexico.

The economy in Cuba represents a major deviation from the pattern in the rest of the region. Following the Castro revolution in 1959, a socialist economy was constructed around sugar exports to the former Soviet Union, and Cuba later joined the communist trading alliance. Government reforms in the 1990s aimed to ameliorate the resulting drastic decline in GDP. Foreign investment was permitted in some state enterprises and government controls of imports and exports were relaxed. There was also some liberalization of agriculture markets. As a result GDP has shown an upturn, although living standards have not yet risen.

Borderline economy (*above*) Mexican workers ending their shift at a Chrysler automobile plant. Manufacturing industry in Mexico is heavily dependent on this and other United States' multinationals who have moved south to take advantage of lower labor costs.

Map of GDP per capita (*below*) The Cayman Islands and Bahamas, due to offshore banking, have by far the region's highest GDP per capita. Mexico City, the region's only major international business center, houses the largest banks and commercial offices.

Profile of inflation (*above*) Linked to the international debt crisis, inflation in Mexico rose and fell sharply in the 1980s. Even at its peak, over 125 percent, Mexico's figure was far from the region's highest. Jamaica has now recovered from a peak of 75 percent in 1991.

Economic indicators

GDP per capita (US$)
- 15 000–20 000
- 10 000–14 999
- 5 000–9 999
- 2 000–4 999
- 500–1 999

no data available

FRAGILE INSTABILITY

Throughout the 1990s the economies of Central America and the Caribbean were still predominantly dependent on aid and borrowed money. Exports were mostly raw agricultural products or mineral resources, and imports were manufactured goods or fuel for energy, so the terms of trade remained weighted against the countries of the region. During the world recession of the 1980s, the prices of commodities dropped in the world market and dependence on the United States deepened. Only a near monopoly of a vital commodity could empower any country to maintain high prices, and no part of the region has ever achieved that. Japanese purchases of Jamaican Blue Mountain coffee have greatly stimulated coffee production, but at the expense of renewed soil erosion. In Central America only the Mexican oil industry controls a primary product vital to the United States in all political and economic climates.

Sporadic warfare also devastated several Central American and Caribbean economies during the recession years of the 1980s. Grenada's tiny economy was turned upside down by the US invasion of 1983, only for the redemocratized government to have financial support from the United States withdrawn in the late 1980s. El Salvador's disintegrating economy was propped up during its guerrilla war by vast amounts of United States aid, and support continued through to the end of the 1990s. In Nicaragua, the United States funded a low-intensity war against the left-wing Sandinista government, consuming half the tiny country's budget. The

Mexico's balance of merchandise trade (*below*)
Mexico produced nearly 5 percent of the world's total oil output in 1996, providing a quarter of government revenue. Manufactured goods have grown in importance as the effects of NAFTA become more pronounced.

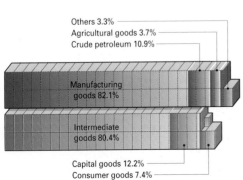

Others 3.3%
Agricultural goods 3.7%
Crude petroleum 10.9%

Manufacturing goods 82.1%

Intermediate goods 80.4%

Capital goods 12.2%
Consumer goods 7.4%

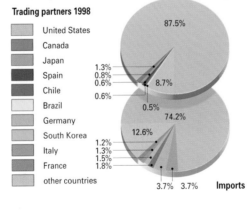

Trading partners 1998

- United States
- Canada
- Japan
- Spain
- Chile
- Brazil
- Germany
- South Korea
- Italy
- France
- other countries

Exports

87.5%
1.3%
0.8%
0.6%
0.6%
8.7%

0.5%
74.2%
12.6%
1.2%
1.3%
1.5%
1.8%
3.7% 3.7% **Imports**

Exports (1996) US$98 bn

Imports (1996) US$89.5 bn

Chamorro government's victory in 1990 established some degree of stability. Nicaragua's economy was subsequently shored up by the World Bank and the International Monetary Fund (IMF) and had just begun to show signs of recovery when Hurricane Mitch hit, late in 1998.

Rescue packages

Efforts to rebuild economic confidence in the region had only limited success. Political volatility had frightened off new investors and made existing investors anxious to move their money elsewhere. In a bid to create stability, Edward Seaga's right-wing government in Jamaica established a policy of friendship with the United States as the main platform of its reforms in the early 1980s; but American financiers and manufacturers could still not be persuaded that investment in Jamaica was a good risk.

Gateway to trade (*left*) A loaded ship passes through the Panama Canal, opened in 1914 to create direct access between the Atlantic and Pacific oceans. Trade is crucial to Panama's economy, equivalent to 80 percent of GDP in 1992.

Small business in Jamaica (*right*) Washing car windows on a street in Kingston, this boy joins the ranks of Jamaica's thriving informal economy. Unemployment remains high in Jamaica – 16.5% in 1997.

The United States also made attempts to improve the situation. President Reagan's Caribbean Basin Initiative (1982) was intended to stimulate United States' investment and open the American market to Caribbean products. However, the United States' sugar and textile lobbies (protecting their own interest) limited the impact of the initiative and much of the aid money involved went to trusted anti-socialist regimes in El Salvador, Costa Rica, Jamaica and other countries of the Commonwealth Caribbean. Costa Rica, Jamaica and the Dominican Republic, all with democratic regimes and skilled labor forces, have benefited from the Caribbean Basin Initiative but the rewards have not been shared more widely.

In Mexico, efforts to regenerate growth in the economy using the revenues from new oil discoveries in the late 1970s failed completely. By 1982 inflation and the bal-ance-of-payments deficit created by the collapse of oil prices put the country under intolerable strain. That year Mexico gave the world a new term – "debt crisis" – when it admitted that it could no longer service its debt of more than $100 billion. Opening up the Mexican economy to capitalist forces and expanding the geographical extent of its duty-free export zone seem to be bringing Mexico out of recession, but the smaller economies of the Caribbean may have problems responding to similar initiatives. Trinidad and Tobago is in the middle of an investment boom following successful economic reforms in 1995, while Jamaica is struggling to meet its stringent financial targets. The fragile economies of these small countries can be damaged by sudden fluctuations in the price of their staple export commodity.

Finding new directions

Increased dependency characterized the late 1990s. Mexico joined the North American Free Trade Agreement (NAFTA) in 1994 and as feared, this has increased its dependence on the United States' economy. This has some advantages: trade between the US, Canada and Mexico grew by 101 percent between 1993 and 1998, and the agreement helped stabilize Mexico during its devaluation crisis in 1994. The United States government is keen to extend NAFTA to other Caribbean and South American countries, but it is feared that this can only increase the power of the world's largest capitalist nation. It is extremely difficult for small countries, such as Jamaica, Grenada, Nicaragua and Cuba to isolate themselves from their traditional trading partners or to negotiate new trading terms. Mexico is pursuing additional trade agreements within Latin America and with the EU in order to widen its markets and lessen dependence on the US. The creation of a single European market in 1992 was viewed by some politicians and businessmen as presenting new trading opportunities, while others feared the emergence of new global trading blocs.

Mexico and other Caribbean countries face the problem of modernizing their economies while controlling their balance of payments and especially the flow of foreign investment. Only Cuba was comparatively successful in the past at confronting capitalist dependency, but the demise of the Soviet Union removed any serious economic challenge within the region.

CARIBBEAN OFFSHORE BANKING

Almost devoid of natural resources to trade, several Caribbean islands have legislation that allows offshore banking. Most activity is concentrated in the Cayman Islands, the British Virgin Islands, Anguilla, the Turks and Caicos Islands, the Bahamas, and the Netherlands Antilles, all of which have unsavory associations with laundering drug money. The Bahamas have been independent of Britain for over 20 years, but the Caymans, British Virgin Islands, Anguilla, and the Turks and Caicos are still dependent, leaving Britain with the responsibility of main-taining some degree of economic supervision.

The key factor in the development of offshore banking has been proximity to the United States. The islands provide tax havens for American investors and for those trafficking in drugs into the United States, generating profits that must be handled clandestinely. Anguilla had 42 banks by the late 1980s; the Cayman Islands recorded 520 banks and trust companies; and the Bahamas boasted 425 banks in 1996, only half of which had more than a name plate and a numbered post office box.

POVERTY AND PREJUDICE

Throughout most of Central America and the Caribbean, wealth is highly concentrated in the hands of the few, retaining the pattern of privilege established during the colonial era when Europeans formed an exclusive elite. Subsequent government policies have tried to redistribute prosperity more widely but with little success. In the late 1990s most inhabitants of the region still lacked access to basic healthcare, social services or education.

Class, race and hierarchy
Everywhere, the class hierarchy remains steeply graded, particularly in unreformed societies (such as El Salvador) where the rural working classes live in hovels on the sides of the roads. In the Caribbean, the class hierarchy has been partly broken down by the welfare policies of colonial and postcolonial governments (especially in the British and French Caribbean), but the quality of life for the majority of people is still very poor.

Up to two-thirds of the urban labor force in the region work as domestic servants, yard boys, shoe shine boys, market traders or unskilled repairmen. Some survive through a range of quasi-legal or illegal activities. The bulk of the higher-grade and better paid jobs in government, financial services, public services, manufacturing or port-side activities are also concentrated in the cities, and those fortunate enough to hold them have access to cheap domestic servants.

The class hierarchy is reinforced by race, color or ethnic and cultural distinctions. In the British and French Caribbean, the white, brown and black populations

Acapulco, Mexico's most luxurious city (*above*) is the center of the country's tourist trade. Most tourists come from the United States, swelling an industry that generated revenue of $5 billion in 1991, creating 650,000 jobs in construction and service industries.

generally correspond with the elite, middle class and the working class respectively. Peasants and manual workers are black or East Indian; white-collar workers are normally brown or mulatto; planters and influential businessmen are white. Decolonization, however, has brought black people into political prominence. Central America has similar correlations between color and class: elite groups are typically European in appearance, though the middle and lower classes may be of mixed race.

At the bottom of the scale is the vast class of impoverished landless peasants,

which in some countries (notably Mexico and Guatemala) is predominantly Amerindian. Since NAFTA was implemented in 1994 the Zapatista rebellion in Mexico has drawn world attention to the extreme poverty of the Amerindians, who have not shared in Mexico's increasing prosperity.

Small exceptions
Only Cuba and Costa Rica have made significant headway in providing a more equal quality of life for all their citizens. During the 1960s and 1970s Soviet aid funded programs in Cuba providing education and healthcare to the mass of the population. Cuba's government also attempted, without much success, to stamp out the racial inequality so prevalent throughout the rest of the region. During the 1980s the Gorbachev regime severely cut back aid to Cuba, and its economy reached a crisis with the dissolution of the Soviet Union in 1991.

Costa Rica, an oasis of democracy and stability since 1920, is unique in Central America because it has a social security system. Its health service and old-age pension schemes are far superior to anything else available in the region, although financial pressures in the late 1990s appeared to be threatening this situation. Health spending absorbed 8.5 percent of GDP in 1995, life expectancy at birth is as good as in the United States and infant mortality is the lowest in Latin America. Government agencies cooperate to bring health services and preventive medicine to

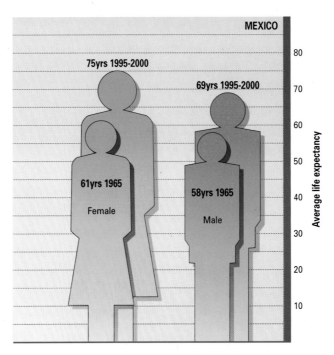

Lessons in hardship (*right*) A young Nicaraguan girl carries her chair home at the end of the school day in one of the poor neigborhoods of the capital, Managua. Seven years' free compulsory education is offered by the government, but the severe shortage of facilities means that it is not unusual for children to bring their own materials and furniture. Trained staff are also in short supply, and only about half of the school-age children can be provided for. Of these, fewer still receive secondary education.

Life expectancy and age distribution (*left*) Mexican women now live an average of 14 years longer than they did in 1965, while men have gained an average of only 11 years. The average number of children per mother in Mexico is 3, contributing to a relatively large segment (35.9 percent) of the population that is under 15 and a low percentage of over 65s (4.1%).

the poor, especially in dispersed rural communities. Two meals a day are served to all preschool and primary school children as well as to expectant and nursing mothers. Costa Rica also has a good education system from primary through to tertiary level and the highest literacy rate (93 percent) in Central America.

If the vast majority of the inhabitants of Central America and the Caribbean are underprivileged, this is even more true of women than of men. Middle-class women are now prominent in the professions, supported by a huge underclass of female servants. Women of the working class, whether peasants or members of the urban poor, are forced to supplement household income by work as seamstresses or craft producers; or work outside the home as servants, factory workers or market stallholders. Women are noticeably absent from the public arena of politics. They are "invisible" even in small administrative units in rural Mexico, where, otherwise, a strong sense of democratic involvement exists.

LEARNING TO READ AND WRITE IN NICARAGUA

The left-wing Sandinista revolutionaries who seized power in Nicaragua in 1979 inherited a society that was 40 percent illiterate. In rural areas, the figure rose to 70 percent. Provision of schooling was at the root of the problem: in rural areas only 5 percent of children finished primary education, compared with 44 percent in urban areas. In 1980, a literacy crusade was launched, funded by foreign governments and nongovernmental organizations. The crusade involved some 100,000 teachers, many of them foreign volunteers, and in just 6 months they cut illiteracy drastically.

The Sandinistas proposed to introduce work-study programs at all levels from kindergarten to university. By the mid 1980s, a seven-fold increase in children enrolled in preschool and special education had been recorded, but only at the expense of engaging untrained teachers. All these achievements were to be engulfed by the low-intensity warfare unleashed by the United States-backed Contras. As early as 1985, about 800 schools had been closed in response to fighting and almost 30 had been totally destroyed. By the time the Sandinistas were defeated in the 1990 election, Nicaragua was desperate for peace at any price.

The informal economy in Mexico

Two factors favor a thriving informal economy in Mexico: the long-standing lack of an effective political opposition to challenge the long-incumbent ruling party, the PRI (Institutional Revolutionary Party), and the chronic shortage of formal-sector employment in the urban areas. This shortage has been made even worse by the debt crisis that has existed since 1982. In some cities more than 60 percent of the labor force is employed "off the record" and avoids paying taxes on earnings. Many simply describe themselves as self-employed; others form shifting work crews, are paid irregular wages and lack any formal job security. The majority of the tasks carried out in this way are technically illegal: stallholders are unlicensed, food sellers disregard public health requirements and construction workers are unprotected by safety regulations.

Even more blatantly illegal transactions are common. Begging, stealing, prostitution, extortion and drug smuggling are rife in the more dangerous sections of Mexico's towns and cities. In view of the general poverty in urban areas and the comparatively vast sums of money that can be made by these illegal activities, it is not surprising that the organizers of crime often act under political protection; or that law enforcement is frustrated by political insiders, if not by the police.

Spreading the rot

Corruption extends from bribing traffic policemen to ignoring real-estate developers who make illegal sub-divisions in new property. The degrees of illegality involved in the informal housing market are legion. Plots of land for building may not even be owned by the developer; and even if the land tenure is legal, development may contravene planning, public health or building requirements. In squatter settlements, the organizer may demand protection money from the squatters and use it to buy electoral votes. Local politicians sometimes impede legalization and slow down the provision of services to maintain their control over the poor: the politically ambitious have no economic leverage over people without needs.

In Mexico City, the world's largest metropolis, almost half the inhabitants in the last two decades have been housed in

Skilled workers (*below*) advertising their availability for work in Mexico City. Only 36 percent of Mexicans were active in the formal economy in 1992, reflecting the extreme shortage of jobs. Corrupt officials often sell jobs – hiring workers in return for cash payments.

Single-party domination (*right*) The PRI has controlled the Mexican economy since 1929. New administrations announce anticorruption measures, but officials continue to line their own pockets as insurance against losing office.

self-built neighborhoods, all illegal in one sense or another. The PRI government that ended with the election of Vicente Fox in 2000 presided over this state of affairs and controlled every kind of state intervention and regulation, including the recent social welfare program known as Solidarity. In this way, the government has been able to retain considerable control over the urban poor without making a vast outlay in state

funds to subsidize formal housing. Most urban Mexicans cannot avoid some element of illegality and corruption in their daily lives, either in the informal labor market or through informal housing.

The PRI was under great pressure, particularly from the United States, to permit fair elections and stop vote rigging, leading to a genuinely plural political democracy that would bring about much-needed

financial reform. However, the police and state officials were suspected of racketeering and offering protection to Mexican drug dealers.

The situation continues to cause grave concern among those Mexicans who campaign for a fairer society, though the victory of Vicente Fox in the 2000 presidential election seemed to offer a fresh start at last. But it is unlikely that the corruption

and illegality that prevailed for so long will disappear quickly. The new government has inherited the challenge of the rebellion of indigenous Amerindian peoples known as the Zapatistas, which began in Chiapas province in 1994 and continued into the 2000s. Amerindians are the poorest of the Mexican poor, and they were by far the worst affected by PRI economic policies since the 1980s.

PEOPLES AND CULTURES

CONQUESTS AND COLONIZATION · THE CULTURAL MOSAIC · SOCIAL STRATIFICATIONS

Central America and the Caribbean islands originally supported a culturally diverse set of peoples who had lived there for at least 12,000 years before the European discovery of the "New World" in 1492. This event sparked off a sustained invasion of the region by Europeans, with devastating effects on the indigenous peoples. The Spanish quickly seized control of Mexico and the Central American isthmus, and their language, religion and customs continue to prevail there today. The scattered islands of the Caribbean were colonized by a number of European nations, but the predominant cultural influence is African, derived from the millions of slaves shipped there to work the sugar plantations. Asians and impoverished Europeans, both brought as laborers, added to the cultural amalgam.

Colorful culture (*above*) Maya women from Guatemala bring textiles and other handicrafts to sell in the markets. Virtually all Amerindian communities have their own style of colorful clothing that distinguishes one from another.

Pride in the past (*right*) The great murals painted by the Mexican artist Diego Rivera (1886–1957) after the 1910 revolution signaled a rebirth of nationalism by celebrating the country's native civilizations and rejecting European ideals.

COUNTRIES IN THE REGION

Antigua and Barbuda, Bahamas, Barbados, Belize, Costa Rica, Cuba, Dominica, Dominican Republic, El Salvador, Grenada, Guatemala, Haiti, Honduras, Jamaica, Mexico, Nicaragua, Panama, St Kitts-Nevis, St Lucia, St Vincent and the Grenadines, Trinidad and Tobago

POPULATION

Over 100 million Mexico

5 million–15 million Cuba, Dominican Republic, El Salvador, Guatemala, Haiti, Honduras

1 million–5 million Costa Rica, Jamaica, Nicaragua, Panama, Trinidad and Tobago

250,000–1 million Bahamas, Barbados

Under 250,00 Antigua and Barbuda, Belize, Dominica, Grenada, St Kitts-Nevis, St Lucia, St Vincent and the Grenadines

LANGUAGE

Countries with one official language (English) Antigua and Barbuda, Bahamas, Barbados, Belize, Dominica, Grenada, Jamaica, St Kitts-Nevis, St Vincent and the Grenadines, Trinidad and Tobago; (Spanish) Costa Rica, Cuba, Dominican Republic, El Salvador, Guatemala, Honduras, Mexico, Nicaragua, Panama

Country with two official languages (Creole, French) Haiti

Other languages spoken in the region include Carib, Nahua and other indigenous languages; creoles and French patois; Hindi (Trinidad and Tobago)

RELIGION

Countries with one major religion (P) Antigua and Barbuda; (RC) Costa Rica, Cuba, Dominica, Dominican Republic, El Salvador, Honduras, Mexico, Nicaragua

Countries with more than one major religion (P, RC) Bahamas, Barbados, Belize, Grenada, Jamaica, St Kitts-Nevis, St Lucia, St Vincent and the Grenadines; (P, RC, V) Haiti; (H, M, P, RC) Trinidad and Tobago

Country in which religion is officially proscribed Cuba

Key: H–Hindu, M–Muslim, P–Protestant, RC–Roman Catholic, V–Voodoo

---

CONQUEST AND COLONIZATION

Christopher Columbus (1461–1506) and the Spanish explorers and conquerors of the New World encountered a variety of indigenous peoples (whom, without distinction, they termed "Indians") practicing many differing ways of life. Among these peoples, chiefdoms existed in what are now the countries of Panama and Costa Rica, seminomadic societies inhabited eastern Nicaragua and Honduras, and a succession of complex empires (notably the Olmecs, Toltecs, Mayans and Aztecs) – each renowned for features such as hieroglyphic writing, advanced calendars, mathematics, monumental buildings and marvelous sculptures – left a cultural legacy in Mexico and Guatemala. On the many islands, settled agricultural villages existed in the Greater Antilles: Cuba, Hispaniola (Haiti and the Dominican Republic), Jamaica and Puerto Rico.

The conquering Spanish immediately and ruthlessly imposed their language, religion, bureaucratic forms of government, architecture, town planning and economic system upon all of these indigenous Amerindian peoples. The Spanish regarded the New World as a wild and hostile environment needing to be tamed, the fruits of which were there for the picking. They extracted all the wealth they could from the land and its people, shipping it back to Spain in fleets of treasure-bearing ships. From the Old World of Europe, new animals, new crops and new techniques for building, mining and agriculture were introduced to Central America and the Caribbean. All these radically altered the traditional ways of life of the original inhabitants.

In the course of being colonized, the Amerindians were treated so harshly that their numbers rapidly plummeted. From a total of somewhere between 50 and 100 million before Columbus's arrival, the indigenous population fell to only some 3 million within the first 100 years of Spanish colonization. Many devastating diseases (smallpox, measles, typhus and

yellow fever) were inadvertently introduced, to which the Amerindians had
no immunity. Forced labor under harsh
conditions and systematic slaughter also
took large death tolls. The Amerindians
who survived mainly did so because they
lived in isolated pockets in remote areas.

By 1600, some 300,000 colonists had
migrated to the region, and many mixed
with the Amerindian population. In rural
areas of Central America a rapidly growing population of racially mixed people
(*mestizos*) took the place of the declining
Amerindians to supply labor on the vast
agrarian estates (*haciendas*), owned by a
small elite of Spanish descent.

The Caribbean experience
The Spanish could not prevent other
European nations from laying claim to the

numerous islands of the Caribbean; many
changed hands several times in the two
centuries after Columbus. Although
Spain continued to control the mainland,
England, France and the Netherlands
were the nations that were principally
involved, with some incursions from
Denmark and Sweden, and later from the
United States. Languages, buildings,
public works, laws, elements of popular
culture and other features imported by
these nations are still found throughout
the Caribbean.

The indigenous peoples of the Caribbean islands – Caribs and Arawaks – were
practically wiped out by disease, slavery
and warfare within a few years of colonization. During the following two centuries, therefore, more than 5 million
slaves from Africa were transported to

meet the labor needs of the emerging,
European-imposed plantation economy;
here, many were kept in degrading conditions. After the abolition of slavery
in the 19th century, laborers from the
Middle East, Europe, China and India
came to bolster the labor force. Many,
particularly the Asian Indians, arrived as
indentured workers who were bound by
contracts to work for as much as 5 to 10
years, virtually as slaves themselves.

Following the Spanish–American War
at the end of the 19th century, the United
States seized Cuba and Puerto Rico, and
later became heavily involved in Haiti
and the Dominican Republic. This
powerful neighbor has continued to have
a significant influence – culturally and
economically, as well as politically – over
most other islands in the region.

THE CULTURAL MOSAIC

The mark of the Spanish empire permeates virtually all of Central America and the Spanish-speaking islands of the Caribbean (Cuba, Puerto Rico and the Dominican Republic). This is especially noticeable in the layout of towns and cities, the elaborate architecture of colonial buildings and churches, the heritage of certain forms of music, and even, in places, the popularity of bullfighting. Yet the greatest remaining influence of Spanish rule is found in the continuing role of the church in these countries.

In the early years of the conquest, the mission to convert the Amerindians to Roman Catholicism motivated the Spanish perhaps as strongly as their lust for gold. In addition to the exercise of political control and enforced labor, the religious conversion of the Amerindians was another way of dominating them. However, over many years, the blending of many pre-Colombian beliefs, practices and symbols with those of the Spanish has given the Roman Catholicism of Central America a character and flavor of its own. Among the Otomi of Mexico, for example, ancient religious shrines are still honored, and shamans intercede with spirits on behalf of villagers who are, nonetheless, devout Roman Catholics. In some places today, Roman Catholic influence is being challenged by North American-backed Protestant evangelical missions. This is especially evident in Guatemala, where already up to half the population has converted to such fundamentalist forms of Christianity in relatively recent times.

Amerindian survivals

Although in most of Central America *mestizos* are in the majority, pockets of Amerindian predominance are also to be found, and Amerindian languages, lifestyles and customs persist in one form or another throughout the region. There is great variety in racial composition from country to country: from Honduras, where *mestizos* account for 92 percent of the population, to Costa Rica, which is 92 percent European, to Guatemala, which has 62 percent Amerindians, the highest proportion in Central America. In Mexico, only 10 percent of the population is recorded as being of pure Amerindian descent, yet there are few Mexicans

without some Amerindian blood, and Nahuatl, Mayan, Zapoteco and Mixteco languages are widespread, especially in southern parts of the country.

While European aspects of society and culture are generally widespread across the region, some facets of Amerindian life nonetheless survive from place to place, especially in the more remote rural districts. Such traits include (in addition to language) types of family and social relationships, patterns of collective land use, beliefs and ritual practices devoted to a series of supernatural beings, the honoring of ancestors, cultivation habits and food preferences, and styles of dress and textile production.

In Belize and along the Caribbean coasts of Nicaragua and Costa Rica, another unique cultural tradition is to be

found. Here, the descendants of escaped African slaves form the majority of inhabitants. They mainly speak a Caribbean dialect of English, and many features of their society and culture are also closer to those of the Caribbean than to their Hispanic and Amerindian neighbors. This kind of heterogeneity found along the Caribbean coast is a mirror of the complex makeup of societies found on islands in the Caribbean Sea itself.

A multicultural region

More than 50 nationalities or groups, many with their own art forms, religions, languages, and social institutions, comprise the multicultural societies of the Caribbean islands. Language diversity is the most immediate sign of this – throughout the islands English, French,

A Voodoo priest (*above*) Haiti's folk religious cult is a mixture of Roman Catholicism and African animism and magic. A priest or priestess leads devotees in a ritual involving song, drumming, dance, prayer and the preparation of food.

Day of the Dead (*left*) Mexico's version of All Souls Day is widely observed. Offerings to ancestors' souls are made at a candlelit vigil, and picnics are held at their graves. Shops sell chocolate skulls and other souvenirs of the day.

Dutch, Hindi and Chinese, as well as a wide variety of *creole* or *patois* variants that have evolved through the blending of these with different African languages, can all be heard. The creation of these Caribbean languages coincided with the emergence of a colorful tradition of oral literature, based upon folkloric stories told from generation to generation. Out of this tradition has come, in turn, a number of important contemporary writers, in both English and French, who have explored the heritage of Caribbean peoples in evocative and entertaining ways.

The Caribbean is also renowned for its unique syncretic religions, such as voodoo in Haiti, pocomania in Jamaica and shango in Trinidad. These bring together the beliefs and practices of Roman Catholicism with facets of traditional West African religions, often involving the inducement of ecstatic states of consciousness and trance, rituals of healing, and the identification of Christian saints with West African (especially Yoruba) gods or supernatural powers.

Because societies in the Caribbean were created by colonial powers wholly for the production of export crops, their populations grew well beyond the capacity of each island to support them. After the ending of slavery a tradition of migration between the islands developed, widening to countries farther afield as regional economic problems intensified. Following World War II, Britain was the principal destination for immigrants from Jamaica, Barbados, Trinidad and other islands then belonging to Britain. Today, the goal for most is the United States.

THE VIRGIN OF GUADALUPE

Perhaps no other symbol encapsulates the identity of a nation so well as Mexico's patron saint, the Virgin of Guadalupe. Her image preceded armies of insurgents in the War of Independence from Spain in 1821, and today it is found everywhere: in homes and churches, taxis and buses, restaurants, bullrings and brothels.

According to legend, at Tepeyac, to the north of Mexico City, in 1531, the Virgin appeared to an Amerindian convert named Juan Diego, asking that a shrine be built in her honor. Diego petitioned the local archbishop unsuccessfully until the Virgin allegedly worked a miracle: producing roses where they could not have grown and marking her image on Juan Diego's cloak. Today, the famous cloak hangs above the altar in the church where his vision was believed to have taken place, and it now attracts hundreds of thousands of pilgrims each year.

In Tepeyac, in pre-Columbian times, there had stood a temple in honor of Tonantzin, the Aztec mother goddess. The pagan Tonantzin was replaced by the Christian Virgin of Guadalupe, thus linking Amerindian beliefs with those of their Spanish conquerors. The Virgin has thus now become the symbol of a single Mexican people.

SOCIAL STRATIFICATIONS

The longest-lasting legacy that European colonialism has given to Central America is a rigid, pyramidal social structure, with a powerful local aristocracy at the top, *mestizos* filling the middle classes, and Amerindians at the bottom. Attempts to wrest social and economic equality from the predominantly white elite have contributed to the endemic political instability of the region, resulting in a history of left-wing revolutions and right-wing military takeovers.

The struggle to survive

Regardless of their ethnic background, impoverished peasants make up the bulk of Central American society. For many, the struggle for survival is hard, whether as subsistence farmers on land where the soil has been eroded and degraded by deforestation or living in the crowded slums of Mexico City. It is among such people that the ideas summed up in the "liberation theology" movement, which calls for direct action to free the poor from dehumanizing social structures, have taken strong hold – as evidenced by the presence of Jesuit Roman Catholic priests in the left-wing Sandinista government of Nicaragua. Others seek to escape from poverty by migrating. Since the 1970s there has been a massive, sometimes illegal, exodus of peasants from all over Central America to the United States.

Social causes and movements will often harness local indigenous symbols to rally popular support. But indigenous culture itself is vulnerable to all kinds of pressure from above. For example, the military-controlled government of Guatemala pursued an overt and hostile program of "cultural genocide" during the 1980s, seeking to drive into extinction all traces of indigenous culture – and often its practitioners as well. Similar policies led to the virtual extermination of traditional indigenous cultures in Costa Rica, El Salvador and Honduras.

Shades of color

In the Caribbean, the plantation took the place of the *hacienda* in determining the social structure. The local plantation represented a complete social and economic unit that controlled practically every aspect of the resident workers' lives, from housing and work routines to marriage patterns and leisure activities. French, British and Dutch colonial rule created a strict hierarchy. In most places, whites formed the ruling and wealth-owning class, the numerically dominant blacks the laboring class, and those of mixed race (variously called mulattos, quadroons or mustees) were sandwiched in the middle – a pyramidal structure not dissimilar to that found on the Central American mainland.

However, in ways unique to the Caribbean, a separate "brown" racial category came to have great importance in determining social status and acceptability. Depending on the society and its part-

More than a game (*above*) The West Indies cricket team unites the islands of the Caribbean. Cricketing prowess represents black pride and independence from former British colonial masters.

A new identity (*below*) A Rastafarian family in Jamaica. Rastafarianism replaced Western religion and culture with a specifically black creed that turned to Africa for its inspiration.

RASTAFARIANISM

During the 1930s a religious movement was born in Jamaica that offered black people a cultural identity and called for an end to the inequalities that determined their place in society. Rastafarianism preached that the only way for black people to escape their poverty was to return to Africa. Adopting the symbolism of Judaism (and holding that the Bible has been deliberately mistranslated by whites), Rastafarians believe that the Africans of the Caribbean are in Babylon, the place of exile, from where a Messiah, or leader, identified as the late emperor of Ethiopia, Haile Selassie (1892–1975) – known as Ras Tafia, the Lion of Judah – will lead them to a promised land in Africa.

Rastafarians use a distinct dialect and obey Biblical injunctions not to cut their hair, wearing it long in dreadlocks, they adopt the distinctive colors of Ethiopia: red, green and gold. The movement's promotion of black pride and black power, and criticism of imperialism and social inequality, mean that its symbols and rhetoric have been borrowed by political parties at home and farther afield.

Rastafarianism has had widespread cultural influence – adherents are found around the world, particularly in the United States and Britain, and many of its usages have been absorbed by urban youth subcultures. This is largely due to the worldwide audience for reggae, which has become the Rastafarians' most successful method of communicating ideas, especially through singers such as Bob Marley (1945–80).

icular ethnic makeup, Chinese, Arabs (invariably called Syrians regardless of national origin) and Jews spread through the middle classes. Sometimes Portuguese and other groups of poor whites maintained a vague status apart from the browns and blacks, but were nevertheless placed in society's lowest ranks. Asians, too, were usually relegated to the bottom rank, largely because of their position in the labor market and their alien language, religion and culture. Only in Dominica and the Netherland Antilles do pockets of full-blooded Caribs and Arawaks survive; inevitably, these also occupy a place at the bottom of society. Since independence, most countries have been struggling to overcome this legacy of colonial rule. However, nearly everywhere, the white rulers of the past have been replaced by a brown elite, while whites often still control some of the most important economic assets.

Trinidad – colonized in turn by the Spanish, French and English – has perhaps the most diverse and complex of all Caribbean societies. Most of the ethnic groups of the Caribbean are represented here. In addition to English, three creole and several Asian languages are spoken, and both the mixed race and African-origin groups, including those that have migrated in recent times from nearby islands such as Barbados and St Vincent, are further subdivided on the basis of whether they are Roman Catholic or Protestant. Those of Asian descent (approximately half the population) are similarly differentiated by religion into Hindus, Muslims and Christians.

These deep-rooted ethnic and cultural differences within the population means there are few common symbols to unite the country. Social and cultural fragmentation is a problem that affects all Caribbean societies. Even though Caribbean peoples share a similar heritage and general social and cultural patterns, most attempts to arrive at some sort of common regional identity have been unsuccessful, partly due to size; the peoples of the small islands insist on maintaining their social and cultural independence.

Yet, especially in the fields of music (particularly reggae, soca and calypso), sport (cricket and soccer), theater and literature, Caribbean peoples are increasingly finding mutual expressions of their common historical roots. The existence of Caribbean communities in other parts of the world, such as New York, Canada and Britain, means that aspects of this distinctive culture are also found worldwide.

Hindus in the Caribbean

Hindu and Tamil languages, spiced Asian food, Indian music and decorated Hindu temples may seem out of place in the accepted picture of Caribbean life, with its dominant creole culture based on the merging of Roman Catholic and African traditions, but they are all to be observed within a variety of thriving Indian communities throughout the islands.

Between 1838 and 1917, more than half a million Indians were brought to the Caribbean. Most came from northern India and settled in the British colonies of Trinidad, Jamaica and some of the smaller islands. Others, from southern India, were transported to the French colonies of Guadeloupe and Martinique. Most of them were Hindus, adherents of the dominant religion of the Indian subcontinent, which consists of a complex system of rites and ceremonies.

Within the first years of their coming to the Caribbean, Indian Hindus built temples and organized the celebration of major festivals. However, in the new environment in which the immigrants found themselves planted, many aspects of Indian culture that had distinguished groups and communities at home, such as languages and their dialects, customs, religious practices and art forms, merged with one another. The result was a diminution in cultural vigor. The most significant feature of Indian culture to become weakened was the caste system. Inextricably linked with Hinduism, it was the traditional method of maintaining social, economic and political distinctions between groups within society – but, transferred to the plantation economy of the Caribbean, it ceased to operate in an effective way.

There were regional variations in the vigor with which Indian cultural identity was preserved. In the smaller islands, where Indian immigrants were few in number, their social and cultural habits were more easily superseded by the local creole ones. Where Indians were more numerous and densely settled, however, many characteristically Indian ways of life were strongly upheld.

Cultural reinvigoration

In recent years, many religious and cultural practices have been revitalized and embellished, largely through the growth of local and national Hindu organizations. These include *yagnas* (week-long sets of ceremonies surrounding readings of the

Hindu sacred books), and the annual Ram Lila, a religious play concerning the life of Lord Rama, one of the main gods of Hinduism. Performances may last for several days, and sometimes involve more than 100 participants. Hindus have also reestablished the performance of important rituals, such as *pujas* (ritual offerings to deities) and the rites-of-passage, which are celebrated to mark the stages of an individual's life.

Strong as their sentiments and activities are, many Caribbean Indians feel alienated and discriminated against. In Trinidad, for example, the sizable Indian community considers itself the victim of attempts to promote a sense of national unity, since such efforts focus on cultural phenomena such as carnival or calypso music, both of which are predominantly associated with Afro-Caribbean culture. The selection of an Indian player to the West Indian national cricket team is likely to cause controversy throughout the cricket-playing parts of the region, since the game is still regarded as belonging to the Afro-Caribbean tradition.

Hindus attest that efforts to create a common Caribbean identity ignore the interests of the minority cultures and religions such as theirs. So long as this is the case, they argue, Caribbean societies will continue to be seriously fragmented through lack of cooperation.

Rites of passage (*above*) The eldest son sprinkles petals on the corpse before the body is cremated and the ashes sprinkled in sacred water, usually a river.

Religious revival (*right*) A devout Hindu prays at the temple. Caribbean Hinduism has been invigorated by better organization and political participation.

A place for worship (*below*) A new temple in Trinidad mixes Caribbean and Indian styles. Hindu temples are shrines for individual, rather than congregational, worship.

Carnival!

Carnival was traditionally celebrated in Christian Europe as a time of feasting and popular fun before the start of the 40-day period of abstinence known as Lent. It was observed in the Caribbean as early as the 18th century, and after the emancipation of slaves was taken over by black Africans, when it resumed its original character as a time of rule-breaking and role reversal. Men dressed as women, slaves became masters, night became day, people hid behind masks, and the streets were filled with music, revelry and drinking, banned at other times of the year.

Carnival had a variety of names throughout the Caribbean – Junkanoo (or John Canoe) in Jamaica, Belize and the Bahamas, and "mas" (short for masquerade) in Grenada. Some were held before Lent, others on New Year's Day or Twelfth Night, 12 days after Christmas. Its associations with disorderly behavior meant that it constantly came into conflict with the authorities and was frequently banned.

After independence, Carnival was made a day of national celebration in many of the islands. Cuba moved its Carnival to July to celebrate the revolution, while Bermuda and Grenada shifted theirs to August for the tourist season – Carnival has become a valuable source of revenue. The traditional mingling of costumed paraders and onlookers and the spontaneous routes taken by the parades were changed to create a more orderly spectacle. In doing so, much of the subversive character of the festivities has been lost, though in Trinidad – the greatest Carnival of them all – the calypso-singing competition still provides an occasion to mock politicians.

A swirl of color Every year, crowds of people fill the streets of Port of Spain in Trinidad to watch the costume parade, attend the dance competitions and listen to the calypsos, steel bands and reggae that make Carnival such a vibrant celebration.

CITIES

Until recently, the population of Central America and the Caribbean was predominantly rural, but the decline of traditional subsistence farming systems (and the decay of the plantation system in the Caribbean) has been the cause of massive movement to the cities. In nearly every country, one major city – usually the capital – predominates over all the rest, acting as a magnet for people seeking an escape from grinding rural poverty. But the enormous, unplanned and rapid growth of urban populations has not been matched by a rise in industrialization, and the cities face vast employment and housing problems. People cope by finding work in the informal sector and live in self-help settlements, but the municipal authorities of the region are hard pressed to supply even basic services and amenities.

COUNTRIES IN THE REGION

Antigua and Barbuda, Bahamas, Barbados, Belize, Costa Rica, Cuba, Dominica, Dominican Republic, El Salvador, Grenada, Guatemala, Haiti, Honduras, Jamaica, Mexico, Nicaragua, Panama, St Kitts-Nevis, St Lucia, St Vincent and the Grenadines, Trinidad and Tobago

POPULATION

Total population of region (millions)			168.3
	Mexico	**Jamaica**	**Honduras**
Population density (persons per sq km)	51.2	243.3	52.4
Population change (average annual percent 1995–2000)			
Urban	+1.89%	+1.73%	+4.84%
Rural	+0.90%	–0.19%	+0.64%

URBAN POPULATION

As percentage of total population 1995	73%	54%	48%

TEN LARGEST CITIES

	Country	Population
Mexico City †	Mexico	8,591,309
Havana †	Cuba	2,143,406
Guadalajara	Mexico	1,647,000
Ecatepec	Mexico	1,619,000
Santo Domingo †	Dominican Republic	1,609,699
Puebla	Mexico	1,270,989
Nezahualcóyotl	Mexico	1,224,500
Ciudad Juárez	Mexico	1,119,000
Tijuana	Mexico	1,115,000
Monterrey	Mexico	1,108,400

† denotes capital city

City population figures are for the city proper.

EXPLOITING THE NEW WORLD

Settled village life based on farming probably began to emerge in Mexico and the Central American isthmus around 7000 BC, and subsequently the development of intensive agricultural techniques supported the rise of urban cultures such as the Maya and the Aztec. At its height, from about 250 to 900 AD, the Mayan civilization boasted more than 40 cities in the area of southern Mexico, Guatemala and northern Belize, with populations of between 5,000 and 50,000. Today most are visible only as creeper-covered ruins emerging from the lowland forests.

The first European city in the Americas – that of Santo Domingo on the island of Hispaniola, today the capital of the Dominican Republic – was founded by the Spanish in 1496, only four years after Christopher Columbus (1451–1506) first set foot in the New World. It was from here that Mexico was conquered, followed by the annexation of the Central American isthmus. Avoiding the forested areas of the mainland, the Spanish swiftly established a network of towns along the coasts or at high altitude. These served as administrative centers from which to oversee the exploitation of the region's resources and to organize the indigenous population to provide forced labor in silver mines or on large agricultural estates (*haciendas*).

In the Caribbean, two major entrepot trading ports, Havana (on Cuba) and Puerto Rico (later known as San Juan, the present-day capital of Puerto Rico), supplied the great bullion fleets that, loaded with silver from the mines of Mexico and Upper Peru, crossed the Atlantic to Spain. Small farms in the hinterland grew foodstuffs for the passing crews – a contrast to the practice on the mainland. From the early 17th century, the British, French and Dutch replaced Spanish power in many Caribbean islands and set up a different settlement pattern. Large sugar cane plantations were established, usually on the coast; urban settlement was limited to a few exporting ports.

When the indigenous peoples of the Caribbean, the Caribs and Arawaks, were wiped out by European diseases and slavery, slaves were imported from Africa to work the plantations. Towns such as Spanish Town in Jamaica and St Pierre in Martinique became the resort of white

elites who resided there seasonally or semipermanently to enjoy the communal comforts of a more sophisticated and protected way of life than their plantations could afford. Similarly, in the mainland cities such as Oaxaca City in southern Mexico or Guatemala City, a small Spanish elite dominated the Amerindian and *mestizo* (mixed) populations. A major common denominator throughout the region was the role of the town as commercial and administrative center – an outpost of the colonizing country, with imposing public buildings in Spanish baroque, English gothic or French provincial styles.

Post-slavery settlement

The ending of slavery between 1834 and 1886 in the Caribbean brought a new element to the settlement pattern. Slave numbers had been greatest in the British and French islands, and on many of them

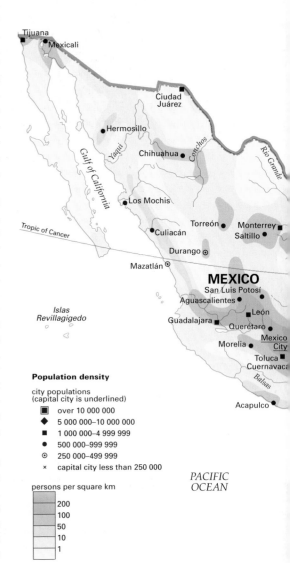

Population density

city populations
(capital city is underlined)

- ■ over 10 000 000
- ◆ 5 000 000–10 000 000
- ■ 1 000 000–4 999 999
- ● 500 000–999 999
- ◉ 250 000–499 999
- × capital city less than 250 000

persons per square km

	200
	100
	50
	10
	1

there was a mass movement of population away from the coastal plantations as large numbers of ex-slaves bought or squatted on plots of land in the previously un-occupied interior. These people worked the land as subsistence farmers, and a new network of inland villages, market centers and towns came into being to serve them.

Although the old colonial ports at first remained at the apex of the urban hierarchy, many declined when the sugar industry was hit by the removal of protective tariffs during the second half of the 19th century. However, a number of new ports developed to export the agricultural produce grown on peasant holdings, such as bananas. Consequently, the settlement pattern is more varied than on the mainland. Here, little has altered in the last 150 years, except that urban centers are now better linked through improved road, rail and air communications.

A bridge with the past (*left*) The arch of Santa Catarina in Antigua, the former capital of Guatemala, and one of the first planned cities in the Americas. It has twice been destroyed by earthquakes, most recently in 1976.

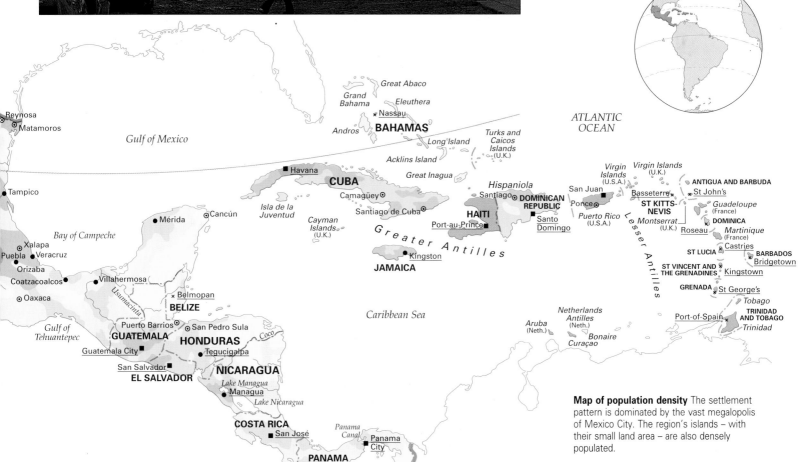

Map of population density The settlement pattern is dominated by the vast megalopolis of Mexico City. The region's islands – with their small land area – are also densely populated.

FACTORS OF GROWTH

Central American cities are growing very rapidly. The most obvious reason is the combination of falling death rates, due to the ability to control epidemic diseases, and a high – though slowly declining – birthrate. As a result of rural overpopulation and poverty, increasing numbers of people have migrated either to the cities or abroad. Urban populations, originally swelled by rural migration, continue to grow since governments are hard pressed to fund the public health programs to reduce fertility rates.

The population of Kingston, Jamaica, has doubled since independence in 1962 and now stands at more than half a million. In mainland Central America a handful of cities now have populations of over 1 million. Mexico City is the world's

CUBA – AN ISLAND APART

Since 1959 urban and rural planning in Cuba has been shaped by socialist principles. The artificially high prices it received for sugar from the former Soviet Union, combined with cheap oil imports, enabled it to carry out ambitious programs that emphasized rural development at the expense of urban growth, in sharp contrast to the trend in the rest of the region. One way it did this was to create "small cities" (*pequeñas ciudades*) – small clusters of modern housing, schools and healthcare facilities in the countryside.

Although the population of Havana, the island's capital, has doubled in the last 30 years, it has grown much less than other cities in the region: over the same period Mexico City's population has increased sixfold. Public health programs account for the lowest fertility rate in the region. There is provision of state-funded housing, with rents fixed as a proportion of income. New housing developments have been built and old residential areas upgraded by "microbrigades" employed and directed by the state. Many town properties belonging to the rich, mainly white, elite when they abandoned Cuba after the revolution have been reallocated to public services, such as hospitals and schools. However, the economic crisis brought about by the demise of the former Soviet Union has reduced living standards for the average Cuban and conditions are unlikely to improve in the near future.

largest metropolis: unofficial estimates place its population as high as 19 million and it is still growing. It is likely to have reached more than 20 million by the end of the century.

A number of other factors help to explain the region's recent rapid urbanization. In the Caribbean, the granting of political independence to the majority of islands since the 1960s has created many new capital cities, with all that entails in the way of extra government and administrative functions. The development of new industries such as bauxite mining, tourism and petroleum extraction, and the introduction of universal education and social welfare programs have increased the pulling power of the cities in all but the smallest of islands.

In some mainland Central American countries the ever increasing economic influence of the United States has been instrumental in promoting urban growth. The region's capitals have taken on many of the aspects of the United States' city. In a number of cities, such as Puebla in central Mexico and Mexico City, joint ventures with United States' firms, using

American technology, have increased employment opportunities. The setting up of the Central American Common Market (CACOM) in the 1970s stimulated growth in centers such as San Salvador and Guatemala City.

No glittering prizes

Most cities in the region, however, especially those in the Caribbean, do not possess a sufficiently varied and thriving industrial base to sustain rapid urbanization. For the majority of rural migrants, city life does not bring the desired economic advantages. A shortage of jobs means that only the very few find work within the formal employment sector – that is, with secure wages, regular hours of work and social security benefits. Most are therefore compelled to live within the informal sector, seizing every chance for work that offers itself, whether as casual laborers, recycling scrap, or cleaning cars or shoes. In many parts of the Caribbean domestic service is the mainstay of the urban female workforce.

Even in Mexico City, which has a more diversified economy than most, more

Rural street life (*above*) A street vendor weighs out his goods near a shop selling locally-produced beer, wine and liquor. Compared to the frenetic pace of Mexico City, the country's small towns and villages have a slow and easy atmosphere.

Castro's children (below) Cuba has one of the lowest population growth rates in the region. Declining birth rates, combined with heavy emigration by young people, mean that the majority of the Cuban population is over the age of 30.

many, the rewards of illegal activities such as robbery or drug pushing are obvious. Given that the cities and towns of Central America and the Caribbean lie across the conduit supplying drugs from South America to the United States, it is not surprising that urban gangs in most are involved in the illicit trade.

Rural decline

Urbanization, especially in the Caribbean, has led to acute rural depopulation and agricultural decline. In Jamaica, for example, sugar and banana production, the traditional mainstays of the economy, have fallen sharply over the past two decades, and Jamaica now has a massive food import bill. These conditions are repeated elsewhere in the Caribbean, especially in Trinidad and the French dependencies of Martinique and Guadeloupe. The lack of amenities in rural communities persuades more people to migrate to the cities, and so the spiral of decline is maintained.

In Mexico, where land reform since the mid 1920s has placed many millions of hectares in the hands of peasant farmers (*ejidatarios*), the problem is not as great since rural communities have been less affected by political and educational pressures for change. However, in some of the countries of the Central American isthmus – such as El Salvador and Nicaragua, which are plagued by endemic political violence – acts of brutality by guerrillas and national soldiers have terrorized parts of the countryside and forced many to flee for safety to the cities.

than 40 percent of the labor force in 1980 operated outside the formal sector. The economic crisis of the 1980s, when governments struggled to repay massive international debts, increased urban unemployment right across the region. In most cities, including Mexico City, the number of those in the informal sector is now likely to be nearer 60 percent. For

In the fast lane (*below*) A cow, a car and a bicycle share the freeway in Santo Domingo, the capital of the Dominican Republic. The road system is part of an American-inspired urban development program that was begun in the late 1950s. Plans were based on an ambitious forecast of economic growth; this has not been fulfilled, and the new roads are underused and left open to any traffic.

OLD AND NEW, RICH AND POOR

All the cities of Central America are showing the strains of unprecedented rapid growth. Mexico City, by far and away the largest, provides a striking example of the chaos that can result from unchecked development. Much of the city's industrialization over the last 50 years has been unplanned, with the result that factories are often poorly located. The city is surrounded on all sides by mountains that trap vehicle and industrial emissions and make air pollution a serious hazard. The area is prone to earthquakes such as the one in 1985 that killed 7,000 people. All these factors add to the problems of a city in which the service and transportation infrastructure is already severely overburdened and where the rate of population increase shows no sign of slowing down.

A blend of influences

Mexico City – built on top of the pre-Columbian capital Tenochtitlan – is the only city of the region that predates the European era. Like cities throughout the developing world, most are a blend of colonial and modern influences. Obvious symbols of former imperial domination

Scrap-heap recycling At the municipal dump in Guatemala City, a family of scavengers search for food and objects to sell among a sea of urban waste. The region's cities do not have a sufficiently developed industrial base to support their increasing populations, so many people are forced to make ends meet however and wherever they can.

such as place-names and statues have been removed or replaced with those of nationalist heroes, and the cathedral and the governor's residence have given way to city skyscrapers.

The smaller towns and cities show more visibly the signs of their colonial origins. In the formerly Spanish cities, for example, the large square flanked by imposing religious and civic buildings still lies at the center. There is considerable mixing of commercial and residential functions with many people living above or behind their place of work, and the areas of poorest housing are confined to the city periphery. In the large cities, by contrast, a century or more of invading modern influences and new technologies, acquired first of all from Western Europe and more recently from the United States, have virtually obliterated the earlier pattern. These new elements include central business districts (CBDs), as well as much greater segregation of commercial, industrial and residential areas.

The general pattern is for residential segregation to increase as cities grow. Elite suburbs of attractively landscaped low-density housing occupy large areas on the outskirts of the city. They are served by out-of-town shopping malls, and by rapid transit systems and expressways. These suburbs are taking on the appearance of affluent ghettos in the midst of a sea of overcrowded tenements and underserviced squatter settlements. In the case of San Salvador, capital of El Salvador, this is almost literally true. After a decade or more of insurgency, the elite barely leave the protection of the suburb, and even travel within it, to ice cream parlor or video arcade, behind the safety of tinted car windows.

The housing crisis

The rapid increase in urban populations has spawned enormous housing problems, which municipal authorities are far from being able to solve. Those living within the informal sector rely on their own efforts to acquire homes. Self-help housing takes many forms throughout the region. In the Caribbean, squatting is rare, but houses are built on rented plots (known as rent yards) without planning permission. Often there is complex subletting of these properties.

In Central America squatter settlements, often lacking services such as

COLLECTIVE CONSUMPTION IN MEXICO CITY

Collective consumption is the term often given to goods and services that individual households cannot obtain on their own; in recent times their *en masse* provision has become increasingly the responsibility of state or local authorities. Services such as electricity, water supply and drainage, as well as housing itself, fall into this category.

In Mexico City the state plays an important role in providing these facilities, not through government housing schemes but through a number of federal agencies that are responsible for legalizing existing informal housing and improving infrastructure. Government action between 1970 and 1980 saw a greater provision of these collective services: house ownership increased from 42 to 54 percent, homes without electricity fell from 9 to 3 percent, those without an interior water supply from 40 to 31 percent, and without sewerage from 25 to 14 percent.

It would be wrong to attribute these improvements solely to altruism on the part of Mexico's ruling Institutional Revolutionary Party (PRI). By legalizing squatters and upgrading services, the state acquires enormous powers of leverage over the mass of people in the world's largest capital. Moreover, once settlements are upgraded and recognized, they provide a tax base from which government funds can be replenished.

City within a city (*above*) One of Mexico City's residential districts, Nizahua-Coyotl, is home to more than 3 million people. The mushrooming growth of the city's population has created a huge urban sprawl, halted only by the mountains that surround the city.

Rooms with a view (*left*) A luxurious riverside mansion in Belize City. The region's cities present stark contrasts between the living conditions of rich and poor. Residential areas are highly segregated; many wealthy citizens rarely venture beyond the borders of their favored areas.

electricity, piped water and sewerage, invade land belonging to someone else, often tucked away alongside rivers, as in San Salvador and Guatemala City. In Mexico City, as well as outright squatting, realtors may illegally subdivide orthodox housing developments. About half the population of Mexico City lives in informal settlements. Most of the houses are in various stages of improvement as their residents strive to get them legally recognized by the municipal authorities and so enable them to be connected to electricity and water supplies.

The cities of Central America and the Caribbean are centers of social inequality based essentially on class, but with strong overtones of ethnicity, color and culture. The residential districts, transportation systems, work places and shopping amenities of the white – or pass-as-white – city conform to the standards of the United States or Europe. The self-help settlements, overcrowded buses, ramshackle repair yards and produce markets of the Amerindian city (in Central America) or black city (in the Caribbean) are by these standards exceedingly deprived. Yet even the urban poor achieve living standards that are often far superior to those they left behind when they migrated from the countryside, and their children can aspire to far better education and healthcare in the cities than is available in the rural villages.

Kingston – poverty and violence

One in four of Jamaica's inhabitants live in the capital, Kingston, the island's capital and major port, and one of the largest cities in the Caribbean. The city was founded in 1692 to house refugees displaced by the earthquake at Port Royal; the rectangular form and grid street layout of the old core city are still clearly discernible today. Although Kingston was originally a planned settlement, its rapid growth since World War II has been anything but controlled. Many of its shanty towns are reminiscent of the makeshift huts that the first inhabitants occupied in the late 17th century.

Kingston's population has doubled since Jamaica became independent in 1962. The rate of increase has, however, been lower than previously predicted: largescale emigration to Britain and, more recently, to Canada and the United States has had a drastic effect. Today, about 20,000 educated Jamaicans a year leave for better-paid jobs abroad. Another factor that has reduced the city's projected growth has been the drop in the birthrate caused by youth emigration and the widespread availability of family planning. There is evidence to suggest that political violence in the capital has led not only to urban depopulation but also to a falling off in the numbers of rural migrants to the city.

Social divisions

Kingston strongly exemplifies many of the urban divisions found in the region: colonialism and independence; formal and informal sectors; affluence and poverty; modernity and backwardness. In Kingston's case there is also a hierarchical social structure based on class, which in turn is strongly correlated with color and culture – these three factors govern the city's patterns of residential segregation.

Old-style colonialism, however, has to some extent been replaced by a kind of Americanized neocolonialism. Out-of-town shopping plazas cater for the upper and middle classes, leaving the old city core to the poorest section of the black population. A modern shopping and service complex has been developed at New Kingston, partially counterbalanced by the redevelopment of the waterfront, which now boasts the Bank of Jamaica, the Conference Center for the Law of the Sea, the National Gallery, and affluent apartments and boutiques.

Even by the standards of the region, Kingston is an exceptionally impoverished city. About one-third of its labor force is unemployed and the informal sector of the labor market has therefore grown enormously to become in some areas of the city the mainstay of the population. A significant, though unquantifiable, part

Kingston rent yard During the 1960s and 1970s, very large numbers of rural Jamaicans moved into the city of Kingston in search of work. Population growth was so fast that planners could not provide enough housing for all the migrants. Alternative housing arrangements – such as rent yards and shanty towns – became increasingly common and still exist in large numbers today. Now the government is supporting a program of agricultural reforms with the aim of redeveloping and repopulating the countryside in an effort to relieve population pressure on the capital.

Land use

- ● important site
- —— major road
- →— major railroad (with terminus)
- central business district
- commercial and mixed
- industrial
- residential
- shanty town
- parks and open spaces
- other

Harbor site The key to Kingston's growth is its excellent, virtually landlocked deepwater harbor. It is enclosed by the Palisadoes, a 13 km (8 mi) landspit that today houses the island's international airport and a complex of tourist hotels and marina. Port Royal, destroyed by an earthquake in 1672, stood at the western end of this spit. The planned city of Kingston replaced it on the north shore, and its residential areas now extend some distance inland. The commercial district abuts the old port area, now redeveloped to take large cruise and cargo ships.

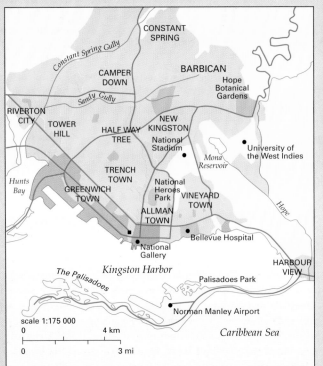

CONSTANT SPRING
Constant Spring Gully
CAMPER DOWN
Sandy Gully
BARBICAN
Hope Botanical Gardens
RIVERTON CITY
TOWER HILL
HALF WAY TREE
NEW KINGSTON
National Stadium
Mona Reservoir
University of the West Indies
TRENCH TOWN
Hunts Bay
GREENWICH TOWN
National Heroes Park
VINEYARD TOWN
ALLMAN TOWN
Bellevue Hospital
National Gallery
Kingston Harbor
The Palisadoes
Palisadoes Park
Hope
HARBOUR VIEW
Norman Manley Airport
Caribbean Sea

scale 1:175 000
0 — 4 km
0 — 3 mi

of the labor force that declares itself unemployed is engaged in illegal and criminal activity. Drug dealing and gang violence, especially in West Kingston, brutalize life to a degree unknown in most other Caribbean capitals.

Only the elite and some of the middle class own property; most housing is rented or located on rented land. Squat-ting is confined to the poorest areas – in Kingston the most striking example of informal housing is the rent yard.

In 1960, 30 percent of the population lived in dilapidated housing, and more than 25 percent in overcrowded accom-modation. Before the destruction caused by Hurricane Gilbert in 1988, 40 percent of dwellings were in need of replacement or upgrading, and 60,000 people required rehousing. That the situation was not worse was due in part to government housing schemes, though these more often than not benefited the clients of which-ever political party was in power. The migration of many people to the Spanish Town area during the years of political violence in the 1970s was also a factor.

GOVERNMENT

The 33 states and dependencies of the Central American region were among the oldest European colonies in the world. Spanish settlement of the island of Hispaniola began as early as 1493; the rest of the region was later colonized by a number of European powers. Mexico and the states of the Central American isthmus (apart from Belize, formerly British Honduras), with Cuba and the Dominican Republic formed part of the vast Spanish American empire. The tiny island colonies of the Caribbean basin changed hands many times as contending European states sought to exploit their rich natural resources. Independence came to the Spanish colonies and to the French colony of Haiti through armed struggle in the 19th century; decolonization in the Caribbean has taken place peacefully since the 1960s.

COUNTRIES IN THE REGION

Antigua and Barbuda, Bahamas, Barbados, Belize, Costa Rica, Cuba, Dominica, Dominican Republic, El Salvador, Grenada, Guatemala, Haiti, Honduras, Jamaica, Mexico, Nicaragua, Panama, St Kitts-Nevis, St Lucia, St Vincent and .the Grenadines, Trinidad and Tobago

Dependencies of other states Anguilla, Bermuda, British Virgin Islands, Cayman Islands (UK); Aruba, Netherlands Antilles (Netherlands); Guadeloupe, Martinique (France); Puerto Rico, US Virgin Islands (USA)

STYLES OF GOVERNMENT

Republics Costa Rica, Cuba, Dominica, Dominican Republic, El Salvador, Guatemala, Haiti, Honduras, Mexico, Nicaragua, Panama, Trinidad and Tobago

Monarchies All other countries in the region

Multi-party states All countries except Cuba, Haiti

One-party states Cuba, Haiti

Military influence Guatemala, Haiti, Honduras

CONFLICTS (since 1945)

Coups Dominican Republic 1961, 1963; El Salvador 1948, 1960–61, 1979; Grenada 1979, 1983; Guatemala 1954, 1957. 1963, 1982, 1983; Haiti 1950, 1956, 1986, 1991; Honduras 1963; Panama 1968, 1988

Revolutions Cuba 1959; Nicaragua 1979

Civil wars Costa Rica 1948, 1955; Dominican Republic 1965–66 (US involvement); El Salvador 1979–92; Guatemala 1967–85; Nicaragua 1962– (US involvement after 1981); Panama 1958–59

Interstate conflicts Nicaragua/Honduras 1957–60; Cuba/USA 1961; El Salvador/Honduras 1969; Grenada/USA 1983

MEMBERSHIP OF INTERNATIONAL ORGANIZATIONS

Caribbean Community (CARICOM) Antigua and Barbuda, Bahamas, Barbados, Belize, Dominica, Dominican Republic, Grenada, Jamaica, St Kitts-Nevis, St Lucia, St Vincent and the Grenadines, Trinidad and Tobago

Organization of American States (OAS) All countries of the region

TWO COLONIAL TRADITIONS

The struggle for independence in Mexico, begun in 1810, was won in 1821. A short-lived Mexican empire was set up, which included the territories of California, New Mexico, Texas and Utah in North America and extended southward as far as the present border of Panama. In 1823 Central America broke away to form a federation. El Salvador was the first of the isthmus states to declare its independence in 1838, and the other remote settlement clusters of Central America became the cores of the independent states of Costa Rica, Honduras, Guatemala and Nicaragua. In 1836 Texas rebelled against the Mexican dictator Santa Anna (1795–1876). Its annexation by the United States in 1845 led to the Mexican–American War, which ended in 1848 with the sale to the United States for $15 million of all territory formerly held by Mexico north of the Rio Grande.

The creation of Panama

Panama, which had been part of the South American viceroyalty of New Granada under Spanish rule, became part of the newly independent state of Colombia. The United States had long sought to construct a canal across the isthmus to secure a sea route between its west and east coasts, and in 1903 underwrote a revolution that secured Panama's independence under United States protection. Work on the Panama Canal began in 1906, and the United States was granted in perpetuity the use, occupation and control of a zone 5 km (3 mi) wide on either side. Panama's protectorate status was ended in 1939; the Canal Zone, which became a focus of anti-US feeling in the 1960s, was formally transferred to Panamanian sovereignty on 1 October 1979. Final transfer of the ownership of the canal itself took place in 2000.

Belize, formerly British Honduras, the only state on the Central American isthmus not colonized by Spain, achieved full internal self-government in 1964. A longstanding territorial dispute with neighboring Guatemala delayed the granting of full independence until 1981, and after that Britain still maintained a military defensive presence there.

Spain was the colonizing power of the larger islands of the Caribbean: Cuba, Hispaniola and Puerto Rico (the Greater

Cuba's revolution, led by Fidel Castro – here cementing friendship with Soviet leader Nikita Khrushchev – affected much of the region.

Armed soldiers go unremarked in El Salvador, scene of some of the worst excesses of political violence in the region. In the early 1980s more than 20,000 civilians were killed as army "death squads" terrorized the population in its campaign against left-wing guerrillas.

Vanished empires Most of the states in the region belonged to the Spanish empire, which overran and destroyed the indigenous Indian cultures in the 16th century. The smaller islands, colonized by several European nations, have generally been more stable.

Antilles). Haiti, occupying the western one-third of Hispaniola, was a French colony. Its independence was achieved with great violence in 1804 (when it became the first independent state in the region and the first black republic in the world). The Spanish colony on Hispaniola, the Dominican Republic, was also ruled by France from 1795 to 1808, and by Haiti from 1822 to 1844, when it was declared a republic. It was briefly reannexed to Spain from 1861 to 1865; it had a troubled history of weak governments, and was occupied by the United States from 1916 to 1924. Haiti was similarly occupied from 1915 to 1934.

Following the Spanish–American War of 1898 Puerto Rico was ceded to the United States, and in 1952 became a Commonwealth voluntarily associated with the United States. Cuba also gained its independence from Spain in 1898, with military assistance from the United States. It became fully independent in 1902, though the United States retained naval bases there and reserved the right to intervene in Cuba's domestic affairs. This it did several times before relinquishing the right in 1934. In 1959 Cuban nationalists, led by Fidel Castro, overthrew the right-wing Batista dictatorship (1935–59). In 1961 Castro declared a Marxist regime in Cuba, following the unsuccessful "Bay of Pigs" invasion attempt made by Cuban exiles with the support of the United States. The Cuban government became a source of support for left-wing groups in the Caribbean and in South America as well as Africa.

An archipelago of island states

The smaller islands of the Caribbean were colonized mainly by Britain, France and the Netherlands, though Denmark and Sweden have both had colonial interests there. The United States purchased the Danish-owned Virgin Islands in 1917.

British plans for decolonization in its Caribbean possessions after World War II involved the creation of a single federal state – the Federation of the West Indies – which it was hoped would incorporate all its colonies. This failed to provide a workable solution to self-government in the area, however, and following Jamaica's defection from the Federation in 1961, the British territories became independent in two waves: Jamaica and Trinidad, and then Barbados, in the 1960s; the remaining (smaller) islands in the 1970s and 1980s.

Britain retains one colony (Bermuda) and also five Caribbean dependencies. Martinique and Guadeloupe are French overseas departments; the Netherlands Antilles form an autonomous part of the kingdom of the Netherlands; the western-most island, Aruba, achieved separate self-governing status in 1986.

DEGREES OF DEMOCRACY

The two distinct patterns of colonial rule, with differing experiences of decolonization, have resulted in contrasting styles of government. Haiti and the former Spanish-ruled states have been characterized by long periods of authoritarian military or civilian dictatorship.

The military factor

In Haiti a long history of military dictatorship was modified in 1956 by the installation – first by election and then by presidential fiat – of François Duvalier ("Papa Doc", 1907–71). In the early 1960s he established a perverted version of black power, using the folk religion, *vodun*, and his private army, the *tontons macoutes*, as a means of social control. After a coup removed his son Jean Claude in 1986, Haiti returned to military rule. Elections were restored in 1990 but peaceful democracy only prevailed in 1996.

Cuba is the only left-wing authoritarian regime in the region. During the 1970s it began to adopt a political system based on that of the Soviet Union. In 1975 the first congress of the Cuban Communist Party was held, and a new socialist constitution was approved by referendum the following year, when Fidel Castro was elected head of state.

Nearly all the Central American mainland states are potentially unstable. Small

THE PRICE OF MEXICO'S POLITICAL STABILITY

Unlike most of Central America, Mexico has been politically stable since 1920. The price has been single-party government by the Institional Revolutionary Party (PRI), which kept a stranglehold on politics and the economy until finally voted out in 2000.

Since World War II the PRI attempted to generate growth through industrialization and the development of the oil industry (nationalized in 1938), while spending substantial amounts on welfare, supplemented by a fluctuating program of land reform. Urbanization was rapid, and a substantial middle and working class grew in Mexico City (with an unofficial population of 19 million) and large towns. Rural dwellers, above all the Amerindian peasants who represent the last of the indigenous population, were largely left out.

Even urban Mexicans became profoundly disaffected with the PRI. At the 1988 election Salinas de Gortari, the PRI candidate, polled barely 50 percent of the votes cast (with almost half the registered electorate abstaining). The massive foreign debt, economic recession since the oil boom of 1978–81, and pervasive corruption could be blamed on no one other than the PRI. However, opposition parties such as the National Action Party (PAN) on the right and the National Democratic Front (NDF) on the left still had little to offer the peasants. A guerrilla group calling itself the Zapatista National Liberation Army launched an armed rebellion in the province of Chiapas on December 31, 1993, coinciding with Mexico's entry into NAFTA, which the Zapatistas described as sentencing the peasants to "death by neglect." The rebellion continued into the 2000s and garnered widespread support with its demands for direct democracy and devolution of authority.

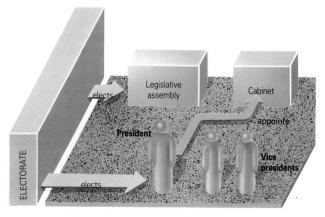

A stable democracy Costa Rica has a unique record of uninterrupted government on the Central American isthmus. Its constitution, dating from 1949, forbids the establishment or maintenance of an army. Elections are held every four years to choose a president and two vice presidents. The candidate who receives the largest vote, provided it is over 40 percent, is elected; if none does so a second election is held. There is a single-chamber assembly of 57 members, also elected for a four-year term. Voting is compulsory.

but powerful, mainly European elites, backed by the army (often with United States support), still seek to maintain power against a large, impoverished lower class, which is often ethnically distinct, demanding a share in government. In several states (El Salvador, Guatemala, Nicaragua) the longterm operation of guerrilla groups has killed many thousands of people, and human rights go largely unrecognized.

Costa Rica, which has the distinction of being the most stable democracy in the isthmus, is the only state that does not have a standing army. Since 1948 it has had uninterrupted democratic government: the president is elected for a four-year term by compulsory adult suffrage. Oscar Arias Sanchez, elected in 1986, won the Nobel Peace Prize in 1987.

In 1966, following United States' intervention, democracy was established in the Dominican Republic after the dictatorship of Rafael Trujillo from 1930 to 1961. Elections in 1978 brought the first peaceful transfer of power for an opposition party, but the Christian Democrats remain the dominant party. Mexico has the longest experience of stable government, but was controlled by one party, the Institutional Revolutionary Party (PRI), since 1929. Mexico's political system was plunged into crisis by the Zapatista rebellion of indigenous peoples, beginning in 1993, which embarrassed the PRI and challenged opposition parties who had hoped to share power within the existing system. In El Salvador the 1989 elections marked the first transition of power from one elected government to another. However, the winning right-wing Arena party had been linked with anti-leftist death squads; the Farabundo Marti National Liberation Front (FMLN) boycotted the elections, and the guerrilla war that had lasted since 1972 continued.

Despite the apparatus of democratic

elections the army remained the final arbiter of power in both Guatemala and Honduras; in Panama the legally elected president was ousted in 1988 by General Manuel Noriega, allegedly a narcotics baron. In early 1989 Noriega declared the Panamanian elections void after observers backed the opposition's claim of fraud. When he refused to yield, the United States removed him by force.

In Nicaragua the right-wing Somoza dictatorship (1934–79) was violently overthrown by the Sandinista National Liberation Front (FSLN). Despite attempts by the United States to undermine the new socialist regime, the Sandinistas won the 1984 elections in a multi-party contest, and Daniel Ortega, the FSLN leader, assumed the presidency. Six years later, in democratic elections, the Sandinistas lost to an alliance of opposition parties and conceded defeat gracefully.

Westminster constitutions

In the former British colonies parliamentary democracy, based on the model of Westminster, has taken deeper root, though the government of Grenada was subject to a left-wing revolution in 1979. Following a further Marxist coup in 1983, an invasion headed by the United States, which feared the creation of a Cuban base on the island, led to the restoration of its former constitution.

In Jamaica the People's National Party (PNP), led by Michael Manley, formed the government between 1972 and 1980. Then the spiraling economic crisis and the rejection of Manley's socialist programs brought its electoral defeat by Edward Seaga's right-wing Jamaica Labor Party (JLP), following a violent campaign in which more than 600 people were killed. The PNP refused to contest Seaga's snap election of 1983 on the grounds that the electoral roll was out of date, but won a peaceful landslide victory in 1989.

Voting day in Guatemala An elector is thumbprinted before he casts his vote. Guatemala's recent political history has been turbulent, with power being contested between rival army factions. The 1985 constitution brought a return to elected government, but the army remained the dominant power and elections were closely controlled.

A popular rebellion An Amerindian woman sells Zapatista dolls in San Cristóbal de las Casas, the first town seized by the Zapatistas at the end of 1993. The dolls are dressed like Subcommander Marcos, spokesman of the Zapatistas, who has become a folk hero. The movement has drawn large numbers of Amerindian women, the poorest of Mexico's poor.

THE GEOPOLITICS OF CONFLICT

Cuba's socialist revolution in 1959 has had widespread repercussions in the region, where the United States still has great influence. Cuba's commitment to assisting left-wing revolutionary movements in neighboring (and more distant) states causes the United States to regard it with suspicion. Puerto Rico, as a Commonwealth of the United States, enjoys a quasi-colonial status; the Dominican Republic and Haiti also lie within its sphere of influence. From 1972 to 1991 Cuba itself was a member of the Eastern bloc's trading organization, COMECON.

Regional cooperation

Factors of geography and historical evolution have determined that with a few exceptions the states of the region fall traditionally into two major groupings. Most of them belong either to the Central American Common Market (CACOM) or to the Caribbean Community (CARICOM – formerly the Caribbean Free Trade Area, CARIFTA). CACOM includes Costa Rica, El Salvador, Guatemala, Honduras and Nicaragua, but not Mexico or Panama. It developed rapidly after 1951, creating important regional manufacturing strategies until Honduras withdrew in 1970, following the "soccer war" – sparked off by a sports event – with El Salvador. The decline in trade that took place after 1980 was due in part to economic factors (exacerbated by the heavy external debts of its member states) and in part to the damaging impact of civil wars in El Salvador and Nicaragua.

CARIFTA was created in 1968 among former British colonies, including mainland Belize and Guyana, as a counterbalance to the threat of West Indian fragmentation following decolonization. It was established as CARICOM in 1973 with the aim of coordinating economic and foreign policy in the region. However, many of the tensions – such as competitive development strategies, inter-island jealousies and distance between member states – that contributed to the breakup of the Federation of the West Indies (1958–62) have resurfaced in CARICOM.

The less developed countries of the Lesser Antilles, which want closer economic integration than do the larger members (Jamaica and Guyana), have

US marines in Grenada The threat of a Marxist government provoked the United States to invade the island in 1983 with a force that included 12 ships and an many as 6,000 marines and rangers.

General Manuel Noriega subverted the democratic process in Panama until US troops removed him from power in 1989 – just one example of US intervention in Central America.

Cuban troops were recalled from Angola as part of the agreement for Namibia's independence in 1989. They had been backing the government forces.

complained persistently that they have been exploited by the others. They have sought coordinated diplomatic representation overseas, and in 1983 formed the Organization of Eastern Caribbean States (OECS). It was on the basis of the defense pact involved in this agreement that the United States was invited by the OECS to take part in the 1983 invasion of Grenada, on the grounds that Cuba was planning to build an airport there to use as a military base. In fact the airport was needed to expand the island's tourist economy, and had been planned while Grenada was still a British colony.

By 1981, when Ronald Reagan became president of the United States, the US administration perceived the Caribbean and Central America as penetrated by Marxist activity from Cuba (backed by the Soviet Union), which had supported the Sandinista revolution in Nicaragua and the left-wing FMLN guerrillas in El Salvador. Through its support for the anti-Sandinista Contra guerrillas, United States' efforts in Central America were therefore directed toward toppling the government.

Frustrated plans for peace

The only counterweight to this policy in the mid-1980s was given by the Contadora Group (named after the island where they first met), which included Mexico, Panama, and two South American states, Colombia and Venezuela. Contadora's 21-point peace plan, which proposed the partial demilitarization of all of Central America to stop the civil wars in El Salvador and Nicaragua, was rejected by the United States. The Arias plan, named for the president of Costa Rica who devised it and signed by five Central American presidents in August 1987, proposed the declaration of a ceasefire and the holding of free elections, but collapsed because of the United States' refusal to halt aid to the Contras.

It was the reduction of aid from the Soviet Union as a consequence of its own economic crisis and its desire to withdraw from its commitments to socialist movements and regimes around the world that indirectly brought the civil war to an end. In the face of mounting economic pressure, the Sandinista government was defeated in national elections in 1990, leading to the demobilization of the army and the disbanding of the Contras.

CUBA'S ROLE IN THE WORLD

Until the revolution of 1959 the dominant influence in Cuba had been the United States, which was hostile toward the Cuba's socialist regime. This, and particularly the United States' part in the Bay of Pigs invasion, contributed to Fidel Castro's declaration of a Marxist–Leninist state, bringing Cuba closer to the Soviet Union. After 1974 a political structure very similar to that of the Soviet Union's Eastern European satellites was set up in Cuba. It was the first non-neighboring state of the former Soviet Union (Vietnam joined in 1978) to become a member of COMECON, the Soviet-led organization to promote economic cooperation between communist states. Cuba's continuing financial dependence on the Soviet Union was very great. One estimate put the total value of Soviet economic aid to Cuba during the early 1980s to be $3.5 billion a year.

In the early years of the regime Cuba was committed to extending the revolution throughout Latin America. Che Guevara (1928–67), the theoretician of the revolution, was killed by Bolivian troops while organizing a guerrilla base there. Cuba joined the nonaligned movement opposed to neocolonialism and imperialism, and gave assistance to left-wing and anticolonial groups elsewhere in the world, particularly in Africa. In 1989 the Cuban troops withdrew from Angola as part of the agreement for South Africa's withdrawal from Namibia, negotiated through the United Nations. Nearer home, the provision of aid to the Marxist regime in Grenada (1979–83) and to the Sandinista government in Nicaragua increased tensions with the United States in the mid-1980s. Despite the cessation of Soviet aid and the end of the Cold War in the 1990s, Cuba is moving only slowly and reluctantly from its position of entrenched communism.

Conflict in Nicaragua

The establishment in 1979 of a socialist government in Nicaragua, after more than a decade of fighting, was seen by many people in the United States as a direct threat to its interests in the region. Nicaragua occupies a strategically pivotal position in the Central American isthmus, from which military control could be established over El Salvador, Guatemala and Honduras to the north, and over Costa Rica and Panama to the south.

The Sandinista government (which took its name from a guerrilla group headed by Augusto César Sandino that had opposed the establishment of US naval bases in 1912) under Daniel Ortega immediately set out to reverse the pro-United States policy of the authoritarian Somoza regime it overthrew. The new government soon introduced extensive economic and land reforms. The part of the economy (about 60 percent) that had been under the direct control of the Somoza family was nationalized. The rest, including many large estates on the Pacific coast, remained in private hands. Nicaragua continued to operate a state-led mixed economy.

Nicaragua's relations with the United States deteriorated rapidly after the election of Ronald Reagan as president in 1981. Alleging that the Sandinista government was supporting anti-government FMLN guerrillas in El Salvador, the Reagan administration immediately cancelled the supply of economic aid, linked to the restoration of human rights, that his predecessor Jimmy Carter (president 1977–81) had inaugurated.

The price of United States' involvement
Active support was given to the Contra guerrillas opposed to the Sandinista government, and in 1984 Nicaragua's harbors were mined by the CIA. Nicaragua was denounced as a Marxist regime, and attempts were made to isolate it diplomatically and financially, and by trade embargo. When the United States Congress refused to allow the continuation of aid to the Contras, other channels were found to direct funds to them. The Iran-gate scandal of 1986 revealed that cash resulting from secret arms deals with Iran to bring about the release of United States' hostages in Lebanon was intended to fund back-door military aid to Nicaragua.

The United States exercises close guardianship over its Central American and Caribbean backyard. Its military support bases in the 1960s reflected its strategic goals of limiting the influence of the Cuban left-wing socialist regime, neutralizing Soviet influence, and protecting the free passage of the Panama Canal.

The US presence in Central America
- ✛ US airfield/airbase
- ★ US training or support unit
- ★ Sandinista base
- Contra area
- other guerrilla area

Nicaragua's civil war A government soldier shoulders his Soviet-supplied rifle. The successful seizure of power by the Sandinistas appeared to give Cuba and the Soviet Union the opportunity to extend their influence on to the Central American mainland. Fearing that one state after another would fall under communist control (the "domino theory"), the US government stepped up its support for the right-wing Contra guerrillas after 1981, and backed the establishment of anti-Sandinista bases in Honduras. An economic blockade and years of civil war caused havoc to the Nicaraguan economy, leading to the rejection of the Sandinista government by voters in 1990.

Nicaraguan "mothers of the disappeared" hold up pictures of their sons who vanished during the bitter years of fighting.

The United States' action against Nicaragua was the latest in a series of interventions in the region, since the onset of superpower hostility after World War II. These included support of the Bay of Pigs invasion of Cuba in 1961, and direct military intervention in the Dominican Republic in 1965 and Grenada in 1983 to prevent the threatened installation of Marxist governments.

Such action has traditionally been defended by invoking the Monroe Doctrine (1823), which stated that interference by any outside power in the affairs of the newly emerging independent states of the American continent would be regarded as an unfriendly act toward the United States itself. In 1904 this was extended by President Theodore Roosevelt (1858–1919) to allow the United States to exer-

cise police power in the region as necessary to defend its interests, and was subsequently used to justify direct action on many occasions. The United States' policy against Nicaragua had repercussions throughout Central America. To assist the Contra rebels United States' bases were maintained in Honduras, from which surveillance planes operated throughout the region.

Nicaragua responded to the hostile and destabilizing actions of the United States by developing its links with Cuba and the Soviet Union, which before 1987 supplied all its oil requirements. Conscript forces were employed to defend the Atlantic coast and the northern border from guerrilla activity, and by the mid-1980s the war against the Ccntras was absorbing more than half the national budget.

Governing the Bahamas

The Bahamas are typical of the smaller member states of the Commonwealth. Governed by the British from 1783 to 1973, it consists of some 700 islands between Florida and Haiti, 30 of which are inhabited. The total population is just under a quarter of a million.

When the Bahamas achieved independence the British monarch remained as head of state, represented by a governor general. The constitution is broadly modeled on that of Britain, with a two-chamber legislature consisting of an elected house of assembly and an appointed senate. The chief executive is the prime minister, who is appointed by the governor general from the party that controls the house of assembly.

Although the legacy of imperial rule lingers on in political institutions and traditions, the economic influence of the neighboring United States is becoming increasingly important. The economy is linked to that of the United States through its dependence on tourism and international banking. The changing situation is symbolized by the fact that the pound sterling is no longer accepted as general currency on the islands, and has been replaced by the US dollar.

A soldier on guard in Nassau, the islands' capital, provides tourists with a reminder of the Bahamas' former links with the British empire.

ENVIRONMENTAL ISSUES

COMPREHENSIVE CHANGES · CLEARANCE AND CONTAMINATION · PROSPECTS FOR THE FUTURE

Environmental concerns have only recently been added to the political agenda of Central America and the Caribbean, but are certain to figure more strongly in future. Some success has been achieved in nature conservation, but the task of tackling the region's other pressing issues is only just beginning. Two key concerns are widespread soil degradation and deforestation in the mountains of mainland Central America and some of the high islands. Deforestation, in turn, has caused flooding and siltation. Other dilemmas include severe air pollution and waste disposal problems in urban areas, the heavy impact of tourism on coastlines and coral reefs, disturbance to the marine ecology from overfishing, and the loss of biodiversity and habitat degradation. The main causes are rapid population growth and poverty.

COUNTRIES IN THE REGION

Antigua and Barbuda, Bahamas, Barbados, Belize, Costa Rica, Cuba, Dominica, Dominican Republic, El Salvador, Grenada, Guatemala, Haiti, Honduras, Jamaica, Mexico, Nicaragua, Panama, St Kitts-Nevis, St Lucia, St Vincent and the Grenadines, Trinidad and Tobago

POPULATION AND WEALTH

	Highest	Middle	Lowest
Population (millions)	100.349 (Mexico)	6.249 (Honduras)	0.038 (St Kitts)
Population increase (1990–95)	2.7% (Honduras)	1.6% (Panama)	0.4% (Cuba)
Energy use (kg/year per person oil equivalent)	6,419 (Trin & Tob)	1,297 (Cuba)	227 (Haiti)
Purchasing power parity (Int$)	$6,999 (Trin & Tob)	$4,396 (Belize)	$1,213 (Haiti)

ENVIRONMENTAL INDICATORS

	Highest	Middle	Lowest
CO$_2$ emissions ('000 tonnes year)	357,834 (Mexico)	29,067 (Cuba)	414 (Belize)
Car ownership (% of population)	30% (Bahamas)	8% (Panama)	1% (Haiti)
Protected territory including marine areas (%)	173% (Dom Rep)	24% (Costa Rica)	0.2% (El Salvador)
Forests as a % of original forest	96% (Belize)	46% (Guatemala)	1% (Haiti)
Artificial fertilizer use (kg/ha/annum)	322 (Costa Rica)	106 (El Salvador)	9 (Haiti)
Access to safe drinking water (% population; rural/urban)	73/99% (Panama)	66/90% (Mexico)	28/50% (Haiti)

MAJOR ENVIRONMENTAL PROBLEMS AND SOURCES

Air pollution: urban high
Land degradation: *types:* soil erosion, deforestation; *causes:* agriculture, population pressure, tourism
Resource issues: inadequate drinking water and sanitation; coastal flooding; coral bleaching and loss
Population issues: population explosion; inadequate health facilities; tourism
Major events: Ixtoc 1 (1979), oil rig fire and leak; Guadalajara (1992), series of gas explosions, frequent hurricanes

COMPREHENSIVE CHANGES

Central America and the Caribbean have always been subject to earthquakes and volcanoes, which bring immediate and dramatic changes to the environment. Some areas have been repeatedly buried under lava and volcanic dust and scorched by fire, while others are prone to landslides and inundation by tidal waves. Such disruption, though immediately devastating, can enrich the environment in the long run – volcanic ash, for example, has created some of the region's most fertile soils.

Thousands of years ago, human activities started to alter the region's natural landscapes. Crop cultivation may have begun as early as 7000 BC in Mexico, displacing the natural vegetation. Later, terraces were carved into many of the hillslopes, and channels dug to bring water for irrigation. But until colonial times – from the 16th century onward – change was small scale. The predominant form of agriculture was slash-and-burn cultivation. By this method, small plots of land were cleared of trees and cultivated for only two or three years before being left fallow to allow the forest to regenerate. The system, still in use in many parts of the region, helps preserve soil fertility and conserves land quality – as long as population densities do not become too high and the land overused.

Environmental change accelerated with the introduction of commercial farming methods by European settlers. Spanish, English, French and Dutch colonists created large plantations of single crops for export. Some plantation crops, such as sugar cane, required total deforestation of the land before planting. Although most were established on the fertile, flatter land of the valleys and coastal plains, some spread onto hillslopes, allowing the thin, unprotected soils to be washed quickly away by the heavy rains.

The modernization and commercialization of farming in the course of the 20th century has placed even greater demands on the region's soil and water resources. After 1945 high-yielding hybrid maize, adopted from the United States to boost production levels, became widespread across much of the mainland. The hybrids require far more nutrients from the soil than native varieties, and this has led to an expensive dependency on fertilizers,

resulting in river and groundwater pollution. In Costa Rica and elsewhere, widespread cattle ranching – established with American investment to supply the United States' huge market for beef – has transformed vast areas of tropical rainforest to poor grassland.

Pressure of numbers

From 1950 to 1970, the region had the highest rate of population growth in the world, at 3.3 percent per annum. Since then rates have slowed but are still high. Densities of population in relation to the supply of farming land are some of the highest in the world. The region averages

475 people per 1000 hectares (2471 acres) with over 2000 people per 1000 hectares in some Caribbean islands notably Haiti, Jamaica, Trinidad and Tobago. Yet the amount of cultivable land – usually 15 to 30 percent of the total land area – is diminishing because of degradation.

The growing number of landless cultivators, who have no option but to squat on and cultivate infertile mountain land, are the main cause of land degradation in the 1990s. Although they practice traditional slash-and-burn cultivation, the population pressure is such that they are forced to overuse the land in order to feed their families. In southern parts of the mainland especially, forests are being

Buried in the jungle (*right*) Temple ruins at Tikal in northern Guatemala. These monuments to the Mayan civilization were deserted in the 9th century and remained undiscovered until the mid 19th century. The Mayans built many such cities, but the forest was able to recover after the decline of their early civilizations. Without proper management, modern civilization will cause permanent damage to the forests.

Map of environmental problems (*below*) Forests in the region continue to be under extreme pressure, with 87 per cent of frontier forests under threat. Where forests have been cleared, erosion and desertification are serious problems. Volcanoes, earthquakes and hurricanes are common natural disasters.

Key environmental issues

- ● major town or city
- 🏭 polluted town or city
- 🔥 major pollution event
- ✛ major natural disaster
- ▲ active volcano
- ～ polluted river
- remaining tropical rainforest
- area of deforestation

area at risk of desertification
- very high
- high
- moderate

removed at an exceptionally rapid rate, and severe soil erosion has set in.

The rapidly growing urban populations also put enormous pressure on the environment, both locally and farther afield. Two-thirds of all the people in the region live in urban areas, while Mexico City has over 25 million. As rural migrants flock to the cities, more and more food is demanded from already overused farmland, while pollution problems are escalating.

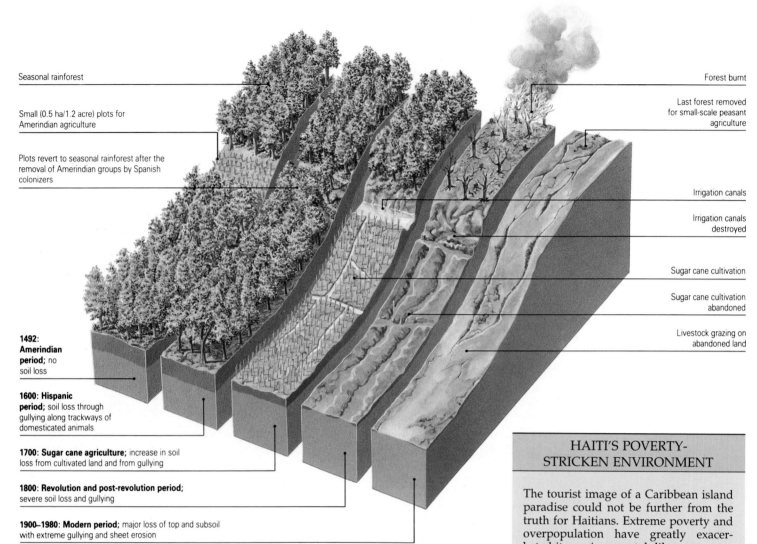

Seasonal rainforest

Small (0.5 ha/1.2 acre) plots for Amerindian agriculture

Plots revert to seasonal rainforest after the removal of Amerindian groups by Spanish colonizers

Forest burnt

Last forest removed for small-scale peasant agriculture

Irrigation canals

Irrigation canals destroyed

Sugar cane cultivation

Sugar cane cultivation abandoned

Livestock grazing on abandoned land

1492: Amerindian period; no soil loss

1600: Hispanic period; soil loss through gullying along trackways of domesticated animals

1700: Sugar cane agriculture; increase in soil loss from cultivated land and from gullying

1800: Revolution and post-revolution period; severe soil loss and gullying

1900–1980: Modern period; major loss of top and subsoil with extreme gullying and sheet erosion

Deforestation in Haiti: the gradual process of deforestation and subsequent erosion from precolonial to modern times. After the arrival of Europeans, each new period of exploitation prepared the way for the devastation that now exists.

CLEARANCE AND CONTAMINATION

Five centuries of increasing environmental deterioration in Central America and the Caribbean have left the region extremely vulnerable to damage from human activities. The consequences of forest loss present some of the region's most intractable problems. Less than 50 percent of the region's natural forests remain and the rate of annual deforestation in the region is 2.1 percent. Many of the forests that remain are being stretched beyond their capacity for survival. This is especially the case along the central spine of the mainland, where illegal logging for valued timber and squatting by landless peasant cultivators is widespread.

Mexico, Nicaragua, Guatemala, Honduras, Panama and Costa Rica all have exceptionally high rates of deforestation. Costa Rica has one of the highest rates in the world at 3.1 percent per annum: of the 1.2 million ha (3 million acres) of forest that remain, 60,000 ha (148,000 acres) dis-

appear every year. In other parts of the region – especially Cuba, the Dominican Republic and northern Mexico – timber removal for fuelwood (for cooking and heating) outstrips natural regeneration.

Disappearing soils

Forest loss quickly leads to land degradation. This involves first a decline in soil fertility and then soil erosion, especially on steep slopes. Tropical soils are heavy in laterites (iron and other oxides), which in normal circumstances are leached downward through the soil. Removal of the tree cover erodes the topsoil, exposing the laterites and making the land unworkable. Guatemala has lost approximately 40 percent of the productive capacity of the land through erosion. In the Caribbean, sugar-cane plantations and factory sugar estates have been especially destructive. Sugar cane does not tolerate shade and

HAITI'S POVERTY-STRICKEN ENVIRONMENT

The tourist image of a Caribbean island paradise could not be further from the truth for Haitians. Extreme poverty and overpopulation have greatly exacerbated its environmental dilemma.

Ruined by years of neglect, economic mismanagement and corruption, Haiti is the poorest country in the western world, with a per capita income of only $250 per year. People attempt to scratch a living from the most marginal of resources. Less than 2 percent of the country remains forested and the rest is under severe threat from people cutting trees for fuelwood and charcoal, desperate for some form of income.

Much of the country is mountainous and severely eroded. The topsoil disappeared long ago, and now the country is losing even its subsoil to erosion as millions of tonnes of it are swept by rain down to the sea every year. Farmers are forced ever higher to find usable land for their crops, but the combination of overcultivation and thin soils means that the new plots are quickly eroded.

Although groundwater is plentiful, safe drinking water is scarce. Most of the population of over 7 million live without piped water, and inadequate sewerage makes the sources they have vulnerable to contamination and disease. In the "cardboard cities" erected by rural emigrants on landfill in the capital, Port-au-Prince, thousands wash in (and drink) a water-sewage mix.

Defiling an underwater paradise A plastic bag on elkhorn coral in the Bahamas is a visible reminder of the environmental threats to coral reefs, which are highly vulnerable to pollution, fishing and physical damage, all related to urbanization, agriculture and tourism.

requires total clearance of the natural vegetation for it to flourish. The soil between individual crop plants is kept as weed-free as possible during cultivation, leaving the exposed soil highly vulnerable to erosion from rainstorms. Barbados, the first "sugar island", had been cleared of all its tree cover and suffered severe soil erosion well before 1700. Haiti, once the richest of the sugar nations, no longer has any topsoil.

In 1952 most of the forest within the Lake Gatún watershed in central Panama was intact. Today much has gone, leaving bare hills on which soil erosion is severe. There are now so few trees to intercept rainwater and stabilize run-off, the discharge of water into the canal system has become irregular. The Panama Canal runs through Lake Gatún and is now threatened by heavy siltation as the stripped soil accumulates in the water as well as from pollution from sewage and industrial

waste. The weather phenomenon El Niño also resulted in the worst drought in Panama's history, reducing water levels in the Canal. In 1998 the Panama Canal Commission reduced the maximum draft of ships passing through, reducing cargo levels, and increased the rates for cargo.

Mining activities also cause forest loss. Former silver mining in Zacatecas, Mexico, denuded the forest for kilometers around, while in Jamaica, huge open-cast bauxite mines have left deep-red gashes against the green forested landscape.

Pollution problems

Pollution in the region is becoming ever more widespread. Levels of air pollution in Mexico City are among the worst in the world, with serious implications for the health of its citizens. In Guadalajara, Mexico's second largest city, at least 191 people were killed in April 1992 when industrial gases were discharged into underground sewerage pipes and caused a series of explosions. Raw sewage discharged from holiday homes around Lake Atitlán, Guatemala, along with fertilizer

run-off, has caused such excessive algal growth in the lake that the oxygen supply has plummeted and 80 percent of the wildlife has died.

The wider Caribbean region is one of the largest oil producers in the world with most of the oil shipped by tanker. Consequently, accidental oil spills plus the cleaning of tanks and bilge are a major source of marine pollution. Other sources include eutrophication from fertilizer run-off, pesticide run-off and siltation from rivers – all due to deforestation.

Coral reefs are especially sensitive to pollution. Sewage discharged from the increasing number of hotels clouds seawater, inhibiting the growth of corals by depriving them of sunlight. Sewage also increases nutrient levels in the water, encouraging the growth of aquatic plants, which smother and kill the coral. Overfishing and sudden declines in algal predators (such as sea urchins) have also encouraged algae to proliferate. Thus, the ecosystem of the coral reef is destroyed, and a new coral reef may take hundreds of years to develop.

PROSPECTS FOR THE FUTURE

Urgent action is required to combat environmental problems in Central America and the Caribbean, but political difficulties and lack of money make effective action hard to achieve. Intergovernmental agreements on the environment have always proved difficult to negotiate, monitor and uphold. Many countries have huge foreign debts: Mexico owes over $145 billion. The scale of such debts often constrains nations in their efforts to direct money towards environmental projects.

Land reform over most of the region would go far to relieving the growing problem of peasant cultivators exhausting marginal farming plots. The majority of the land is in the hands of a few landowners, leaving the bulk of the rural population to make a living from the remaining land, which is of inferior quality. Land issues have been the root cause of the wars in Guatemala, El Salvador and Nicaragua. Today, the World Bank Central America land program is supporting better land distribution and strengthened property rights. Many other social problems hinder the resolution of environmental problems, including population growth, poverty, and lack of education (particularly in how to deal with environmental problems).

The return of trees

Some positive action, however, has started in most countries of the region, notably in the designation of protected parks and reserves. Often eco-tourism has provided the spur for conservation. The demands of wildlife tourism, for example, have led to a new forest preservation plan in the Petén area of northern Guatemala.

In Costa Rica, where tourism is now the biggest industry, action on the deforestation issue has been taken a stage further, from protection of the remaining forests to the actual reforestation of previously cleared and often degraded land. Efforts to recreate the dry forests of the Guanacaste National Park in the Pacific lowlands are being paralleled upslope in the Monteverde cloud forest of the central mountains. Here, a project has been launched to buy bare, abandoned farming plots and replant them with forest trees to prevent soil erosion on the slopes. The

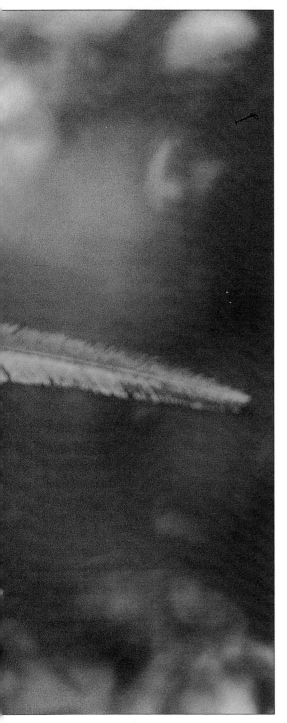

COSTA RICA'S PATH TO SURVIVAL

Since the 1970s Costa Rica has led the way in forest conservation in Central America. The government has worked closely with farmers, conservation bodies and foreign banks to overcome the country's devastating record of deforestation by incorporating surviving forests into protected areas. In 1996, they introduced a series of forestry laws that aimed to reward people involved in forest conservation. Another scheme involved creating a green corridor between the Monteverde cloud forest and another preserve to save fast-disappearing species of plants and animals.

The privately owned Monteverde reserve is a remarkably complex ecosystem. It straddles the mountains that divide the Caribbean and Pacific parts of the country, and along the steep slopes are clearly defined zones of climate and vegetation, each forming a distinct habitat. However, land outside the protected area has been extensively deforested to make way for cattle ranching, and conservationists have seen their efforts thwarted as forested areas have been reduced to islands of refuge amid bare grazing land. Several bird and mammal species that breed in the protected highlands have been deprived of their lowland wintering grounds, and have disappeared from the area.

Local biologists, galvanized into action by threats to the habitat of the rare Umbrella bird, formed the Monteverde Conservation League to expand the area of protected forests by linking individual forest stands along a network of forested "paths". These would allow migratory access through woodland. The League negotiated with farmers to buy and reforest land between the Monteverde forest and another reserve, creating a continuous refuge of over 21,000 ha (51,900 acres).

Symbol of conservation (*left*) A brilliantly colored male quetzal, the national bird of Costa Rica, is just one of thousands of species benefiting from the region's conservation programs.

A self-appointed conservationist (*below*), tending his patch in the rainforest of Panama. The Kuna Indians' way of life, based on harvesting the many resources of the forest without overexploiting them, is in harmony with nature: the Kuna are natural conservationists of their home in the Kuna Yala Reserve.

local community has saved part of the cloud forest which, in turn, now attracts about 50,000 tourists a year.

The Panamanian government has also encouraged tree planting in deforested upland areas, and has discouraged – through more vigilant policing – illegal logging and settlement in pristine forests of the Chocó, in the far east of the country. Communities in the interior of Haiti have been encouraged to become involved in reforestation schemes set up by environmental groups. Meanwhile, in Jamaica, the government has insisted that bauxite mining companies restore land that has been degraded and abandoned after intensive exploitation. The mining companies must first replace the topsoil and then either reforest the areas or plant them with pangola grass, which provides good feed for cattle. Badly eroded land in both Jamaica's Yallah's valley and Barbados' Scotland district has been remolded and terraced with the help of large subsidies from the government.

Marine protection

Many countries have established marine reserves to protect coral reefs, and while some have set up underwater trails for tourists, others are closed to visitors for full conservation. Overfishing is increasingly being controlled by military patrols in the Caribbean Sea, sanctioned by the international Law of the Sea convention, signed in Jamaica in 1982. In 1999, the nations of the wider Caribbean adopted a regional treaty to protect the marine environment from pollution, from land-based sources such as sewage and run-off.

Despite some successful conservation programs and the passing of environmental legislation and agreements – including the debt-for-nature programs that began in the late 1980s, allowing selected nations to write off part of their debt in exchange for conservation – the Caribbean region had not made significant environmental progress in the late 1990s. The enforcement of environmental policies is hampered by financial shortages, institutional weakness, inadequate monitoring and control mechanisms, lack of public awareness, and above all, poverty.

Crisis in Mexico City

Few cities in the world so graphically illustrate the environmental hazards of urban overcrowding as Mexico City, where the population in 2000 was over 25 million. The city already has severe problems of air pollution, access to clean water and the disposal of sewage and waste. Its crisis reflects the widespread problems of high rural-urban migration, rapid urban growth and poor infrastructure that beset much of the developing world.

Shaky foundations

Mexico City's environmental plight is not helped by its geography. The city lies in a dry mountain basin on lake beds deposited in the old Lake Texcoco. The beds are spongy and vulnerable to subsidence when water is extracted from underneath them. They also accentuate the effects of earthquake tremors, as in 1985, when the Guerrero-Michoacan quake claimed 7,000 lives, demolished at least 1,000 buildings in the center and caused over $4 billion damage. Except for the rainy season from July to September, when floods can occur, the climate is arid and surface water resources are limited.

Subsidence of the lake beds caused by past water extraction (up to 8 m or 26 ft in places) is now so great that both water and sewage pipes have been dislocated. Moreover, most local sources of groundwater have now either dried up or become contaminated by sewage seepage. Today, water supplies are pumped over 1000 m (3,200 ft) over the mountain rim from adjacent high valleys, costing millions of dollars a year.

Sewage is also expensive to manage. A new deep system of sewers is being laid 40 m (130 ft) below ground level so as to avoid subsidence effects. Much of the raw sewage from this is piped north for many kilometers along the city's Gran Canal, and then tunneled through the mountain rim and out of the basin. Providing water and sewage services costs the city about $1 billion a year and still nearly 40 percent of homes in Mexico City have not been provided with piped water or sewerage. Even if the city authorities could supply these utilities, they would still have to cope with the influx of 400,000 new immigrants every year, most of whom squat on public land, with no access to clean water or waste facilities.

Noxious air

Mexico City's most intractable environ-

Mexico City site

- Lake area in 1519
- Present-day lakes
- Urban areas

0 ——— 20 km
0 ——— 10 mi

Lake Zumpango

Lake Xaltocan

Sierra las Cruces

Lake Texcoco

Mexico City

Sierra del Ajusco

Iztaccihuatl
(5,286 m/17,343 ft)

Popocatepetl
(5,452 m/17,887 ft)

A city threatened by its location (*above*) Mexico City is built on gradually subsiding lake beds that exacerbate the effects of earthquake tremors. The surrounding mountains trap air pollution and also make water supply a major problem.

Smoking rubble (*left*) of a collapsed hotel is extinguished by firefighters after the Mexican earthquake of 1985. Mexico City is located at the junction of two great mountain chains – the area of greatest seismic activity in the country.

Traffic in Mexico City (*right*) accounts for 60 percent of solid-particle air pollution. During rush hour, visibility can drop to less than three city blocks. Lead-free petrol has been introduced but still pollution-related illnesses kill over 70,000 city dwellers annually.

mental hazard, however, is its air pollution, which is probably the worst in the world. The surrounding high mountain rim traps air contaminants in the city basin, preventing their dispersal by air currents. Contaminants, including carbon monoxide, hydrocarbons, sulfur dioxide and nitrogen oxides, are emitted by the city's 3 million motor vehicles and 30,000 factories, most of the latter burning highly polluting low-grade, sulfur-rich fuel. Ozone levels have been recorded at 10 times the normal atmospheric levels, caus-

ing the government to temporarily close schools.

The Mexican government launched a 5-year pollution reduction program. It also imposed the "Today Don't Drive" law to reduce city traffic and pollution. The law banned cars one day a week, the day depending on the last digit of their license plate. Rather than reduce the number of vehicles on the road, it had the opposite effect as people bought additional cars to get the plates which allowed them to drive every day.

GLOSSARY

Acid rain Rain or any other form of PRECIPITATION that has become more acid by absorbing waste gases (for example, sulfur dioxide and nitrogen oxides) discharged into the ATMOSPHERE.

Acid soil Soil that has a pH of less than 7; it is often PEATY.

Added value A higher price fetched by an article or RESOURCE after it has been processed, such as crude oil after refining.

Agricultural economy An economy where most people work as cultivators or PASTORALISTS.

AIDS Acquired Immune Deficiency Syndrome, a disease that damages the body's immune system, making people more susceptible to disease. Human Immunodeficiency Virus (HIV) is one of the viruses that can lead to AIDS.

Air pollution The presence of gases and suspended particles in the air in high enough concentrations to harm humans, other animals, vegetation or materials. Human activity is the source of most pollution.

Alkaline soil Soil that has a pH of more than 7; chalk or limestone soils.

Alpine (1) A treeless ENVIRONMENT found on a mountain above the tree line but beneath the limit of permanent snow. (2) A plant that is adapted to grow in the TUNDRA-like environment of mountain areas.

Amphibian An animal that lives on land but whose life cycle requires some time in water.

Apartheid A way of organizing society to keep different racial groups apart. Introduced in South Africa by the National Party after 1948 as a means of ensuring continued white political dominance, it was dismantled in the 1990s.

Aquifer An underground layer of permeable rock, sand or gravel that absorbs and holds GROUNDWATER.

Arctic The northern POLAR region. In biological terms it also refers to the northern region of the globe where the mean temperature of the warmest month does not exceed 10°C (50°F).

Arid (climate) Dry and usually hot. Arid areas generally have less than 250 mm (10 inches) of rain a year.

Atmosphere The gaseous layer surrounding the Earth. It consists of nitrogen (78 percent), oxygen (21 percent), argon (1 percent), tiny amounts of carbon dioxide, neon, ozone, hydrogen and krypton, and varying amounts of water vapor.

Atoll A circular chain of CORAL reefs enclosing a lagoon. Atolls form as coral reefs fringing a volcanic island; as sea levels rise or the island sinks a lagoon is formed.

Autonomy The condition of being self-governing, usually granted to a subdivision of a larger STATE or to a territory belonging to it.

Balance of payments A statement of a country's transactions with all other countries over a given period.

Balance of power A theory of political stability based upon an even distribution of power among the leading STATES.

Basalt A fine-grained IGNEOUS ROCK. It has a dark color and contains little silica. Ninety percent of lavas are basaltic.

Bible The book of scriptures of CHRISTIANITY and JUDAISM. The Jewish Bible contains many books in common with the Christian version describing historical events and prophetic teachings, but the latter also includes accounts of the life and teachings of Jesus Christ.

Biodegradable (of a substance) easily broken down into simpler substances by bacteria or other decomposers. Products made of organic materials such as paper, woolens, leather and wood are biodegradable; many plastics are not.

Biodiversity The number of different species of plants and animals found in a given area. In general, the greater the number of species, the more stable and robust the ECOSYSTEM is.

Biomass The total mass of all the living organisms in a defined area or ECOSYSTEM.

Biosphere The thin layer of the Earth that contains all living organisms and the ENVIRONMENT that supports them.

Biotechnology Technology applied to biological processes, including genetic engineering, the manipulation of the genetic makeup of living organisms.

Birthrate The number of births expressed as a proportion of a population. Usually given as the annual number of live births per 1,000 population (also known as the crude birth rate).

Black economy The sector of the economy that avoids paying tax.

Bloc A group of countries closely bound by economic and/or political ties.

Boreal Typical of the northern climates lying between the ARCTIC and latitude 50°N, characterized by long cold winters and short summers. Vegetation in these regions is dominated by BOREAL FOREST.

Boreal forest The name given to the CONIFEROUS FORESTS or TAIGA of the northern hemisphere.

Brown coal A peat-like material, also known as lignite, which has a lower energy value than more mature forms of coal.

Buddhism A religion founded in the 6th and 5th centuries BC and based on the teachings of Siddhartha Gautama; it is widely observed in southern and southeast Asia.

Bureaucracy The body of STATE officials that carry out the day-to-day running of government. It may also refer to a system of a ministration marked by the inflexible application of rules.

Capital Machinery, investment funds or an employment relationship involving waged labor.

Capitalism A political and economic system based on the production of goods and services for profitable exchange in which labor is bought and sold for wages. Capitalist economies can be more or less regulated by governments. In a capitalist mixed economy the government owns some of the country's utilities and industries and also acts as a major employer.

Cash crop A crop grown for sale rather than for SUBSISTENCE.

Caste A system of rigid hereditary social divisions, normally associated with the Hindu caste system in India, where an individual is born into the caste of his or her parents, must marry within it, and cannot leave it.

Caucasian (1) A racial classification based on white or light skin color. (2) An inhabitant of the Caucasus region or the Indo-European language of this people.

Cereal A cultivated grass that has been bred selectively to produce high yields of edible grain for consumption by humans and livestock. The most important are wheat (*Triticum* sp.), rice (*Oryza saliva*) and maize (*Zea mays*).

CFCs (chlorofluorocarbons) Organic compounds made up of atoms of carbon, chlorine and fluorine. Gaseous CFCs used as aerosol propellants, refrigerant gases and solvent cleaners are known to cause depletion of the OZONE LAYER.

Christianity A religion based on the teachings of Jesus Christ and originating in the 1st century AD from JUDAISM; its main beliefs are found in the BIBLE. The Roman Catholic, Orthodox and Protestant churches are its major branches.

CITES (Convention on International Trade in Endangered Species) An international agreement signed by over 90 countries since 1973. SPECIES (FAUNA and FLORA) placed in Appendix I are considered to be in danger of EXTINCTION, and trade is prohibited without an export permit. Signatory countries must supply data to the World Conservation Union, which monitors IMPORTS and EXPORTS. Appendix II species may be threatened with extinction if trade is unregulated.

City-state An independent STATE consisting of a single city and the surrounding countryside needed to support it. Singapore is an example of a modern city-state.

Class (1) A group of people sharing a common economic position, for example large landowners, waged laborers or owners of small businesses. (2) (in zoology and botany) A rank in the taxonomic hierarchy coming between phylum and order. *See* CLASSIFICATION.

Classification A system of arranging the different types of living organisms according to the degree of similarity of their inherited characteristics. The classification system enables organisms to be identified and may also reveal the relationships between different groups. The internationally accepted classification hierarchy groups organisms first into divisions, then phyla, CLASSES, orders, FAMILIES, GENERA, SPECIES and SUBSPECIES.

Collectivization The organization of an economy (typically communist) by collective control through agencies of the state. *See* COMMUNISM.

Colonialism The political practice of occupying a foreign country for settlement and economic exploitation.

Colony A territory under the sovereignty of a foreign power.

COMECON The Council for Mutual Economic Assistance, formed in 1947 as an organization to further trade and economic cooperation between communist countries. It had 10 members before its collapse in 1989: the Soviet Union, Bulgaria, Czechoslovakia, Hungary, Poland, Romania, East Germany, Mongolia, Cuba, and Vietnam.

Commonwealth A loose association of STATES that were members of the former British EMPIRE, with the British monarch at its head.

Communism A social and economic system based on the communal ownership of property. It usually refers to the state-controlled social and economic systems in the former Soviet Union and Soviet-bloc countries and in the People's Republic of China. *See* SOCIALISM.

Coniferous forest A forest of mainly coniferous, or cone-bearing trees, frequently with evergreen needle-shaped leaves and found principally in the TEMPERATE ZONES and BOREAL regions.

Conservation The use, management and protection of NATURAL RESOURCES so that they are not degraded, depleted or wasted. *See also* SUSTAINABILITY.

Constitution The written statement of laws that defines the way in which a country is governed.

Consumer goods Goods that are acquired for immediate use, such as foodstuffs, radios, televisions and washing machines.

Continental climate The type of climate associated with the interior of continents. It is characterized by wide daily and seasonal ranges of temperature, especially outside the TROPICS, and by low rainfall.

Continental drift The theory that today's continents, formed by the breakup of prehistoric supercontinents, have slowly drifted to their present positions. The theory was first proposed by Alfred Wegener in 1912.

Continental shelf An extension of a continent, forming a shallow, sloping shelf covered by sea.

Coral A group of animals related to sea anemones and living in warm seas. Individuals, called polyps, combine to form a COLONY.

Culture (1) The beliefs, customs and social relations of a people. (2) The assumptions that a people make in interpreting their world.

Cyclone A center of low atmospheric pressure. Tropical cyclones are known as HURRICANES or typhoons.

Dead lake (or Dead river) An area of water in which dissolved oxygen levels have fallen as a result of acidification, overgrowth of plants or high levels of pollution, to the extent that few or no living things are able to survive.

Debt The financial obligations owed by a country to the rest of the world, usually repayable in US dollars. Total external debt includes public, publicly guaranteed, and private long-term debt.

Decolonization The transfer of government from a colonial power to the people of the COLONY at the time of political independence.

Deforestation The felling of trees and clearing of forested land to be put to other uses.

Delta A large accumulation of sediment, often fan-shaped, deposited where a river enters the sea or a lake.

Democracy A form of government in which policy is made by the people (direct democracy) or on their behalf (indirect democracy). Indirect democracy usually takes the form of competition among political parties at elections.

Desert A very ARID area with less than 25 cm (10 in) rainfall a year. In hot deserts the rate of evaporation is greater than the rate of PRECIPITATION, and there is little vegetation.

Desertification The creation of desert-like conditions usually caused by a combination of overgrazing, soil EROSION, prolonged DROUGHT and climate change.

Devaluation A deliberate reduction by a government in the exchange value of its own currency in gold, or in relation to the value of another currency.

Developed country Any country with high standards of living and a sophisticated economy, in contrast to DEVELOPING COUNTRIES. Various indicators are used to measure a country's wealth and material well-being: the GROSS NATIONAL PRODUCT, the PER CAPITA consumption of energy, the number of doctors per head of population and the average life expectancy, for example.

Developing country Any country that is characterized by low standards of living and a SUBSISTENCE economy. Sometimes called THIRD WORLD countries, they include most of Africa, Asia and Central and South America.

Dictator A leader who concentrates the power of the STATE in his or her own hands.

Divide see WATERSHED.

Dominant species The most numerous or prevailing SPECIES in a community of plants or animals.

Dormancy A period during which the metabolic activity of a plant or animal is reduced to such an extent that it can withstand difficult environmental conditions such as cold or DROUGHT.

Drought An extended period in which rainfall is substantially lower than average and the water supply is insufficient to meet demand.

EC *See* EUROPEAN COMMUNITY.

Ecology (1) The study of the interactions of living organisms with each other and with their ENVIRONMENT. (2) The study of the structure and functions of nature.

Ecosystem A community of plants and animals and the ENVIRONMENT in which they live and react with each other.

Effluent Any liquid waste discharged into the ENVIRONMENT as a byproduct of industry, agriculture or sewage treatment.

Emission A substance discharged into the air in the form of gases and suspended particles, from automobile engines and industrial smokestacks, for example.

Empire (1) A political organization of STATES and territories in which one dominates the rest. (2) The territory that constitutes such a group of states.

Endangered species A SPECIES whose population has dropped to such low levels that its continued survival is threatened.

Endemic species A SPECIES that is native to one specific area, and is therefore often said to be characteristic of that area.

Environment (1) The external conditions – climate, geology and other living things – that influence the life of individual organisms or ECOSYSTEMS. (2) The surroundings in which animals and plants live and interact.

Erosion The process by which exposed land surfaces are broken down into smaller particles or worn away by water, wind or ice.

Ethnic group A group of people sharing a social identity or **culture** based on language, religion, customs and/or common descent or kinship.

Euro The common currency of the EUROPEAN UNION, introduced in 1999. The euro operates at a fixed rate alongside the national currencies of member states until 2002, when it will supersede them. To enter the euro trading zone countries needed to meet financial convergence criteria set out in the Maastricht Treaty of 1992. Eleven countries did so: Austria, Belgium, Finland, France, Germany, Ireland, Italy, Luxembourg, the Netherlands, Portugal and Spain. Membership in the euro zone involves ceding control of monetary policy to the European Central Bank, which some countries – notably Britain – remain reluctant to do.

European Community (EU) An alliance of western European nations formed to agree common policies on trade, aid, agriculture and economics. The founder members in 1957 were France, West Germany, Belgium, Holland, Luxembourg and Italy. Britain, Ireland and Denmark joined in 1973, Greece in 1981 and

Spain and Portugal in 1986. East Germany became a member when it was reunited with West Germany in 1990. It became the EUROPEAN UNION with the Maastricht Treaty of 1992.

European Union (EU) The former EUROPEAN COMMUNITY, created by the Maastricht Treaty, which was signed in 1992 and implemented from 1993. The treaty gave the European parliament wider powers, setting the agenda for achieving for full monetary and political union. Austria, Finland and Sweden joined the EU in 1995.

Evolution The process by which SPECIES develop their appearance, form and behavior through the process of NATURAL SELECTION, and by which new species or varieties are formed.

Exotic (animal or plant) Not native to an area but established after being introduced from elsewhere, often for commercial or decorative use.

Exports Goods and services sold to other countries, bringing in foreign exchange.

Extinction The loss of a local population of a articular SPECIES or even the entire species. It may be natural or be caused by human activity.

Family A taxonomic term for a group of related plants or animals. For example, the family Felidae (cat family) includes the lion, the tiger and all the smaller cats. Most families contain several GENERA, and families are grouped together into orders. *See* CLASSIFICATION.

Famine An acute shortage of food leading to widespread malnutrition and starvation.

Fault A fracture or crack in the Earth along which there has been movement of the rock masses.

Fauna The general term for the animals that live in a particular region.

Feudalism (1) A type of society in which landlords collect dues from the agricultural producers in return for military protection. (2) A hierarchical society of mutual obligations that preceded CAPITALISM in Europe.

First World A term sometimes used to describe the advanced industrial or DEVELOPED COUNTRIES.

Fjord A steep-sided inlet formed when the sea floods and covers a glaciated U-shaped valley. *See* GLACIATION.

Flora The plant life of a particular region.

Fossil fuel Any fuel, such as coal, oil and NATURAL GAS, formed beneath the Earth's surface under conditions of heat and pressure from organisms that died millions of years ago.

Free trade A system of international trade in which goods and services are exchanged without TARIFFS, QUOTAS or other restrictions.

GATT The General Agreement on Tariffs and Trade, a treaty that governs world imports and exports. Its aim is to promote FREE TRADE, but many countries impose TARIFF barriers to favor their own industries and agricultural produce.

GDP *See* GROSS DOMESTIC PRODUCT.

Genus (pl. genera) A level of biological CLASSIFICATION of organisms in which closely related SPECIES are grouped. For example, dogs, wolves, jackals and coyotes are all grouped together in the genus *Canis*.

Ghetto A slum area in a city that is occupied by an ETHNIC minority. The word originally referred to the area of medieval European cities to which Jews were restricted by law.

Glaciation The process of GLACIER and ice sheet growth, and their effect on the landscape.

Glacier A mass of ice formed by the compaction

and freezing of snow and which shows evidence of past or present movement.

Global warming The increase in the average temperature of the Earth that is believed to be caused by the GREENHOUSE EFFECT.

GNP *See* GROSS NATIONAL PRODUCT.

Greenhouse effect The effect of certain gases in the ATMOSPHERE, such as carbon dioxide and METHANE, in absorbing solar heat radiated back from the surface of the Earth and preventing its escape into space. Without these gases the Earth would be too cold for living things, but the burning of FOSSIL FUELS for industry and transportation has caused atmospheric levels of these gases to increase, and this is believed to be a cause of GLOBAL WARMING.

Green Revolution The introduction of high-yielding varieties of seeds (especially rice and wheat) and modern agricultural techniques to increase agricultural production in DEVELOPING COUNTRIES. It began in the early 1960s.

Gross Domestic Product (GDP) The total value of a country's annual output of goods and services, with allowances being made for depreciation. Growth in GDP is usually expressed in constant prices to offset the effects of inflation. GDP is a useful guide to the level of economic activity in a country.

Gross National Product (GNP) A country's GROSS DOMESTIC PRODUCT plus income from abroad.

Groundwater Water that has percolated into the ground from the Earth's surface, filling pores, cracks and fissures. An impermeable layer of rock prevents it from moving deeper so that the lower levels become saturate . The upper limit of saturation is known as the WATER TABLE.

Growing season The period of the year when the average temperature is high enough for plants to grow. It is longest at low altitudes and latitudes. Most plants can grow when the temperature exceeds 5°C (42°F).

Habitat The external ENVIRONMENT to which an animal or plant is adapted and in which it prefers to live, usually defined in terms of vegetation, climate or altitude – eg grassland habitat.

Hard currency A currency used by international traders because they think it is safe from DEVALUATION.

Hinduism A body of religious practices, originating in India in the 2nd millennium BC, that emphasizes ways of living rather than ways of thought. Its beliefs and practices are based on the Vedas and other scriptures and are closely intertwined with the culture of India's people.

HIV (Human Immunodeficiency Virus) *See* AIDS.

Hunter-gatherers People who obtain their food requirements by hunting wild animals and gathering the berries and fruits from wild plants.

Hurricane A tropical CYCLONE, usually found in the Caribbean and western North Atlantic.

Hybrid An animal or plant that is the offspring of two genetically different individuals. Hybrid crops are often grown because they give higher yields and are more resistant to disease.

Ice age A long period of geological time in which the temperature of the Earth falls, and snow and ice sheets are present throughout the year in mid and high latitudes.

Igneous rock Rock formed when magma (molten material in the Earth's crust) cools and solidifies.

Imperialism The process whereby one country forces its rule on another country, frequently in order to establish an EMPIRE.

Imports Goods and services purchased from other countries.

Import substitution industry Any industry that has been set up (mainly in DEVELOPING COUNTRIES) to manufacture products that used to be imported. Import substitution industries are normally simple ones with an immediate local market, such as the manufacture of cigarettes, soap and textiles. They are protected during their start-up phase by high TARIFFS on foreign rivals.

Indigenous peoples The original inhabitants of a region, generally leading a traditional way of life.

Inflation The general rise in prices when the supply of money and credit in an economy is increasing faster than the availability of goods and services.

Islam A religion based on the revelations of God to the prophet Muhammed in the 7th century AD, which are contained in the Qu'ran. Islam is widely practiced throughout North Africa, the Indian subcontinent, the Middle East and parts of Southeast Asia.

Judaism A religion founded in 2000 BC among the ancient Hebrews and practiced by Jews; its main beliefs are contained in the BIBLE.

Labor force The economically active population of a country or region, including the armed forces and the unemployed. Full-time homemakers and unpaid caregivers are not included.

Leaching The process by which water washes nutrients and minerals downward from one layer of soil to another, or into streams.

Legislature The branch of government responsible for enacting laws.

Mammal A vertebrate animal of the CLASS Mammalia, with a four-chambered heart, fur or hair, and mammae (nipples) for feeding its young on milk. Except for monotremes, mammals do not lay eggs but give birth to live young.

Mangrove A dense forest of shrubs and trees growing on tidal coastal mudflats and estuaries throughout the tropics.

Maquis The typical vegetation of the Mediter-ranean coast, consisting of aromatic shrubs, laurel, myrtle, rock rose, broom and small trees such as olive, fig and holm oak.

Maritime climate A generally moist climate close to the sea, whose slow cooling and heating reduces variations in temperature.

Market economy An economy in which most activities are transacted by private individuals and firms in largely unregulated markets.

Marxism The system of thought derived from the 19th-century political theorist Karl Marx, in which politics is interpreted as a struggle be-tween economic CLASSES. It promotes communal ownership of property when it is practiced, so is popularly known as COMMUNISM.

Methane A gas produced by decomposing organic matter that burns without releasing pollutants and can be used as an energy source. Excessive methane production from vast amounts of animal manure is believed to contribute to the GREENHOUSE EFFECT.

Migrant workers Part of the LABOR FORCE which has come from another region or country, looking for temporary employment.

Monetarism An economic philosophy that sees INFLATION as the main menace to economic growth and proposes a direct relationship between the rate of growth of the money supply of a country and its subsequent rate of inflation.

Monsoon (1) The wind systems in the TROPICS that reverse their direction according to the sea-sons. (2) The rain caused by these winds.

Montane The zone at middle altitudes on the slopes of mountains, below the ALPINE zone.

NAFTA The North American Free Trade Agreement, signed by Canada, Mexico and the United States, and implemented on 1 January 1994, lowering trade barriers between them, though many in the US and Canada feared the massive loss of jobs to less expensive Mexico.

Nation A community that believes it consists of a single people, based upon historical and cultural criteria and sharing a common territory. Sometimes used interchangeably with STATE.

Nationalism An ideology that assumes all NATIONS should have their own STATE, a NATION-STATE, in their own territory, the national homeland.

Nation-state A STATE in which the inhabitants all belong to one NATION. Most states claim to be nation-states; in practice almost all of them include minority groups.

Natural gas A FOSSIL FUEL in the form of a flam-mable gas that occurs naturally in the Earth. It is often found with deposits of petroleum.

Natural resources REOURCES created by the Earth's natural processes including mineral deposits, FOSSIL FUELS, soil, air, water, plants and animals. Most natural resources are harvested by people for use in agriculture, industry and economic activities.

Natural selection The process by which organisms not well suited to their ENVIRONMENT are eliminated by predation, parasitism, compe-tition, etc, and those that are well suited survive, breed and pass on their genes.

Nomad A member of a (usually pastoral) people that moves seasonally from one place to another in search of food, water or pasture for their animals. *See* PASTORALIST.

Nonrenewable resource A NATURAL RESOURCE that is present in the Earth's makeup in finite amounts (coal, oil etc) and cannot be replaced once reserves are exhausted.

OECD (Organization for Economic Cooperation and Development) An international organization set up in 1961 to promote the economic growth of its (now 24) member countries.

One-party system A political system in which there is no competition to the government PARTY at elections (eg communist and military regimes) and all but the government party is banned.

OPEC The Organization of Petroleum Exporting Countries, an 11-member cartel that is able to exercise a degree of control over the price of oil.

Ozone layer A band of enriched oxygen or ozone found in the upper ATMOSPHERE. It absorbs harmful ultraviolet radiation from the Sun. The heat this creates provides a cap for the Earth's weather systems.

Pangea The supercontinent that was composed of all the present-day continents and therefore included both Gondwanaland and Laurasia. It existed between 250 and 200 million years ago. *See also* CONTINENTAL DRIFT.

Parliamentary democracy A political system in which the LEGISLATURE (parliament) is elected by all the adult members of the population and the government is formed by the PARTY that commands a majority in the parliament.

Party An organized group seeking political power to implement an agreed set of policies.

Pastoralism A way of life based on tending herds

of animals such as sheep, cattle, goats or camels; often NOMADIC, it involves moving the herds as the seasons change.

Peat Soil formed by an accumulation of plant material incompletely decomposed due to low temperature and lack of oxygen, usually as a result of waterlogging.

Per capita Per head of population.

Permafrost Soil and rock that remains permanently frozen, typically in the POLAR REGIONS. A layer of soil at the surface may melt in summer, but refreezes in colder conditions.

Pesticide Any chemical substance used to control the pests that can damage crops, such as insects and rodents. Often used as a general term for herbicides, insecticides and fungicides.

pH A measurement on the scale 0–14 of the acidity or alkalinity of a substance.

Plateau A large area of level, elevated land. When bordered by steep slopes it is called a tableland.

Polar regions The regions that lie within the lines of latitude known as the ARCTIC and Antarctic circles, respectively 66°32′ north and south of the Equator. At this latitude the sun does not set in midsummer nor rise in midwinter.

Polder An area of level land at or below sea level obtained by land reclamation. It is normally used for agriculture.

Poverty line A measure of deprivation that varies from country to country. In low-income economies a certain percentage of the population lacks sufficient food and shelter. In the industrial world people are considered to be poor if they earn less than 60 percent of the average wage.

PPP Purchasing power parity – a way of measuring income or GDP for different countries based on standardized dollar values, rather than the conventional method of converting different currencies according to official exchange rates. By taking away the currency exchange factor, PPP is less prone to fluctuations that may distort the comparisons between countries.

Prairie The flat grassland in the interior of North America between 30°N and 55°N, much of which has been plowed and is used to grow CEREALS.

Precipitation Moisture that reaches the Earth from the ATMOSPHERE, including mist, dew, rain, sleet, snow and hail.

Predator An animal that feeds on another animal (the PREY).

President A head of state, elected in some countries directly by the voters and in others by members of the LEGISLATURE. In some political systems the president is chief executive, in others the office is largely ceremonial.

Prey An animal that a PREDATOR hunts and kills for food.

Productivity (1) A measure of economic output in relation to the quantity of economic inputs (labor, machines, land, etc) needed for production. (2) The amount of weight (or energy) gained by an individual, a SPECIES or an ECOSYSTEM per unit of area per unit of time.

Quota A limit imposed on the amount of a product that can be imported in a given time.

Radioactivity The emission of alpha-, beta- and gamma particles from atomic nuclei. This is greatest when the atom is split, as in a nuclear reactor. Prolonged exposure to radioactive material can cause damage to living tissue, leading to cancers and ultimately death.

Rainforest Forest in which there is abundant rainfall all year long – in tropical as well as TEMPERATE ZONES. Rainforests probably contain half of all the Earth's plant and animal species.

Refuge A place where a SPECIES of plant or animal has survived after formerly occupying a much larger area.

Resource Any material, source of information or skill that is of economic value to industry and business.

Runoff Water produced by rainfall or melting snow that flows across the land surface into streams and rivers.

Salinization The accumulation of soluble salts near or at the surface of soil in an ARID climate. Salinization can also occur when water used for irrigation evaporates; the land becomes so salty that it is worthless for cultivation.

Savanna A HABITAT of open grassland with scattered trees in tropical and subtropical areas. There is a marked dry season and too little rain to support large areas of forest.

Second World A term sometimes used to describe the DEVELOPED socialist countries (including the former Soviet Union and former Soviet bloc).

Semiarid land Any area between an ARID DESERT and a more fertile region where there is sufficient moisture to support a little more vegetation than can survive in a desert. Also called semidesert.

Separatism A political movement in a STATE that supports the secession of a particular minority group, within a defined territory, from that state.

Service industries Industries that supply services to customers or to other sectors of the economy: typically banking, transport, insurance, education, healthcare, retailing and distribution.

Shanty town An area of very poor housing consisting of ramshackle huts and other simple dwellings often made from waste materials and with inadequate services.

Shifting cultivation A method of farming prevalent in tropical areas in which a piece of land is cleared and cultivated until its fertility is diminished. The farmer then abandons the land, which restores itself naturally.

Slash-and-burn farming A method of farming in tropical areas in which the vegetation cover is cut and burned to fertilize the land before crops are planted. Often a feature of SHIFTING CULTIVATION.

Socialism An economic system and political ideology based upon the principle of equality between people, the redistribution of wealth and property, and equal access to benefits such as healthcare and education.

Solar energy The radiant energy, produced by the Sun, that powers all the Earth's processes. It can be captured and used to provide domestic heating or converted to produce electrical energy.

Specialization (in natural history) The evolutionary development of a SPECIES, leading to narrow limits of tolerance and a restricted role (or niche) in the community.

Species The basic unit of CLASSIFICATION of plants and animals. Species are grouped into GENERA and variations may be categorized into SUBSPECIES in descending order of hierarchy.

State The primary political unit of the modern world, usually defined by its possession of sovereignty over a territory and its people.

Steppe An open grassy plain with few trees or shrubs, characterized by low and sporadic rainfall, with fluctuating temperatures during the year.

Subsistence A term applied to systems in which producers can supply their own needs for food, shelter, etc but have little or no surplus to trade.

Subspecies A rank in the CLASSIFICATION of plants and animals between SPECIES and variety. It often denotes a geographical variation of a species.

Subtropical The climate zone between the TROPICS and TEMPERATE ZONES. There are marked seasonal changes of temperature but it is never very cold.

Succession The development and maturation of an ECOSYSTEM, through changes in the types and abundance of SPECIES.

Sustainability The concept of using the Earth's NATURAL RESOURCES to improve people's lives without diminishing the ability of the Earth to support life today and in the future.

Taiga The CONIFEROUS FOREST and PEAT landbelt that stretches around the world in the northern hemisphere, south of the TUNDRA and north of the DECIDUOUS forests and grasslands.

Tariff A tax on imported goods or services.

Taxonomy The scientific CLASSIFICATION of organisms.

Temperate zone Any one of the climatic zones in mid latitudes, with a mild climate. They cover areas between the warm TROPICS and cold POLAR REGIONS.

Terrestrial (of a plant, animal etc) spending its entire life cycle on the land.

Third World A term first used to refer to ex-COLONIES that were neither fully capitalist (FIRST WORLD) nor fully socialist (SECOND WORLD). Now used to refer to the poorer, less industrialized countries of the developing world.

Tribe A group of people united by a common language, religion, customs and/or descent and kinship; often used to describe the social groups of peoples who have no developed STATE or government and whose social organization is based on ancestry and extended family systems.

Tropics The area of the Earth lying between the Tropic of Cancer (23°30′ N) and the Tropic of Capricorn (23°30′ S).

Tundra The level, treeless land lying in the very cold northern regions of Europe, Asia and North America, where winters are long and cold and the ground beneath the surface is permanently frozen. *See also* PERMAFROST.

Urbanization (1) The process by which city populations grow as the rural population diminishes. (2) City formation and growth.

Water table The uppermost level of underground rock that is permanently saturated with GROUNDWATER.

Watershed The boundary line dividing two river systems. It is also known as a water-parting or divide, particularly in the United States, where the word watershed refers to a river basin (the area drained by a river and its tributaries).

Welfare state A social and economic system based on STATE provision of healthcare, pensions and unemployment insurance. These services are financed by contributions from the working population, and access is intended to be available to all, free of charge.

Wetland A HABITAT that is waterlogged all or enough of the time to support vegetation adapted to these conditions.

INDEX

Page numbers in **bold** refer to extended treatment of topic; in *italics* to caption, maps or tables

Acknowledgments

CONTRIBUTORS

General Advisory Editor
Professor Peter Haggett, University of Bristol, UK

COUNTRY PROFILES

Advisory Editor
Dr Thomas D. Boswell, University of Miami, USA

Writers
Asgard Publishing Services:
  Philip Gardner
  Allan Scott
  Michael Scott Rohan
  Andrew Shackleton
John and Barbara Baines
Ann Furtado

REGIONAL PROFILES

Advisory Editors

Professor Ken J. Gregory, Goldsmith's College, London, UK
Physical Geography

Robert Burton, Huntingdon, UK
Habitats and their Conservation, Animal Life

Professor D.M. Moore, University of Reading, UK
Plant Life

Dr John Tarrant, University of East Anglia, UK
Agriculture

Dr Ian Hamilton, London School of Economics, UK
Industry

Dr Stuart Corbridge, University of Cambridge, UK
Economy

Dr Alisdair Rogers, University of Oxford, UK
Peoples and Cultures

Professor John Rennie Short, Syracuse University, USA
Cities

Dr Peter Taylor, University of Newcastle upon Tyne, UK
Government

Dr Michael Williams, University of Oxford, UK
Environmental Issues

Writers
Dr R.P.D. Walsh, University College, Swansea, UK
Physical Geography

Dr Gina C. Green, Oxford Forestry Institute, Oxford, UK
Habitats and their Conservation

Jill Bailey, Oxford, UK
Animal Life

Dr C.D. Adams, The Natural History Museum, London, UK
Plant Life

Dr Guy M. Robinson, University of Edinburgh, UK
Agriculture

Dr David Fox, University of Manchester, UK
Industry

Dr Colin Clarke, University of Oxford, UK
Economy, Cities, Government

Dr Steven Vertovec, University of Oxford, UK
Peoples and Cultures

Dr Janet Momsen, University of Newcastle upon Tyne, UK
Government

Dr David Watts, University of Hull, UK
Environmental Issues

Updated edition:

Editorial Director: Graham Bateman
Project Manager: Lauren Bourque
Cartography Manager: Richard Watts
Cartography Editor: Tim Williams
Editorial Assistant: Rita Demetriou
Picture Manager: Claire Turner
Picture Research: Alison Floyd
Design: Martin Anderson
Typesetting: Brian Blackmore
Production: Clive Sparling, Nicolette Colborne

Further reading

South America, Central America and the Caribbean 2000 (Europa Publications Ltd., London, 8th edn., 2000)

Ahmed, B., & Afroz, S., *The Political Economy of Food and Agriculture in the Caribbean* (Ian Randle Publishers Kingston, 1996)

Buxton, J., & Philips, N., *Case Studies in Latin American Political Economy* (Manchester University Press Manchester, 1999)

Chamberlain, M., (Ed.), *Caribbean Migration: Globalised Identities* (Routledge, London, 1998)

Domínguez, J.I., *Democratic Politics in Latin America and the Caribbean* (Johns Hopkins University Press, Baltimore, MD, 1998)

Griffith, I.L., & Sedoc-Dahlberg, B.N., (Eds.), *Democracy and Human Rights in the Caribbean* (Westview Press, Boulder, CO, 1997)

Grossman, L.S., *The Political Ecology of Bananas, Contract Farming, Peasants and Agrarian Change in the Eastern Caribbean* (University of North Carolina Press, Chapel Hill, NC, 1998)

Faber, D.J., *Environment Under Fire: imperialism and the ecological crisis in Central America* (Monthly Review Press, New York, 1993)

LaFeber, W., *Inevitable Revolutions: the United States in Central America* (W.W. Norton, New York, 2nd rev. edn., 1993)

Marshall, D.D., *Caribbean Political Economy at the Crossroads: NAFTA and Regional Developmentism* (Macmillan, Basingstoke, 1998)

Orlove, B., (Ed.), *The Allure of the Foreign: imported goods in postcolonial Latin America* (University of Michigan Press, Ann Arbor, 1997)

Pérez Sáinz, J.P., *From the Finca to the Maquila: labor and capitalist development in Central America* (Westview Press, Boulder, CO, 1998)

Richardson, B.C., *The Caribbean in the Wider World, 1492-1992: A Regional Geography* (Cambridge University Press, Cambridge, 1992)

Vertovec, S., *Hindu Trinidad: religion, ethnicity and socio-economic change* (Macmillan Heinemann ELT, Oxford, 1992)

Wilkinson, P.F., *Tourism policy and planning: case studies from the Commonwealth Caribbean* (Cognizant Communication Corporation, New York, 1997)

Useful websites:
www.centralamericadaily.com
www.virtualhouse.org
www.census.gov/statab
www.igc.org
www.worldwatch.org

www.cia.gov/cia/publications/factbook
www.hurricane.com
www.globalissues.org
www.whyfiles.news.wisc.edu